JURY DUTY

Reclaiming Your Political Power and Taking Responsibility

MICHAEL SINGER

 PRAEGER

AN IMPRINT OF ABC-CLIO, LLC
Santa Barbara, California • Denver, Colorado • Oxford, England

Library of Congress Cataloging-in-Publication Data

Singer, Michael, 1942–
    Jury duty : reclaiming your political power and taking responsibility / Michael Singer.
        p. cm.
    Includes bibliographical references and index.
    ISBN 978–1–4408–0269–0 (cloth) — ISBN 978–1–4408–0270–6 (ebook)
1. Jury—United States. I. Title.
KF8972.S57   2012
347.73′752—dc23   2012014067

ISBN: 978–1–4408–0269–0
EISBN: 978–1–4408–0270–6

16 15 14 13 12   1 2 3 4 5

This book is also available on the World Wide Web as an eBook.
Visit www.abc-clio.com for details.

Praeger
An Imprint of ABC-CLIO, LLC

ABC-CLIO, LLC
130 Cremona Drive, P.O. Box 1911
Santa Barbara, California 93116-1911

This book is printed on acid-free paper (∞)

Manufactured in the United States of America

Contents

Acknowledgments   v

Introduction   vii

PART I   THE BASICS OF THE JURY SYSTEM

Chapter 1   How the Jury System Works   3

Chapter 2   What the Jury System Costs   13

Chapter 3   Citizens as Jurors in the Justice System   29

PART II   MYTHS ABOUT THE JURY SYSTEM

Chapter 4   The Myth of Improved Trial Outcomes   43

Chapter 5   The Myth of Promoting Democratic Citizenship   61

PART III   THE JURY AS POLITICAL INSTITUTION

Chapter 6   The Long History of the Nullification Power   75

Chapter 7   The Jury as Safeguard against Government   87

Chapter 8   The Worth of the Jury System   99

PART IV   GOVERNMENT OBSTRUCTION OF THE JURY

Chapter 9   Obstruction of the Jury in the Trial Process   111

Chapter 10 Obstruction of the Jury in the Sentencing Process   123

PART V   JURY RESPONSIBILITY

Chapter 11 Discretion and Responsibility   145

Chapter 12 Conscientious Fulfillment of Jury Duty   157

Chapter 13 Juror Responsibility for Unjust Prison Conditions   173

Notes   187

Bibliography   217

Index   235

Acknowledgments

I am most particularly grateful to Courtney W. Howland. She read and incisively commented on numerous drafts, and generously devoted countless hours to discussing the jury and its responsibilities over several years. The evolution of this book owes much to her comprehensive, constructive, and judicious criticism. Her balanced judgments and invaluable insights are reflected throughout.

I also thank Jack H. Friedenthal and Frank H. Stewart. Each of them made extensive and perceptively critical comments on an earlier version. Their well-judged critiques have substantially influenced the structure of the book. Charles S. Ingoglia gave helpful comments on an earlier version.

Valentina Tursini, as acquisitions editor at Praeger, was an inspiration. It is thanks to her understanding and guidance that this book developed into its present form. Steve Catalano has been an admirably responsive and supportive editor throughout.

Finally, I thank the Dickson Poon School of Law of King's College London for providing me for the past twelve years with the great privilege of a stimulating and supportive scholarly environment.

Michael Singer

Introduction

A young man committed a battery on a younger boy in the street and was prosecuted for it. He demanded a jury trial, but was refused this and convicted in a trial before a judge alone, who sentenced him to serve sixty days in the parish prison and fined him $150. This might not sound very significant. Yet this apparently insignificant case drew the attention of the Supreme Court of the United States, which insisted that the young man had a right to a jury trial after all.

The incident occurred in Louisiana in the 1960s. The young man was black, and he saw two of his younger boy relatives conversing with four white boys. He didn't like the look of the encounter—there was extreme racial tension in the area—and so took his young relatives peacefully away in his car. As he left, he either touched (by his own admission) or slapped (as the prosecution alleged) one of the white boys on the elbow.

There was no injury, not even a mark on the boy's skin. But still, the young man's own admission would have been enough to make him guilty as charged. The reason is that the exact charge, which was simple battery, has a very broad scope in law. Intentionally touching a person on the elbow without his consent can be enough to meet the legal definition of simple battery. But prosecutors generally focus their limited resources on more serious crime. The vast majority of the insignificant day-to-day incidents that technically constitute simple battery are not prosecuted. Normally, battery is prosecuted only when it is a more serious violation. However, even an insignificant, technical violation of the law is enough for a prosecutor and a judge who want to harass someone, whether on racial grounds or otherwise.

The Supreme Court understood that harassment—specifically, racial harassment—was the motivation for this prosecution. It declared: "A right to jury trial is granted to criminal defendants in order to prevent oppression by the Government. . . . The framers of the constitutions strove to create an independent judiciary, but insisted upon further protection against arbitrary action. Providing an accused with the right to be tried by a jury of his peers gave him an inestimable safeguard against the corrupt or overzealous prosecutor and against the compliant, biased, or eccentric judge."[1]

What difference, though, could a jury make, since the young man would, after all, have been guilty as charged? The difference is that the jury has political roles that go beyond its regular trial task of applying the law to the facts to reach its verdict. The jury has the absolute, unquestionable power to acquit any criminal defendant, regardless of what the law might say and the evidence might be. This power is what the Supreme Court relied on in insisting that the young man had a right to a jury trial. A jury could recognize that the prosecution was brought only for purposes of harassment, and could then decide to vote to acquit.

The Louisiana government knew this. Its legislature promptly passed, and its governor signed, a change in the law of simple battery specifically designed to circumvent the Supreme Court's holding. The same Louisiana court then attempted to try the young man again without a jury, but the federal courts again intervened to prevent this. The state was never willing to risk trying him before a jury.

Power entails responsibility. The Supreme Court relied on this too. The clear sense of its opinion is that the jury in a criminal case has not only the power but also the responsibility to safeguard against arbitrary government action, whether on the part of legislature, executive, prosecutor, or judge. Once a jury recognized that the Louisiana prosecution was brought only for purposes of harassment, it would be under the obligation to take this strongly into account in reaching its verdict.

As the Supreme Court said, the function of the jury system is to prevent oppression by the government. This applies to the federal government as well as the state governments. The jury is there to stop government going too far. That is its function, that is its power, and that is its responsibility. As this book explains, there is no other valid justification for the jury system.

A justification is needed for the jury system because society expends substantial resources on it. Part I of this book assesses the expenditure. This part begins with a brief account of the origins of the jury system in England and its further development in America, and then describes stage by stage the procedure of a jury trial, criminal and civil, in America. It then gives the first-ever assessment of the dollar cost of the American jury system. A realistic assessment must incorporate the value of juror time, the cost of personnel to manage the jury system and of facilities for jurors, various additional costs of a jury trial, and other factors. The assessment comes to over two billion dollars per year.

Part I also looks at what the American citizenry thinks of the jury system and of the justice system as a whole. Surveys show wide public distrust of the justice system. There is widespread public noncompliance with the jury summons, which authority figures ascribe to irresponsibility but which more reasonably indicates that people who distrust the justice system see it as legitimate to reject jury duty.

Some people have argued that there are justifications for the jury system apart from its political roles. These supposed justifications include claims that the jury system improves trial outcomes, in that a jury is supposedly more competent, fair, and consistent than a judge, and also supports community values and interests better than a judge. They also include claims that in a range of ways jury duty promotes democratic citizenship—specifically by providing an education in citizenship, offering participation in the system of government, fostering social community, and maintaining regard for the justice system. Part II closely examines all of these various arguments and finds that in general there is no sufficient basis for any of them.

Only the political roles of the jury system remain as a possible justification of its cost to American society. It might be argued that a jury composed of a group of average citizens is incapable of fulfilling these political roles. This book does not adopt such an attitude. But in any event, anyone who argues that the average jury is incapable of fulfilling its political roles is in effect arguing against the jury system itself, since nothing other than its political roles can justify it.

Part III looks at these political roles of the jury, which are based on its power to acquit regardless of the law and the evidence—its so-called *nullification power*. The jury has exercised this power in a range of cases over the centuries, particularly during periods of social change and conflict. These have mainly been cases raising concerns of injustice in the law or injustice in the likely punishment that the law would impose. Some of these cases have long been justly famous, as when mid-nineteenth-century New England juries refused to convict individuals who had broken the law by helping escaped slaves to reach freedom in Canada.

When the nullification power is analyzed in its historical and social context, it appears as a deeply established political principle and not merely a legally granted right. This positions the jury system as a vital political institution within the system of checks and balances that orders the continuing relationship between government and the people. The jury system as political institution has been criticized as anachronistic, inconsistent, threatening anarchy, and a license for unjust acquittals, but these criticisms are exaggerated. The conclusion of this part of the book is that the political roles of the jury continue to justify society's expenditure on the jury system.

The subject of part IV is government obstruction of the jury. Despite the Supreme Court's insistence on the vital function of the jury as safeguard against government, judicial decisions remain ambivalent toward the political roles of the jury. Judges celebrate the jury's exercise of the nullification power in a number of important cases, while at the same time developing a range of practices to obstruct the jury's exercise of this power. These practices are employed throughout the trial process. Extensive *voir dire* scrutiny of prospective jurors tries to eliminate anyone disposed to exercise the nullification power. During the trial, judges inhibit the jury from exercising its nullification power by concealing from the jury that it possesses this power, exerting pressure on the jury not to exercise the power, and creating a threatening atmosphere against the exercise of the power.

There is also obstruction of the jury in the sentencing process. The way this works is that judicial discretion over sentencing is so broad that the judge can impose punishment that thwarts the jury's verdict. In particular, even if the jury convicts the defendant only on a relatively minor offense, the judge can still base the sentence on major offenses of which the jury has acquitted him or that were not even charged.

The judicial practices discussed in this part undermine the vital political roles of the jury that represent the value of the jury system to American society. The conclusion of this part of the book is that judges should accept responsibility for conducting trials and guiding the jury in ways that foster rather than obstruct these roles.

Part V focuses on jury responsibility in criminal cases. It first discusses an important category of societal roles: those that incorporate discretion to bypass specific obligations of the role without loss of effectiveness in fulfilling the role. The roles of police and prosecutor are significant examples of this kind of role. To fulfill a role of this kind conscientiously requires complying with the specific obligations of the role as a regular matter, but also imposes responsibility to recognize weighty reasons for the exercise of the discretion incorporated into the role.

Jury duty is also a role of this kind. It is the nullification power that grants discretion to bypass the judge's instructions without loss of effectiveness in fulfilling the role of juror. Because of this, conscientious fulfillment of jury duty requires the jury to follow the judge's instructions in general, but also imposes responsibility to take severe injustice into account in reaching its verdict, and possibly then to refuse to convict despite the law and the evidence.

This part concludes with an important aspect of jury responsibility. Juries for centuries have exercised the nullification power to prevent unjust punishment, and have recognized their responsibility to do so. But not enough attention is currently being paid to systemically unjust conditions of imprisonment as constituting unjust punishment. American prison conditions today are systemically unjust in ways that government has recognized, and for which it has acknowledged its responsibility. Systemic overcrowding and systemically inadequate medical care result in injustice for many inmates throughout the American prison system. Rape is pervasive throughout the prison system, with many inmates being victims of rape by other inmates or by guards. A guilty verdict from the jury will foreseeably result in the judge committing the defendant to prison, with all of these systemically unjust conditions.

A jury that fulfills its role conscientiously will take the prospect of systemic unjust prison conditions into account in reaching its verdict. This, of course, does not mean that jurors will exercise the nullification power to acquit in every case, so that no one is ever sent to prison. But it does mean that conscientious jurors will consider in every criminal case whether the overall benefit of society truly requires that the individual defendant in the case should have to face the prospect of systemic unjust prison conditions.

Part I

The Basics of the Jury System

Chapter 1

How the Jury System Works

The American jury system originally derived from the English jury system, which itself grew out of the need to have legal decisions that the populace could respect as legitimate. To understand how the jury system could meet this need, we need to begin with the English jury in medieval times. When a jury in a local community in medieval England decided a case, people could accept that decision as representing the community view and not merely a decision imposed by the remote authority of a judge.

It was important that the community should respect legal decisions, because the community had to live with their consequences. In many cases, English medieval legal process was not greatly concerned with subtleties of legal interpretation. The average criminal trial lasted thirty minutes, with the judge generally accepting the facts as the prosecution presented them. But it was still up to the jury to decide whether to convict or acquit. The jury would largely base its verdict on the defendant's character, reputation, and degree of peer support. If these were good enough to give a fair chance of successfully reabsorbing him into the community, the jury would likely acquit him—even if he had done what he was charged with having done—rather than convict him to face the very severe penalties imposed at that time.[1]

As time went by, there were increasingly many cases in which legal interpretation was important. In those cases, too, community support could give legitimacy to the decision. A good illustration comes from an area of continuing importance from medieval times to the present day: commercial regulation.

The illustration comes from commercial fishing, which has been regulated for many centuries. A key aspect of regulations has always been the setting of minimum mesh sizes for fishing nets, to protect young fish. On countless occasions, fishermen have complained of other fishermen violating mesh-size regulations. The problem is that it is difficult to measure the mesh of fishing nets in any objective way. If the net is opened out to measure the mesh, the measurement will vary according to how hard the net is pulled (for example, by hand) or pushed (for example, by inserting a wedge) to open it out. Many prosecutions of violations of mesh-size regulations have failed because courts found the evidence of mesh size unacceptably subjective.

In the last decade, an intergovernmental organization has developed a sophisticated electronic gauge that applies a precise preset force to the net.[2] But no such device was available to the mayor and aldermen of London in the mid-fourteenth century, when, in a typical case, fishmongers brought to them eight fishing nets that they had found set in the Thames river and that, they claimed, had a mesh finer than the regulation two inches. Yet these officials needed a decision on the nets that would command the respect of the fishing and fish-trading community.

The mayor promptly passed the responsibility for the decision to a specialist jury. He called in "such of the more discreet fishmongers of the City as had knowledge as to nets ... [who then] were sworn to survey, examine, and measure the meshes of the nets." They found four of the nets to be "false," and these were destroyed; they found the other four to be "good," and these were returned to their owners. As the historian James Masschaele explains: "By bringing respected fishmongers into the adjudication process, the mayor increased the likelihood that the offending fishermen would accept the legitimacy of the ruling. More importantly, he increased the likelihood that other fishermen who did not have a direct stake in the matter would treat the decision as legitimate ... [rather than] as a capricious imposition."[3]

Juries nowadays are mostly composed not of specialists but of members of the general public. A number of political systems around the world have brought members of the general public into their judicial trial processes, in some form of jury system. Some have done so continuously for centuries. Others have experimented with a jury system but have since abandoned it. Yet others have adopted a jury system relatively recently and continue to use it. The form of jury system varies enormously among the various judicial systems.[4]

The longest continuing commitment to a jury system is that of the English system.[5] This jury system is rooted in the common-law structure, in which the law develops through court decisions as well as legislative and executive acts. Aspects of the English jury system persist today in several of the countries that were substantially shaped by the English legal system. These include America—the United States—whose jury system is the subject of this book.

The common-law jury systems vary, and some have changed considerably over the years, but they still share certain important characteristics. In all of them, there are legal provisions governing the selection of jurors that aim to make the jury in some sense representative of the populace at large. The jury sits in the courtroom as a body, physically separate from the judge, the attorneys, and the parties. At the conclusion of the proceedings, it retires to deliberate in private. When it has decided on its verdict, it returns to the courtroom to deliver it.

CONSTITUTIONAL AND RELATED COMMITMENTS TO THE JURY SYSTEM

For the Founders of the American Republic, the jury system was essential to the society and government that they sought to establish. In 1771, John Adams, later the second president of the United States, wrote approvingly of the English jury system:

> Of the legislature, the people constitute one essential branch [the House of Commons]. . . . In the administration of justice, too, the people have an important share. Juries are taken, by lot or by suffrage, from the mass of the people, and no man can be condemned of life, or limb, or property, or reputation, without the concurrence of the voice of the people. As the constitution requires that the popular branch of the legislature should have an absolute check, so as to put a peremptory negative upon every act of the government, it requires that the common people, should have as complete a control, as decisive a negative, in every judgment of a court of judicature.[6]

This commitment to the jury system found expression in the federal Constitution. Article III, Section 2 and the Sixth Amendment to the Constitution together establish the right of the accused to a jury in a criminal trial. Also, the Fifth Amendment requires a grand jury indictment for any serious criminal offense. The Seventh Amendment declares the right to a jury trial in civil cases.[7] These provisions are directly applicable to the federal justice system.

As far as the states are concerned, the Supreme Court has interpreted the Fourteenth Amendment to the federal Constitution (denying the states the power to "deprive any person of life, liberty, or property, without due process of law") to mean that the states must also comply with the Sixth Amendment guarantee of a jury in criminal trials, at least for serious offenses.[8] In addition, the individual states have their own constitutional provisions regarding the grand jury and regarding jury trial in criminal and civil cases.

Although the American jury system derived from the English system, the jury is now less firmly rooted in England than in America. In fact, the jury system is now more firmly rooted in America than anywhere else in the world. Remarkably, most of the world's jury trials—as much as 80 percent of all criminal and civil jury trials—now take place in America.[9]

In England the grand jury has been abolished, there are few jury trials in civil cases, and only serious criminal cases are at all likely to result in a jury trial. It is not even certain that, under the unwritten constitution in England, the defendant in a criminal case has any constitutional right to a jury trial. The *Criminal Courts Review*, an influential recent government-sponsored report on the English criminal trial system, insists that there is no such right. Yet despite this, it recognizes the continuing strong English commitment to the jury system as "a hallowed institution" of society.[10]

Although the American and English social and legal systems now differ in many ways, the English jury system is still seen as relevant to the American experience. American courts may still refer in their opinions to English legal precedent regarding the jury system. For this reason, there will be a number of references to the English jury in this book.

The jury system, then, is constitutionally mandated in America and a hallowed institution in England. Even so, it is reasonable to ask what, if anything, makes the jury system worthwhile to society. Societies develop and change, and social institutions do not always retain their earlier social value. William Dwyer, for many years a federal district judge of deservedly high reputation, gave a wise assessment: " 'What have you done for us lately?' is asked of all democratic institutions, and we need to look at whether the jury succeeds today, in the real world. No matter what the federal and state constitutions say, the jury will survive only if it works."[11]

Dwyer's assessment does not even go far enough. It is not enough to be concerned with whether the jury system simply works. As with any social institution, we need to be satisfied that it works well enough, and offers a sufficient benefit to our society, to justify its costs. That is why this book starts its assessment of the jury system with an estimate of its costs, in the next chapter. Subsequent chapters can then assess whether what the jury does, or what it ought to be doing, can justify those costs to society. But first, we should take a look at the trial framework in which the jury does its job.

AMERICAN JURY-TRIAL PROCEDURE

Strictly speaking, there is no such thing as a single American jury-trial procedure, because each of the states, as well as the federal system, has its own separate jury-trial system with its own procedure. But these various systems are still similar enough in their basic features to allow for a general overview, limited here to the main points of trial procedure.

In all the states and in the federal system, most legal actions, criminal or civil, do not result in a jury trial. In a criminal action, the prosecutor might exercise her broad discretion not to prosecute (see chapter 11). Even if she does prosecute, the case is often resolved by plea bargain: the defendant pleads guilty in exchange for a concession, usually a reduced sentence. Sometimes the defendant will plead guilty without any bargain, hoping this will induce the judge to be lenient.

The defendant in a criminal case has a constitutional right to a jury trial for any serious offense. However, he can declare a preference for a bench trial (that is, before a judge alone, without a jury), and some jurisdictions permit him to exercise this choice. Others require the consent of the prosecution, the judge, or both.[12] Overall, failure to prosecute, guilty pleas, and bench trials resolve most criminal actions.

Many civil legal actions do not allow for a jury at all, for reasons that stem from the development of the English legal system. In earlier centuries, England operated several quite separate court systems in parallel at the same time. In only one of these, the common-law courts (or simply called the law courts), jury trial developed. In civil actions, these courts were largely concerned with claims for monetary damages for such matters as injury or breach of contract. Other court systems dealt with various actions not involving or going beyond monetary damages, including injunctions (orders to someone to do or cease doing something), divorce, and probate. In the development of American legal systems, this division regarding jury trial in civil matters was largely adopted. As a result, there are no jury trials in divorce and other family-law cases or in probate and related estate cases. Also, a jury is never involved in deciding whether to issue an injunction.

Even if a jury trial is possible in a civil action, the parties are still free to agree on having a bench trial. Many do so. Overall, the great majority of civil actions that go to trial have a bench trial, either because there is no right to a jury trial or because the parties have agreed on a bench trial.

A jury trial requires jurors. Each court system maintains a list of persons who may be required for *jury duty* (also called *jury service*). The list is generally compiled from one or more of three databases: registered voters, residential real-property taxpayers, and driver's license holders. Various categories of people are, or have been in the past, excluded from the list.[13]

Court officials nowadays usually select persons for jury duty by drawing names at random from the list and mailing a *jury summons* to each. The summons specifies the place and date for jury duty. If this does not yield enough people, more may be obtained by presenting summonses to any nearby persons, including spectators in the courthouse or passersby outside, requiring them to serve at once. Such a juror is called a *talis* (bystander) juror.[14]

Persons who respond to a jury summons report to the courthouse on the appointed day and wait to be called. When called for a trial, they are questioned to determine their fitness to serve, in a process called *voir dire*. The jurisdictions vary in how *voir dire* is carried out.[15] However, they all permit extensive questioning that can be quite invasive of the privacy of prospective jurors. This is unique to the American jury system. In other countries with a common-law jury system, questioning of prospective jurors is strictly and narrowly limited.

For the attorney of either party, the goal of *voir dire* questioning is to ensure a sympathetic jury by *challenges* against unsuitable prospective jurors. Either party can challenge any prospective juror *for cause*. That is, the attorney argues to the judge that *voir dire* questioning has shown the prospective juror to be biased or otherwise unfit to be a juror in the trial. The judge then decides whether or not to grant the attorney's request and dismiss the juror.

Also, each party is allotted a number of *peremptory* challenges to dismiss prospective jurors without giving a reason. The number varies from one jurisdiction to another and from one kind of case to another within a jurisdiction. The federal constitution forbids using peremptory challenges, in federal or state trials, to discriminate on the basis of race or sex in jury selection (see chapter 7). An attorney might use a peremptory challenge against a prospective juror if the judge has rejected his challenge for cause, or if for any reason—or even on a hunch—he feels that the prospective juror may be unsympathetic to his case.

The process of *voir dire* and challenges to prospective jurors goes on until a jury of the required number is selected. The number of jurors is generally between six and twelve, but varies from one jurisdiction to another, and from one kind of case to another within a jurisdiction. The jurors swear to an oath read by the clerk of the court (see chapter 12).

The trial now begins. The judge instructs the jury on trial procedure and the requirements of jury duty. Each party then makes its opening statement to the jury. The party that brought the case to court goes first: this is the prosecution in a criminal trial and the plaintiff in a civil trial.

The party that brought the case to court—prosecution or plaintiff—presents its evidence, calling witnesses, presenting documents, and so forth. When this party calls a witness, it asks the witness questions in what is known as *direct examination*. The other party (the defendant) may then question the witness on issues raised in direct examination; this is known as *cross-examination*. After this, each party may be permitted further limited questioning of the witness in what is known as *redirect examination* and *recross-examination*.

When the prosecution in a criminal trial, or the plaintiff in a civil trial, has finished presenting its evidence, the defendant may request the judge to grant a trial verdict in its favor, on the ground that the evidence that has been presented is insufficient to support any verdict against the defendant. The request, and the judge's ruling on the request, can take various forms, depending on the jurisdiction. If the judge grants the request, the trial is over, with a verdict in favor of the defendant and without the jury having been involved in the decision.

Otherwise, the trial process is now reversed. The defendant party presents its evidence, and its witnesses are subject to direct examination, cross-examination, redirect examination, and recross-examination.

When the defendant party has finished presenting its evidence, either party in a civil case, and the defendant in a criminal case, may request the judge to grant a trial verdict in its favor, on the ground that the opposing party's evidence is insufficient to support any other verdict. If the judge grants the request, the trial is over, without the jury having been involved. However, in a criminal jury trial, only the jury can render a guilty verdict, so the prosecution cannot request the judge to give a trial verdict in its favor without the jury being involved.

The trial process may be interrupted, possibly many times, for discussions between the judge and the attorneys on matters that the jury is not supposed to hear. In addition, the judge may address the jury at various times during the course of a trial.

If the judge has not granted any party's request for a trial verdict in its favor, the trial continues. In some cases, each party may present further evidence in rebuttal of the other party's case. When the evidentiary part of the trial is finally concluded, each party presents its closing arguments. The judge then has the final word. She states the issues in the case and the law that applies to them. She also explains which facts are in dispute and tells the jury that it alone must decide those facts on the basis of the evidence presented at trial. She may further instruct the jury on its responsibilities in applying the law to the facts that it determines.

Either party may now request the judge to declare a *mistrial*. In fact, this request can generally be made at any point during the course of the trial. The basis for a mistrial is usually impropriety or error in the conduct of the trial, juror misconduct, or a misfortune such as the death of a juror. If the judge declares a mistrial, the trial proceedings are null and void. The party that brought the case to court must decide if it wants to start again with a new trial. If the judge denies the request, the trial continues.

The jury now goes to its jury room, where it deliberates privately until it reaches a verdict. In a criminal case, the defendant may be charged with more than one offense. On each of the charges, the only verdict available to the jury is guilty or not guilty. In civil cases, the jury must decide on each of the plaintiff's claims against the defendant and on any counterclaims that the defendant has made against the plaintiff as part of the case, and usually will also determine the award of damages to be paid on any claim that it finds justified.

In federal criminal trials and most state criminal trials, the verdict must be unanimous: for each of the charges against the defendant, every single juror must agree on guilty or agree on not guilty. Some states allow non-unanimous verdicts in criminal cases, although a high majority is always required for a guilty verdict. The requirements are overall less strict in civil cases.[16]

If a jury has difficulty in agreeing on a verdict, the judge will usually encourage it to keep trying. But sometimes a jury finds it impossible to reach a verdict, and this results in a mistrial.

The jury's announcement of its verdict normally ends its role in the trial. But the verdict takes effect only when the judge takes the formal step of *entering judgment*. Either party in a civil case, or the defendant in a criminal case, may request the judge not to enter judgment, despite the jury's verdict. The form of such requests, as well as the range of grounds on which they can be made, varies from one jurisdiction to another.

In civil cases, the powers of the judge to refuse to enter judgment despite the jury's verdict vary from one jurisdiction to another but may be quite considerable. In some jurisdictions, she can alter the terms of the jury's award of damages. Generally, if she considers the verdict to be against the weight of the evidence, she can reject the verdict and order a new trial. Either party in a civil case can appeal the trial verdict, and then the appellate court may also have considerable power to alter the terms of the jury's award.[17]

When the jury reaches a verdict of not guilty on a charge in a criminal case, that determination is final. The defendant has been acquitted of the charge, and there is no appeal or other challenge available to the prosecution.

When the jury has reached a verdict of guilty on one or more charges in a criminal case, the final stage is sentencing. The judge alone determines the sentence at a special *sentencing hearing*, which is preceded by an investigation into all matters that might affect the judge's decision. Following conviction and sentencing, the defendant can appeal against the conviction and can also appeal against the sentence. In some jurisdictions, the prosecution can also appeal against the sentence.[18]

An appeal must have a legal ground, which will often be that the judge in the trial court made an error in applying the law. It is not possible to appeal on the ground that the jury wrongly determined facts that were in dispute. Regarding the facts that are within the jury's province to determine, the jury's decision is final. Another way of putting this is that an appeal is not a retrial on the merits of the case.

There is a narrow exception to this principle. An appellate court can reverse a jury's verdict of guilty (or a jury verdict in a civil case) if it finds that the evidence was insufficient to support the verdict. This is a high barrier to surmount for the party that is appealing. An appellate court set out the standard of review for appeals on this ground against a criminal conviction: "We review the sufficiency of the evidence *de novo*, viewing the evidence in the light most favorable to the jury's verdict, accepting all reasonable inferences that support the verdict, and reversing only if no reasonable jury could have found the defendant guilty beyond a reasonable doubt."[19]

An appeal from a federal trial normally goes to the appropriate federal appellate court (the circuit court). From the circuit court, a further appeal may be sought in the Supreme Court, which serves as the highest appellate court in the federal system. However, the Court's jurisdiction is largely discretionary, and it declines to hear most of the cases that it has the authority to hear.

An appeal from a state trial normally goes to the appropriate state appellate court. From the appellate court, a further appeal may be sought in the highest court in the state system (which in most, but not all, states is called the supreme court of the state). However, these courts also largely have discretionary jurisdiction and decline most cases. From the highest state court, a further review of any case involving federal constitutional or statutory law may be sought in the Supreme Court—which, again, declines to hear most cases.

A further challenge to a trial judgment may be available to a convicted defendant who is being held in custody: a petition for a *writ of habeas corpus*. The writ of habeas corpus originated in English common law and was adopted into the American system. In formal terms, a writ of habeas corpus is an action requiring officials who are holding a person in custody to appear before the court to justify holding him in custody. In practice, the writ is a procedure for a convicted defendant to raise any of a specified range of legal issues regarding his conviction and confinement.

A common example is a person convicted in a state court who petitions the federal courts for a writ of habeas corpus on the ground that the state trial proceedings violated his federal constitutional rights. It is also possible for a person to petition for a writ of habeas corpus on the ground that his conditions of incarceration violate his constitutional rights. Before approaching the federal courts, he must normally exhaust all possibilities of appeal in the state judicial system. If the court grants the writ, it has a broad range of remedies at its disposal, including, ultimately, ordering the release of the person from custody.

Chapter 2

What the Jury System Costs

Chapter 1 promised an assessment of the cost of the American jury system. This chapter gives the first-ever such assessment.

A difficulty in assessing the cost of the jury system is that only very limited data regarding expenditures related to the jury system have been collected and made available. In fact, no specific cost information at all is collected for most items of expenditure on the jury system. This is true in every state system and the federal system. Because of the lack of data, it is not currently possible to name a definite sum of money and make a reliable assessment that the jury system costs this much, no more and no less.

Yet it does turn out to be possible to name a definite sum of money and make a reliable and useful assessment that the jury system costs *at least* this much. Another way of expressing this is that it is possible to arrive at a reliable and useful *lower-bound* assessment of the cost of the jury system. The idea of a lower bound is borrowed from the quantitative sciences and applied here as follows: a lower-bound estimate for a particular amount is an estimate that might be less than the actual amount, but is certainly not more than the actual amount.

The first step toward achieving the lower-bound assessment of the overall cost of the jury system is to reach reliable lower-bound estimates for each of a range of specific costs of the jury system. This requires searching out information from a range of government and other sources and applying it appropriately.

An illustration will show how this is done. One of the many items for which an estimate will be needed is the cost of producing and mailing a jury summons. The Postal Service publishes general mailing rates that depend on the type of item being mailed, the standard of service provided, and also on whether the sender is a private individual, a business, or a charitable organization. It does not publish a rate specifically for jury summonses. However, its lowest published rate of any kind is currently a little over ten cents per item.[1] If the cost of paper and printing are bundled into this, and it is rounded down, a confident estimate is that ten cents is a lower bound for the cost of producing and mailing a jury summons.

The actual cost could be substantially more than this. The cost of mailing a jury summons might well not be lower than the cost of mailing anything else, and the cost of paper and printing is actually more than zero. But the cost is surely *at least* ten cents per jury summons. That is, ten cents is a lower-bound estimate for the cost of producing and mailing a jury summons.

This was a very straightforward illustration for a relatively small item of expenditure on the jury system. However, for some of the items of expenditure considered in this chapter, more effort is needed to obtain the relevant information, and computation is needed to apply it appropriately.

When lower-bound estimates for the various specific costs have been reached, all that is needed to obtain an assessment of the cost of the entire jury system is to add these lower-bound estimates together. Of course, it would hardly be possible to include every kind of expenditure that the jury system entails. However, this does not prevent the assessment being reliable *as a lower bound*. That is, it is still true that our society devotes to the jury system *at least* the total of the expenditures that *are* taken into account in this chapter.

THE COST OF JUROR TIME

The great majority of American jury trials are in state rather than federal courts. The primary source of quantitative information on them is the Court Statistics Project. This is a collaborative effort by two nonprofit organizations, the National Center for State Courts and the Conference of State Court Administrators, together with the Bureau of Justice Statistics of the federal Department of Justice. The National Center for State Courts publishes the information in its *State-of-the-States Survey*. This includes data obtained from state sources, as well as data estimates regarding a number of states that publish little or no information even about such basic matters as the number of jury trials that they hold.

The Courts Statistics Project finds that state courts issue nearly thirty-two million jury summonses per year, but the number of recipients actually empanelled as trial jurors is about one and a half million.[2] So each year summonses are sent to more than thirty million people who do not ultimately serve as jurors.

One reason why so many more people are summoned than ultimately serve is that many prospective jurors are rejected in *voir dire*. Another reason is that many people who receive a summons either do not attend for jury duty, or do attend but are found not to be qualified. A further reason is that quite often a case scheduled for jury trial is dealt with by a settlement or plea agreement at the last minute, so that the prospective jurors for that case are suddenly no longer needed.

Some county jurisdictions within the states do now try to estimate their needs for jurors day by day. When they see that more people than are needed have been summoned for jury duty, they try to inform the surplus by telephone or e-mail that they need not report.[3] However, many jurisdictions still just register every recipient of a jury summons who arrives at the courthouse, and then simply leave the surplus—this being most of them—to pass the day or days as best they can.

Plainly, the populace as a whole spends a great deal of time on jury duty. To estimate how much time would require knowing the average length of jury trials, but this information is not available on a national, or even a statewide basis. The best that can currently be done is to trawl through the websites of a range of individual city and county judicial authorities, as their jury-information web pages often give a rough estimate of the average length of jury duty. Most of these authorities estimate the average length of jury trials as between two and four days. Very few estimate below two days. Some require a much greater time commitment, possibly extending over more than one trial.[4] Even one trial can be a lengthy commitment, with many lasting for several months.

The estimate of between two and four days seems then to be optimistic, especially as it comes from judicial authorities who have an interest in not discouraging prospective jurors. So taking the bottom of this optimistic range—two days—as the average length of a jury trial is certainly a conservative lower bound. It follows that a lower bound for the total number of person-days devoted to jury duty in trials is at least three million each year.

The total time that the populace devotes to the jury system also includes the time spent by the more than thirty million people each year who are summoned but do not ultimately serve. But not all of these commit any significant time to the jury system. Many people simply ignore the summons. Of those who do complete and return the summons form, some are found not to be qualified (for example, they might not satisfy a residency requirement). Of those who are found to be qualified, some simply do not report to the courthouse on the appointed day.

The remaining individuals—those who respond to the summons, are found to be qualified, and report for jury duty on the appointed day—make up the *jury yield*. The average jury yield is around 46 percent of those summoned. So over twelve million people each year are "surplus": they fall within the jury yield, but are not ultimately selected to serve in a trial.[5]

An individual who falls within the jury yield is required to remain at the courthouse for a specified period of time. If she has not been empanelled on a jury by the end of this period, she is dismissed from jury duty. The various jurisdictions differ greatly as to how long a period they specify. Some require only one day of attendance, so that any prospective juror who has not been empanelled on a jury by the end of the day is dismissed from jury duty. But a good number require a week of attendance: any prospective juror who has not been empanelled on a trial jury at the end of his first day of jury duty must attend again the next day, and continue doing so for a week. A few jurisdictions require even more than a week.

However, achieving a reliable lower-bound estimate requires estimating conservatively at every stage. So let us assume that every person available for jury duty is either empanelled or dismissed by the end of the first day of attendance. That is, each of the twelve million or more "surplus" people each year is taken as devoting no more than one day to the jury system.

Some of the surplus people may in fact devote less time than a day. Recall that some jurisdictions operate a system for informing individuals who have been summoned for jury duty as to whether they will actually be needed. It is fair to say that someone who is notified that he should not report devotes no appreciable time to the jury system. But no information is available as to how well these systems operate, and many jurisdictions have no system of this kind. Certainly, no more than half of the total surplus persons could possibly be notified in time. It follows that at least half of the total surplus persons devote at least one day to the jury system. This means that the persons who are available for jury duty, but are not ultimately empanelled to serve in a trial, devote a total of at least six million person-days each year to the jury system.

So the total time that the American citizenry devotes to jury duty is at least nine million person-days each year. This does not include service in federal trial juries, or federal and state grand juries. Also, the estimates have been conservative at every stage, so the figure of nine million person-days each year certainly understates the actual amount of time committed.

To estimate the cost of this total time commitment to the jury system requires an assessment of the value of a person's time. A substantial proportion of the people who perform jury duty are in paid employment. This proportion can be estimated from employment statistics provided by the Bureau of Labor Statistics of the federal Department of Labor regarding the entire civilian population of working age. These statistics show that, although the percentage of the civilian population in paid employment varies during periods of higher or lower national unemployment, it has not fallen below 57 percent.[6]

There are no national statistics regarding what percentage of people summoned for jury duty are in paid employment. Some limited data from individual states suggest that it is higher than the overall percentage of the civilian population in paid employment.[7] This is really not surprising. The list of persons who can be summoned for jury duty is compiled from one or more of three databases: registered voters, residential real-property taxpayers, and driver's license holders. Anyone in paid employment very probably appears in at least one of these databases. But this is not necessarily true for people not in paid employment. So the list of persons who can be summoned for jury duty likely contains a higher proportion of people in paid employment than does the general population.

It is also likely that the percentage of the jury yield in paid employment is higher than the percentage of the civilian population in paid employment. In earlier years, members of a number of professions and occupations were excused from jury duty, either automatically or on claiming that their work was essential to the community. However, current policy disfavors both forms of exclusion (see chapter 9), so relatively few people are likely to be excused on the basis of occupation. But people may well be excused on personal grounds. For example, someone who is caring full-time for a child or a sick relative, and has no substitute caregiver available, may be excused from jury duty. So the sector of the populace that devotes time to the jury system likely contains a higher proportion of people in paid employment than does the general population.

It is therefore a conservative assumption that, on average nationwide, at least 57 percent of people summoned for jury duty, and at least 57 percent of people selected to serve on a jury panel in a trial, are in paid employment.

The Bureau of Labor Statistics of the federal Department of Labor provides statistics on the average cost nationwide of a person in paid employment. Currently, wages and salaries average $20.91 per hour worked. In addition, the cost of a range of benefits must be taken into account. These include legally required benefits, such as Social Security, Medicare, unemployment insurance, and workers' compensation, as well as life, health, and disability insurance, and paid leave benefits. Currently, these costs average $9.21 per hour worked. So the total average cost of a person in paid employment is slightly over $30 per hour worked. The nationwide average working week remains consistently above thirty-four hours.[8] This gives an average working day of at least six working hours, so that the average daily cost of a person in paid employment is currently at least $180.

This does not take account of a great range of overhead costs of employment. Overhead includes providing and maintaining workspace, uniforms and tools, employee training, personnel management related to the employment, and so forth. There are no nationwide statistics regarding any of these overhead costs. Following a conservative approach to achieving a lower-bound cost estimate, total overhead is assessed here at a nominal $10 per day for each person in paid employment.

When a person in paid employment devotes time to the jury system, the cost of that person's time, now estimated at $190 per day on average, is a cost of the jury system. This is a cost of the jury system regardless of whether any given employer pays an employee's wages while that employee is performing jury duty, and regardless of whether government makes payment to jurors for jury duty. The reason is simply that when a person is engaged in the jury system, she is not doing the work that she would otherwise have done. As a result, the value of that work is lost to society. So for a person whose work is valued at $190 per day on average, $190 is the amount that is lost to society for any day that she is engaged in the jury system.[9]

Another way of putting this is that in estimating the cost of the jury system to our society as a whole, the particular pocket from which any part of this cost is paid is irrelevant. Regardless of who pays the cost, or how costs are transferred from one pocket to another, it is still a cost of the jury system.

The time that people who are not in paid employment devote to the jury system must also be taken into account. This includes the time of the many people who normally spend their days in such activities as maintaining a home and caring for family members, or undertaking voluntary work in the community, as well as those independently engaged in creating works of literature, music, or art. All of this work is valuable. If, on a given day, a person who normally does such work is instead engaged with the jury system, the economic value of their normal work must be ascribed to the cost of the jury system. However, there are also people whose usual days produce no economic value at all, and this must be taken into account in estimating an average. To maintain a conservative estimate of costs, only a nominal sum—$5 per hour (far less than federal minimum wage), amounting to $30 per day—will be taken as a lower bound for the average economic value of each day for a person not in paid employment.

Suppose now that we take an average one hundred members of the populace who are devoting time to the jury system. Again, on average, at least fifty-seven of them will be in paid employment at a daily cost of $190. So the daily cost of all fifty-seven of them is $10,830. The remaining forty-three will not be in paid employment, and the daily cost of each of these has been taken as a nominal $30. The daily cost of all forty-three will then be $1,290. The sum total of the daily cost of all the one hundred people is therefore $10,830 plus $1,290; that is, $12,120. So the average daily cost of each person is one-hundredth of this; that is, $121.20, conservatively rounded down to $120.

Overall then, the cost of the three million person-days spent serving on jury panels amounts to at least $360 million each year. The cost of the six million person-days devoted to the jury system by persons who are summoned but do not ultimately serve on a panel amounts to at least $720 million each year.

ADMINISTRATIVE COSTS OF THE JURY SYSTEM

The overall cost of the jury system includes its administrative costs. These are generally government costs, in the sense that they are normally paid from government accounts on the authority of government officials. However, as explained earlier, if any given item is actually a cost of the jury system, then the particular pocket from which the item is paid for is irrelevant. In fact, even if a public benefactor defrayed the entire cost of the jury system for a year, the amount that the benefactor disbursed from her own private funds would still be the cost of the jury system to our society as a whole.

A large item among the administrative costs of the jury system is the cost of employees. There are 3,144 counties in America, each with its own court or courts. Each of these counties must administer its jury system, requiring a complex of jury managers, jury clerks, bailiffs, and others. There are no nation-wide—or even statewide—statistics collected on how many people the various counties employ for this. However, study of the advertisements for positions under the rubric of "Jury Management Job Descriptions" on the website of the National Center for State Courts gives some sense of the range and number of employees required.[10]

There are 1,582 counties with a population of less than twenty-five thousand. A conservative estimate is that each of these manages its jury system with, on average, half the time of a single employee; so the sum total of their requirements is the equivalent of 791 full-time employees. There are 1,035 counties with a population between twenty-five thousand and one hundred thousand. A conservative estimate is that each of these requires on average at least a single full-time employee for this; so in total they require 1,035 full-time employees. There are 415 counties with a population between one hundred thousand and five hundred thousand. A conservative estimate is that each of these requires on average at least three employees, amounting to 1,245 in all. There are 112 counties with a population over five hundred thousand. A conservative estimate is that each of these requires on average at least six employees, amounting to 672 in all. The lower-bound estimate for the sum total of employees required to manage the jury system is then 791, plus 1,035, plus 1,245, plus 672. This is 3,743.

The jury management job descriptions on the website of the National Center for State Courts give some sense of the salaries of these employees. They range from slightly less than the average American wage for junior positions to very much more than this average for senior positions. Overall, it is reasonable to estimate the average cost for salary and benefits of a jury-system employee to be the same as the average for all state and local government workers. The Bureau of Labor Statistics of the federal Department of Labor declares this to be currently a little over $40 per hour worked, including benefits.[11]

Even assuming short working days and many vacation days, there are at least 1,500 working hours in a year. So the nationwide average annual cost of salary and benefits for a jury-system employee may be conservatively estimated at $60,000, even ignoring overhead costs. A conservative estimate for the total annual cost of employees required to manage the jury system is then 3,743 times $60,000, which is $224,580,000.

Another administrative cost of the jury system is that of facilities for pro-spective jurors attending at the courthouse, as well as for jury deliberations. A couple of simple rooms may suffice in a courthouse in a small, peaceful county, but counties with larger populations and cities require extensive accommodations. All of these facilities entail day-to-day running costs for building maintenance; for furnishings and toilet facilities; for light, heat, and air conditioning; and for cleaning and security services.

To assess the cost of all these jury facilities realistically would require a nationwide professional physical survey of courthouses. To remain conservative, the assessments here will be at a level that is surely no more than the most basic day-to-day running costs for the facilities. For each of the 1,582 counties with a population of less than twenty-five thousand, it is very conservative to estimate the cost of jury facilities, on average over the year, as $100 per week—or about $5,000 per year. Using now the same proportions in relation to the size of counties as in estimating employee numbers, for each of the 1,035 counties with a population between twenty-five thousand and one hundred thousand, a conservative estimate for the annual cost of jury facilities is $10,000. Similarly, for each of the 415 counties with a population between one hundred thousand and five hundred thousand, a conservative estimate for the annual cost of jury facilities is $30,000. For each of the 112 counties with a population over five hundred thousand, it is $60,000. The total annual cost of jury facilities is then $37,430,000. Note that this includes no provision for the substantial costs of hotel accommodation when a jury in a criminal case is sequestered.

There is also a cost entailed in producing and mailing nearly thirty-two mil-lion summonses per year. As discussed earlier, ten cents per summons is a lower-bound estimate for this. The total annual cost of mailing summonses is then over $3 million.

Rounding down, the lower-bound estimate for the total annual administra-tive cost of the jury system is now $265 million.

TRIAL COSTS OF THE JURY SYSTEM

Various procedures specific to a jury trial take up time that is not required with a bench trial, and this additional trial time is costly.

The extensive American *voir dire* process is notorious for taking up a great deal of time. More than sixty years ago, the Supreme Court complained: "one of the features which has tended to discredit jury trials is interminable examination and rejection of prospective jurors." The situation may well be worse now. In a major trial nowadays, *voir dire* may even involve several attorneys at the same time, since while one is doing the actual questioning, others "are paying less attention to the answers jurors are giving from the jury box and more attention to their computer screens as they furiously type the prospective jurors' names into . . . search engines" to investigate them.[12]

In a recent case, *voir dire* took forty-three days of court time, with nine hundred prospective jurors being questioned to select the twelve jurors plus three alternates required. Although this is unusually long for jury selection, there is no suggestion that it is the longest period on record. Certainly, it is quite common for jury selection in court to take two or more days. It surely averages at more than two hours, and this period will be taken here as a conservative lower-bound estimate.[13]

Additionally, the process of a jury trial is quite different from that of a bench trial. Attorneys in a jury trial must dramatize their presentation to keep the attention and interest of the jury;[14] doing this in a bench trial would merely try the patience of the judge. Attorneys in a jury trial, and the judge also, must take pains to ensure that the jury understands what is going on, which can demand a good deal of time-consuming repetition.

The judge's summing-up, incorporating various instructions that she needs to give to the jury, also takes up significant time. For example, in the frequent situation of a criminal trial involving eyewitness identification testimony, the trial judge is expected to give special detailed instructions to avoid the danger of the jury relying too easily on such inherently weak testimony.[15]

All this takes up time in a trial. The conservative estimate here is to allow for each of the two parties an average period of one hour for additional time, beyond what would be required in a bench trial, spent examining and cross-examining witnesses, and one half hour for addressing the jury, and also to allow an average period of one half hour for the judge's summing-up. So, overall, this conservatively estimates the average total additional time required for a jury trial over a bench trial, including *voir dire*, at five and a half hours.

Every trial requires the continuing presence of a judge and of court officials, including a clerk or reporter and a bailiff or security guard. The great majority of trials also require the continuing presence of at least one attorney for each of the two parties.

In general, private parties pay the fees for their own attorneys, but the salaries and benefits of judges and other court officials are paid out of government accounts. The fees for court-appointed defense attorneys are also paid out of government accounts. But recall that in estimating the cost of the jury system to society, it makes no difference whether a private party or government pays any part of that cost.

These costs will vary enormously. At the high end, civil litigation between large corporations will require several highly paid attorneys for each party continuously present in the courtroom. Their fees alone may easily amount to several thousand dollars per hour. At the low end, criminal trials of indigent defendants are far cheaper. Some of the states pay meager salaries to public prosecutors and only a low fixed sum per case to court-appointed defense attorneys. Yet even here, the cost of judge, court officials, and attorneys, including salaries, benefits, fees, and overhead, will certainly reach into many hundreds of dollars per hour. As an average over all jury trials, civil and criminal, $400 per hour is surely a conservative lower-bound estimate of the total cost of all these persons together.

This gives an average additional cost per trial on account of the jury system of five and a half hours at $400 per hour, amounting to $2,200. About 150,000 jury trials take place each year.[16] So a lower-bound estimate of the total annual additional trial costs on account of the jury system is $330 million.

THE JURY-TRIAL CONSULTING INDUSTRY

There is a major industry devoted to consulting and research on every aspect of jury trials. A typical firm claims to have studied more than fourteen thousand jury trials over the past twenty-five years. A litigating party that hires this or any similar firm can call on numerous services. The firm will create profiles of the local populace and develop questionnaires for the party's attorneys to use in *voir dire*. It will provide a so-called shadow jury that matches the profile of the actual jury, and have these shadow jurors sit as members of the public in the courtroom. The party's attorneys can audition their witnesses in front of the shadow jury to polish their presentation, and can interview the shadow jurors each evening to obtain feedback on such matters as the effectiveness of the attorneys' presentation and witness testimony.[17]

There are many such firms, and they command substantial fees.[18] From the point of view of society, the entire jury-trial consulting industry constitutes a cost of the jury system. This is because resources such as the time and skill of everyone engaged in this industry are being channeled into the jury system, rather than being deployed elsewhere in our society.

A full decade ago, it was estimated that "trial consulting has mushroomed into a $400 million industry [annually] with over 700 practitioners and over

Table 2.1   The Annual Cost of the American Jury System

Cost of person-days spent serving on jury panels	360,000,000
Cost of person-days spent by persons summoned for jury duty who do not ultimately serve	720,000,000
Administrative costs of the jury system	265,000,000
Trial costs of the jury system	330,000,000
Cost of the jury-trial consulting industry	400,000,000
Total	$ 2,075,000,000

For each listed item of expenditure on the jury system, this chapter derives a conservative lower-bound estimate. Adding these estimates yields an assessment of the annual cost of the jury system at over $2 billion each year. This does not include a range of additional costs that are not readily quantifiable.

400 firms."[19] It has surely mushroomed further since then, but to maintain a conservative approach, the estimate for the current annual cost of this industry will be taken as the decade-old estimate of $400 million.

ASSESSMENT OF THE COST OF THE JURY SYSTEM

Adding together the lower-bound estimates for the various items of expenditure that have been considered gives an assessment of the current annual cost of the American jury system. This appears in Table 2.1. It amounts to over $2 billion per year. This may be small relative to the American economy as a whole, but it is large enough to make it worth considering what benefit the jury system brings to our society. In any event, this assessment certainly underestimates the actual full economic cost of the jury system, as explained next.

COSTS NOT READILY QUANTIFIABLE

There are further costs of running the jury system that were not included previously because no adequate data are readily available to quantify them. It is possible to cover only a sampling of them.

Study, Research, and Skills Development

Investigation and study of the jury system give rise to costs that must be ascribed to the jury system. For example, within the National Center for State Courts, the Center for Jury Studies employs several staff to conduct projects and publish reports on the jury system. Government bears part of the cost of this entity, with various voluntary contributors bearing the remainder of the cost.[20] As explained earlier, the fact that a voluntary contribution serves to defray an expense of the jury system does not affect the status of that expense as a cost of the jury system to our society.

Individual states also conduct their own studies of their particular jury systems, as do nongovernment entities within states.[21] All the costs of these are costs of the jury system.

The National Center for State Courts joins with other government entities in sponsoring conferences on the jury system. "In early 2001, a three-day 'jury summit,' sponsored by the National Center for State Courts, drew nearly four hundred judges, administrators, and academics to New York City."[22] The costs of organizing this conference, the value of the time of the participants, the cost of hotel accommodation in New York City,[23] and the cost of preparing and distributing the report are all further costs of the jury system.

Another cost is that of developing skills for arguing to the jury. This occupies a large proportion of the curriculum in trial-advocacy courses and seminars at law schools and in programs of continuing legal education. Also, law school courses and seminars on constitutional law, civil procedure, criminal procedure, and evidence all may include topics on the jury system. Substantial administrative, professorial, and student time and other resources are devoted to the jury-related aspects of these courses and programs. All of these resources constitute a further cost of the jury system to our society.

Litigation attorneys have to keep up with research on jury-trial strategies. The National Center for Jury Studies produces an online newsletter and regular columns in various court-related periodicals, and dozens of books are published on jury-trial strategy. The time that attorneys and others spend in reading these various publications is a further cost of the jury system.

The books published on jury-trial strategy are a tiny segment of the total output of publications relating to the jury system—of which this book is one. There are even entire books, as well as numerous articles in law journals, devoted to discussion and critique of the jury-trial consulting industry.[24] Books and articles on constitutional law, civil procedure, criminal procedure, and evidence may also include topics on the jury system.

The time and other resources spent in producing these countless books and articles (or topics in books and articles) constitute a further cost of the jury system. This is because resources such as the time and skill of editors, authors, and others are being channeled into the jury system, rather than being deployed elsewhere in our society.

Rules of Trial Procedure and Evidence

Many of the rules of trial procedure and evidence exist solely because of the jury system. Many judges distrust juries, and this distrust has strongly influenced the rules that govern the conduct of trials. For example, the complex rules that determine whether evidence may be admitted or must be excluded "are designed in part to protect the lay jury from beguilement and inflammation."[25]

Recent developments in the English legal system demonstrate the influence of the jury system on the rules governing the conduct of trials. The recent abolition of jury trial for most civil disputes in England has resulted in a considerable simplification of rules of evidence and trial procedure in those cases.[26]

So a substantial part of the societal resources devoted in any way to the rules of trial procedure and evidence constitute a further cost of the jury system to our society. To get some idea of this, consider how the federal rules are crafted.[27] The Judicial Conference of the United States, an organ of the federal judiciary, is required by statute to carry on a continuous study of the operation of the federal courts, including the rules of civil and criminal procedure and of evidence. The Judicial Conference has established a standing committee, assisted by several advisory committees, all composed of federal judges, practicing lawyers, law professors, state chief justices, and representatives of the Department of Justice. Administrative and legal support is provided for these committees.

Any proposal for amendment of the rules goes through a time-consuming process involving a minimum of seven stages of formal comment and review, with public hearings. Plainly, this is a costly undertaking in terms of time and other resources. It seems impossible to obtain a monetary estimate for the proportion of these resources that can be attributed to the jury system, but it is clearly substantial.

Further Legal Proceedings

A considerable number of appeals from a jury-trial verdict raise some matter regarding the jury. For example, many disputes arise over jury selection, over the trial judge's instructions to the jury, over the trial judge's removal of a juror during deliberations for alleged misconduct, or over juror misconduct discovered during or after the trial. Disputes also arise over the division of fact-finding responsibilities between the jury in the trial and the judge in the sentencing hearing (see chapter 10). In many cases, some matter related to the jury is a crucial ground, or even the sole ground, for an appeal from the trial court's decision.

There are also many cases where some jury-related matter is the basis of a habeas corpus challenge in federal district court to a criminal conviction in state court. These federal district court proceedings take place before a judge without a jury, so that the costs of them have not been included in the quantified estimates of the costs of the jury system. The federal district court decision is, of course, subject to appeal. There are cases that have gone through all three levels of federal courts—district court, appellate court, and Supreme Court—on a habeas corpus challenge, on the sole issue of whether the judge's instruction to the jury was proper. The entire cost of all of these further judicial proceedings is a cost of the jury system.[28]

A recent case of misconduct involving the jury illustrates how costs can multiply. The defendant was convicted of rape and murder in a Georgia state trial, and sentenced to death. After the trial, defense counsel learned that "either during or immediately following the penalty phase, some jury members gave the trial judge chocolate shaped as male genitalia and the bailiff chocolate shaped as female breasts."[29] The resulting issues of trial fairness have been raised in the state appellate court, state supreme court, federal district court, federal appellate court, and the Supreme Court. At the time of writing, the Supreme Court has vacated the judgment of the federal appellate court and remanded the case to that court for further consideration.

So this misconduct by jurors is responsible for absorbing the resources of our society in at least six judicial proceedings, apart from the original trial proceedings. The misconduct in this case is bizarre, but the number of subsequent judicial proceedings is quite typical. All the costs of and associated with these proceedings are further costs of the jury system.

Various other legal proceedings also result from the jury system. For example, a number of indigent criminal defendants, particularly in capital-murder cases, have applied to the court for a jury-trial consultant paid from public funds, claiming this to be part of their constitutional right to counsel.[30] The cost of the resulting judicial procedures is a further cost of the jury system.

Juror Hardship

The lower-bound estimate obtained earlier of the cost of time spent serving on juries included the value of work and other activities that could not be undertaken during the period of jury duty, However, it did not take into account a range of burdens that jury duty imposes.

The disruption of normal life is itself a burden on jurors, particularly in long trials. This disruption entails costs beyond simply the value of work not done. Some of these costs will be direct monetary costs, while others appear as emotional stresses that would need to be interpreted in monetary terms to be incorporated into a cost estimate. In any event, all of them are costs of the jury system that have not previously been taken into account.

Also, some trials can impose a particular emotional stress. The National Center for State Courts explains: "Some cases expose jurors to evidence that must be considered as beyond any juror's consideration of reality, and they may be asked to make decisions ... that are beyond any decision they have ever considered before. Yet we expect them to set this aside and return to their daily life as if this can be rationally put behind them."[31] Such stresses certainly impose a social cost, but this would need to be interpreted in monetary terms to be incorporated into a cost estimate.

Overall, it is safe to conclude that the real cost of the jury system is far more than the assessment of readily quantifiable costs, which came to about $2 billion per year. The real cost may well be at least several times more than this.

Chapter 3

Citizens as Jurors in the Justice System

Although a jury summons is an order from government to participate in the justice system, a person who serves on a trial jury does not become part of government for the duration of the trial. He remains a private citizen. As explained in chapter 1, it is this that allows the jury system to give legitimacy to trial decisions.

The importance of the jury being composed of private citizens has long been recognized. Over a hundred and fifty years ago, the Supreme Court distinguished jury trial "as a determination of the rights of the subject or citizen by his fellow subjects or citizens . . . [rather than] by the action of mere officials or creatures of the government."[1]

As this Court opinion makes clear, there is a separation between the people and the government. This is true even though America, as a republic and representative democracy, may aspire to live up to Abraham Lincoln's inspired declaration of "government of the people, by the people, for the people."[2] This declaration expresses a relationship, actual or desired, between the people and the government, but does not pretend that the people and the government are one and the same. In fact, the entire American constitutional system, with its separation of powers, is predicated on the need to constrain the powers of government in relation to the people, and this acknowledges the distinction between the two.

The position of judges may at first seem ambiguous. A judge may appear to be separate from both the government and the people when she adjudicates a civil dispute between private parties. She may appear to be on the side of the people against government when she intervenes against the government executive in favor of individual citizens, and on the side of government against the people when she refuses to intervene. Yet in all these cases the judge acts as an official of government. As a member of the Supreme Court has acknowledged: "Judges, it is sometimes necessary to remind ourselves, are part of the State—and an increasingly bureaucratic part of it, at that."[3]

A judge who intervenes against the government executive in favor of individual citizens performs the crucial function of constraining government power within the bounds of the constitutional and legal framework (that is, the constitutional and legal framework as the judiciary interprets it). In this way, the judiciary maintains the constitutional state. But it does so as one branch of government in relation to another branch of government. The judge may well defer to the government executive in the next case. This does not mean that the judge has "changed sides." It is merely part of the normal process of government in a constitutional state in which the executive, legislative, and judicial powers of the government are separated.

So a person who serves on a jury does so in a context defined and to a great extent controlled by government. That context is the entire justice system. Surprisingly little direct information is available as to what the citizenry, as prospective jurors, think of the justice system, and of the jury system itself. Rather, views about the justice system, and the jury system within it, are mostly found in statements by government officials such as prosecutors and judges, in publications of government departments, and in publications of institutions that are closely associated with government. Institutions of this kind include state bar associations, as well as organizations such as the American Legislative Exchange Council that include government officials and private-sector policy advocates together in their membership.

Another way of putting this is that views on the justice system, and particularly on the jury system, mostly come from *authority figures*. Of course, there is no precise definition of an authority figure. However, it is still helpful to include institutions associated with government, along with government itself, as being the main sources of the views that have been expressed.

It is reasonable to give the views of authority figures a presumption of respect. Many authority figures have valuable expertise and experience, so it is fair to pay attention to their views and try to understand their position. Yet this presumption of respect should not be pressed too far. The citizens of a democracy have the responsibility to maintain a critical attitude toward authority and should not be excessively respectful of the views of authority figures. So it is appropriate to begin with the limited direct information available on the views of the citizenry itself.

PUBLIC ATTITUDE SURVEYS

The main sources of direct information on the views of the American citizenry are two nationwide surveys of public attitudes and one more local survey. One of the nationwide surveys was carried out by the American Bar Association (ABA) in the late 1990s, the other by the *Economist* journal in 2008. The local survey was carried out recently by the supreme courts and bar associations of Pennsylvania and Texas.

The *Economist* survey, which was carried out in both America and England, polled the views of one thousand adults in each of the two countries, selected as a sample of the general populace. The survey asked respondents to specify their level of trust for politicians, public administrative officials, and judges. Very few respondents were willing to give the desirable response, "trust a great deal," for any of these government officials. A mere 9 percent of American respondents gave judges a great deal of trust. English judges fared better, but even so only 16 percent of respondents gave them a great deal of trust. The figures for politicians, national and local, and for public administrative officials were even worse: no more than 3 percent of respondents in either country had a great deal of trust in any of these government officials.[4]

The ABA survey polled the views of one thousand American adults, selected as a sample of the general populace. The survey asked respondents to specify their level of confidence in various parts of the American system of government. Again, only a minority of respondents were willing to give the desirable response, "extremely/very confident," for any part of government. No more than about 25 percent of respondents had this degree of confidence in federal, state, or local executive or legislative branches of government.[5]

The justice system overall fared slightly better, but still only 30 percent of respondents were extremely/very confident in it. Respondents were also asked to specify their level of confidence in particular parts of the justice system, such as the judiciary, state and local courts, and federal courts. There was not much variance from the 30 percent figure, although there was a little more confidence in the federal courts than state and local courts. The Supreme Court was the subject of a separate question and turned out to be the most highly regarded of all institutions, with 50 percent of respondents extremely/very confident in it.

The survey also asked questions relating to the fairness of the justice system. Only 39 percent of respondents agreed with the statement, "In most cases, the courts treat all ethnic and racial groups the same," while 47 percent explicitly disagreed. Only 33 percent of respondents agreed with the statement, "Courts try to treat poor people and wealthy people alike," while 55 percent explicitly disagreed.[6] When respondents were presented with similar statements for law enforcement officials and police instead of the courts, their responses were virtually identical.

In addition, respondents were presented with the statement, "The justice system needs a complete overhaul." A full half of them agreed. This aptly summarizes the low opinion that a large proportion of the respondents held regarding the justice system.[7]

Only two very general questions in the ABA survey related to the jury system. When respondents were presented with the statement, "Juries are the most important part of our judicial system," 69 percent agreed. When respondents were presented with the statement, "The jury system is the most fair way to determine the guilt or innocence of a person accused of a crime," 78 percent agreed.[8]

The Pennsylvania and Texas surveys focused on the integrity of judges. These states are among the many where judges at all levels are elected in expensive campaigns. Both surveys found that over 80 percent of the public believe that contributions to the election campaigns of judges influence their court decisions.[9]

It appears then that a substantial majority of the populace view the justice system overall as unworthy of great trust or confidence, and not very likely to be fair. At the same time, they view the jury system as the most important and the fairest aspect of this generally unsatisfactory justice system. What is not clear from these surveys is whether people view the jury system as sufficient to redeem the shortcomings that they perceive in other parts of the justice system. The following discussion will develop a different way to explore this question.

PUBLIC NONCOMPLIANCE WITH THE JURY SUMMONS

Jury duty is compulsory, yet an enormous number of people do not comply. Some of them ignore the jury summons entirely. Others fill out and return the summons form as required, but then do not report to the courthouse on the appointed date. The level of noncompliance is so high that many jurisdictions, particularly in major cities, have difficulty in finding enough jurors to run their trial systems.

Among the many reports on this situation, one commentator declares that, following increases in no-show rates, nationally as many as two-thirds of the Americans summoned each year fail to report for jury duty, with some jurisdictions reporting as high as an 80 percent no-show rate. Another confirms that in some states turnout is as low as 20 percent. Yet another observes that poor juror turnout in several jurisdictions has reached crisis levels, with, in some urban jurisdictions, fewer than 10 percent of all summoned citizens showing up in court. Specific reported no-show rates are 65 percent of those summoned in Richmond, Virginia, 80 percent in Dallas and Houston, and 82 percent in the District of Columbia.[10]

These reports show an astonishing level of noncompliance. Recall, though, that the average "jury yield" nationwide is near 46 percent (see chapter 2). It follows that the overall national noncompliance level cannot be higher than 54 percent, and so the highest reported levels of noncompliance—on the order of 90 percent—cannot possibly occur in very many jurisdictions. It seems most likely that there is a somewhat higher level of compliance in some rural districts, which to a degree offsets very high levels of noncompliance in some urban districts.

However, it is clearly no exaggeration to estimate the overall national noncompliance level at 50 percent. This means that jury service is a legal obligation that a full half of American citizens bluntly disregard. More than thirty million jury summonses are issued each year, so every year more than fifteen million Americans disregard the jury summons.

THE RESPONSE OF AUTHORITY TO NONCOMPLIANCE

Jury trials require a continuing supply of jurors, so the widespread noncompliance with the jury summons is a serious problem for the justice system. Government authorities, as well as authority figures closely associated with government, have tried various ways to deal with this problem, but none of them have been very successful.

One approach has been to try to reduce the burden and improve the experience of jury duty, in the hope that this will make people less reluctant to perform jury duty. The *Criminal Courts Review*, although focusing on the problem in England, makes a number of proposals for improvement in the treatment of jurors that are equally relevant to the American situation. It suggests improving information for prospective jurors, shortening the length of jury duty by improving the efficiency of the system, improving facilities for jurors and prospective jurors, increasing compensation for jurors and prospective jurors, and showing appreciation to jurors for their service.[11]

Experience has shown that measures of this kind do work, but only to a very limited degree. Consider one of the most successful documented examples of this approach: "When fees [paid as compensation to jurors] are raised to a reasonable level, the increase in turnout is dramatic. El Paso, Texas, recently showed what can be done. Its juror response rate rose from 22 to 46 percent when the daily pay was raised from $6 to $40."[12] Certainly, more than doubling the juror response rate is a dramatic improvement. The trouble is that even the increased juror response rate comes nowhere near to solving the problem of noncompliance.

The fact is that even after juror compensation was raised, more than half the citizenry of El Paso continued to ignore the jury summons. The achieved response rate of 46 percent is still only the overall average nationwide level, which is the level that gives rise to continuing problems of juror supply. Even if improving the conditions of jury duty could solve the problem of noncompliance with the jury summons (which is frankly improbable), this would require a far greater increased expenditure on juror accommodation and compensation than either public funds or litigants could sustain.

A quite different approach to the problem of noncompliance is to impose penalties. There are statutory penalties for noncompliance in every state and in the federal justice system, but, for reasons to be discussed shortly, they are rarely enforced. However, from time to time a report does appear of some local jurisdiction trying to tackle the problem of noncompliance by actually imposing penalties. For example, a report from one district informs that noncompliance "had been a common problem because people were aware that nothing would happen to them. . . . Now, people are calling in to schedule their jury service after watching their neighbors get a visit from the sheriff." Another report, equally assured that imposing penalties will deal with the problem of noncompliance, declares: "By the time we arrest a few people, the response rate for jury service will go up further."[13]

Certainly, when people face the immediate prospect of a severe penalty for noncompliance with a jury summons, they will comply, even if very reluctantly:

> Madeline Byrne was making a quick trip to the grocery store to buy some cheese when a sheriff approached her car in the parking lot and slipped something through her open window.
>
> Byrne didn't get the cheese, but she did get a jury summons.
>
> The 64-year-old woman was ordered to report for jury duty a little more than an hour later at the Lee County courthouse in Sanford, North Carolina. When Byrne protested, the sheriff told her: "Be there or you'll be in contempt."
>
> "I wasn't too happy," said Byrne, one of at least a dozen people handed summonses at random in March [2007] outside a Food Lion and Wal-Mart.[14]

Some authority figures believe that the penalties for noncompliance should be more severe. Along these lines, the American Legislative Exchange Council has drafted a legislative proposal that it calls the Jury Patriotism Act. Several states have wholly or partly enacted it into law, or are considering doing so. The Council's proposal for the Act declares: "The intent of the model act is to communicate to jurors the importance of jury service and to notify them that shirking one's civic obligation to serve will be severely punished. Those who fail to appear for jury service will have a criminal record, a threat sufficient to cause one to pause before ignoring a juror summons."[15]

Yet despite legislative proposals such as this and occasional spates of local enforcement activity, it is rare that anyone actually suffers a penalty for noncompliance with a jury summons. Most jurisdictions take no action at all against people who ignore the jury summons. An obvious reason is that it is simply impracticable to enforce the penalties for noncompliance. More than fifteen million Americans every year disregard the jury summons. Government does not have the resources to pursue more than the tiniest proportion of these, so most of the time the risk of punishment for noncompliance is far too low to make much difference to how people regard a jury summons.

Another, more fundamental reason is that enforcing, or even threatening, severe penalties for noncompliance with the jury summons is likely to be counterproductive. As law professor and experienced public defender Randolph Jonakait explains, "lawyers and litigants are concerned that people too much coerced into jury duty will be hostile and bad jurors whose efforts to listen and deliberate carefully will be suspect."[16] Likewise, the *Criminal Courts Review*, although focusing on the problem of noncompliance in England, makes valid points that are equally relevant to the American situation:

> It is vital for the criminal justice system and public confidence in it that everyone qualified for jury service does it with a good will and regards it as time well spent.... Jurors who are unhappy with their lot may lack the will or the ability to do their job properly; and, as the largest section of the public closely exposed to the workings of the ... [court system], they are likely to make poor ambassadors for it.[17]

This explains why an important study on improving juror response rates in the District of Columbia proposes, as its first recommendation, "that the courts use positive means to encourage participation in the jury system. The imposition of available sanctions for delinquent jurors should be administered cautiously."[18] In fact, most jurisdictions, most of the time, are well aware that enforcing or threatening severe penalties to press people into jury duty is likely to be counterproductive. As a result, the fact that there are penalties for noncompliance on the statute books does not have much overall long-term effect on the level of compliance.

Another approach that authority figures have taken to the problem of noncompliance with the jury summons is to malign the people who do not comply. One writer contrasts them with the "good citizens" who do comply. Dwyer dismisses them as "shirkers." The Jury Patriotism Act characterizes noncompliance as "shirking one's civic obligation." The very title of this act equates noncompliance with a lack of patriotism. This is plainly intentional, as the American Legislative Exchange Council proposal for this act declares with emotive fervor: "The privileged should not be allowed to escape jury duty, *as some escaped military service in Vietnam*."[19] However, as the following discussion will explain, such character traits as shirking and lack of patriotism cannot fully explain the widespread noncompliance with the jury summons.

WHY PEOPLE OBEY OR DISOBEY THE LAW

Authority figures like to believe that a full half of Americans do not comply with the jury summons simply because they regard jury duty as a burden that they can likely avoid without being penalized. But is this really how all these people regard the legal obligation to perform jury duty?

Researchers in social behavior draw a well-established distinction between *instrumental* and *normative* perspectives on why people obey the law. The following discussion of this distinction and its significance in society draws on groundbreaking work by law and psychology professor Tom Tyler.

The instrumental perspective is that people decide whether to obey the law solely on the basis of a cost-benefit analysis. They weigh up the costs and benefits likely to derive from obeying the law and the penalties likely to ensue for not obeying the law. They will then obey the law if, but only if, the net cost of obeying is less than the net cost of disobeying.[20] In blunt terms, this perspective is that people will violate the law whenever they can get away with it to their advantage.

This is essentially the perspective that so many authority figures believe explains widespread noncompliance with the jury summons. It is because they believe this that their attempts to increase compliance focus on the purely instrumental factors of reducing the burden of jury duty and threatening penalties for noncompliance. However, as previously discussed, this approach has very little effect on the overall level of compliance.

The normative perspective is in sharp contrast. According to this perspective, whether someone obeys the law depends on her own internal normative sense. There are two aspects to this. One is that a person will obey the law in general if she considers the government to be legitimate—that is, to have the right to promulgate laws. The other is that she will obey a specific law if she considers that law to be just and morally right.[21]

Tyler's key finding, based on careful studies conducted to high professional standards, is that the instrumental perspective is insufficient to explain why people obey the law. Rather, he finds that in practice:

> Normative concerns are an important determinant of law-abiding behavior. . . . The most important normative influence on compliance with the law is the person's assessment that following the law accords with his or her sense of right and wrong; a second factor is the person's feeling of obligation to obey the law and allegiance to legal authorities. . . . People

generally feel that law breaking is morally wrong, and that they have a strong obligation to obey laws even if they disagree with them.[22]

It is really just as well that people do internalize the obligation to obey the law, because otherwise society could not function. As Tyler explains, "in democratic societies the legal system cannot function if it can influence people only by manipulating rewards and costs. This type of leadership is impractical because government is obliged to produce benefits or exercise coercion every time it seeks to influence citizens' behavior. These strategies consume large amounts of public resources and such societies would be in constant peril of disequilibrium and instability."[23]

Similarly, philosophy professor Mortimer R. Kadish and law professor Sanford H. Kadish insist on the "distinction . . . between modes of social control that operate by the threat of sanctions and modes of social control that operate by virtue of their authority." As they explain, the operation of the law must rely mainly on the authority of law rather than the threat of sanctions under the law, at least in a democratic society "where government has no impenetrable shield to protect it from the governed and very modest resources at best to carry out its threats."[24]

Of course, instrumental factors do have some influence on the extent to which people—Americans or anyone else—obey the law. If compliance with a law is burdensome, more people will violate the law if the penalty is slight and unlikely to be imposed than if the penalty is severe and likely to be imposed. This is obvious, and it would be disingenuous to suggest otherwise.

Yet it is nonetheless true that the vast majority of Americans have a strong internalized normative sense of commitment toward the law that leads them generally to obey it. In the main, we are law-abiding citizens. It is simply not true that a full half of Americans are unpatriotic shirkers who will violate the law whenever they can get away with it to their advantage. On the contrary, when we recognize our legal obligations, we do not need to watch our neighbors get a visit from the sheriff before we comply. American society could not function otherwise.

However, a full half of these generally law-abiding citizens do not have any strong internalized normative sense of commitment to jury duty. They do not feel that it is morally wrong to break the law regarding jury duty, although they do feel that it is morally wrong to break other laws. They do not feel that government has a legitimate demand on them for jury duty, although they do feel that government has a legitimate demand on them regarding other laws. These people do not *shirk* jury duty; they *reject* jury duty.[25]

Authority figures have focused their attention on what might be amiss with people who fail to comply with the legal obligation of jury duty. But it is also fair to ask what might be amiss with jury duty, given that it fails to engender the kind of internalized normative sense of commitment that other legal obligations do. In other words, what makes people reject (rather than merely shirk) jury duty?

NORMATIVE FACTORS IN THE REJECTION OF JURY DUTY

Judges and other authorities are generally very reluctant to recognize that people might reject (rather than merely shirk) jury duty. However, they have acknowledged this in some limited settings.

One well-known setting in American courts concerns the Amish. The tenets of this group reject most forms of participation in the justice system, including jury duty. These tenets are certainly normative positions, which stem, in this case, from religious beliefs. Amish individuals called for jury duty routinely request excusal on the basis of these views. Judges do not normally berate these individuals as "shirkers" but instead routinely grant the request.[26]

Some other countries and regions have provisions dealing with objections to jury duty. The usual form is that the judge has discretion to grant or refuse a prospective juror's application for excusal. This was the case in England with a Practice Direction concerning "conscientious objection" that prescribed that "[e]ach such application should be dealt with sensitively and sympathetically." Provisions of this kind are found in some Australian states and New Zealand, Hong Kong, and Scotland. These provisions have been applied to excuse members of certain religious groups from jury duty, in much the same way as with the Amish in America.[27] But there appears to be no information regarding what other objections to jury duty have been raised and how judges have responded.

There is another setting in American courts where normative factors can be seen to result in excusal from jury duty, although here the court rather than the juror initiates the process. This setting concerns murder cases in which the death penalty may be imposed. In some states, prospective jurors may be questioned in *voir dire* about their attitude to the death penalty. Anyone who admits to principled objections to execution, and professes himself unwilling to set aside his objections under any circumstances, is simply excluded from the jury in the given case. This results in a so-called death-qualified jury.[28]

Going beyond the specific settings of exemption on the basis of membership of particular religious groups or principled objection to execution, it is not difficult to conceive of other normative factors that could lead people to reject jury duty. The surveys of public attitudes discussed earlier showed that most people do not have strong confidence in the American justice system, do not feel that in most cases the courts treat all ethnic and racial groups the same, and do not feel that courts try to treat poor people and wealthy people alike. The great majority believe that contributions to the election campaigns of state judges influence their court decisions. Overall, a full half of those surveyed felt that the justice system needs a complete overhaul.

Among commentators, Paul Butler, a law professor and former federal prosecutor, describes American criminal justice as "one particularly destructive instrument of white supremacy." Henry Louis Gates Jr. notes with approval the saying, "When white folks say 'justice,' they mean 'just us.' " Many others have expressed similar attitudes.[29]

For any of the many people who hold negative views of the American justice system, the prospect of jury duty must raise difficult normative issues. The jury system gives legitimacy to trial decisions, and surely anyone who believes that the justice system is unfair is bound to have mixed feelings about helping, as a juror, to give it legitimacy. As Butler declares: "The American criminal justice system is so dysfunctional that it presents well-intentioned people with a dilemma. Should good people cooperate with it?"[30]

According to the ABA Survey, a large majority of people view the jury as the most important and the fairest aspect of the judicial system. This presents the question of whether people view the jury system as sufficient to redeem the shortcomings that they perceive in other parts of the justice system. Plainly, for someone summoned for jury duty this will depend on what he sees as his potential role. In particular, it will depend on whether he believes that, as a juror, he will be able to influence the trial in which he participates toward a fair outcome. As parts III, IV, and V will explain, the jury does have the power to make a fair trial outcome more likely, and even has the responsibility to do so. People who are aware of this capacity of the jury may affirmatively wish to perform jury duty, so as to exert a meaningful influence on the justice system (see chapter 12).

However, many authority figures, and particularly judges, instruct jurors that their role is strictly defined by the court, and that this role is narrow, limited, and essentially powerless (see chapter 9). In blunt terms, people are led to believe that jury duty is a relatively insignificant role that is closely controlled by a justice system that they do not respect. It is then hardly surprising that many people do not develop an internalized normative sense of commitment to jury duty as a legal obligation.

People are not likely to form a commitment to participate in a system that they do not respect, unless perhaps they feel that they might be able to influence it to the good. As a compelling example, John Martin, a federal district judge who resigned in 2003, wrote at the time: "When I took my oath of office 13 years ago I never thought that I would leave the federal bench . . . [but] I no longer want to be part of our unjust criminal justice system."[31] We know that a large proportion of the American populace shares this judge's view that the criminal justice system is unjust. A good number of them are bound to share his resulting preference not to participate in it, as a normative basis for rejecting jury duty.

Part II

Myths about the Jury System

Chapter 4

The Myth of Improved Trial Outcomes

The regular trial task of juries is to determine the facts and apply the law to them to reach a verdict. But this is a task that judges also regularly perform. Most trials are bench trials, where the judge sits alone without a jury, and in these trials it is the judge who determines the facts and applies the law to them to reach a verdict. In assessing whether the jury system offers a sufficient benefit to our society to justify its costs, an immediate question, which this chapter considers, is whether juries perform this regular trial task better than judges.

This chapter does not deal at all with the political roles of the jury. These roles, which go beyond the jury's regular trial task of applying the law to the facts to reach its verdict, are considered in parts III, IV, and V.

Authority figures have made a variety of claims that juries do perform their regular trial task better than judges and so achieve better trial outcomes overall. A particular claim is that juries are overall more competent in assessing evidence, and another is that juries are overall fairer to the parties. This chapter assesses these and the various other claims, and shows that there is insufficient evidence to support any of them.

Note first, though, that this concerns only a small minority of trials, because substantial evidence shows that in the great majority of cases judge and jury would reach identical decisions. So in all these cases judge and jury would achieve equally good—or equally bad—trial outcomes.

The evidence comes from a serious of studies. In 1966, law professors Harry Kalven and Hans Zeisel published the results of a survey of trial judges conducting jury trials. After the jury retired to deliberate, but before it delivered its verdict, the participating judge specified how he would have decided the case. Over five hundred judges participated, covering more than thirty-five hundred criminal trials and four thousand civil trials. In almost four-fifths of both criminal and civil cases, judge and jury reached the same verdict.

There were problems with the methodology of this survey. Also, trials have changed in the fifty years since the survey data were collected. There are now more scientific evidence and more complex expert testimony, and more women and persons of color now serve on juries. For these reasons, several researchers carried out similar surveys with improved methodology in the 1990s and 2000s. All these surveys showed a level of agreement between judge and jury comparable to that found by Kalven and Zeisel.[1] So the question of whether jury trials offer improved outcomes is relevant only to the roughly one-fifth of jury trials—about thirty thousand each year—in which judge and jury would likely reach different verdicts.

THE JURY AS PEERS

The jurors in a criminal trial are often referred to as the "peers" of the defendant. In fact, arguments in favor of the jury system based on the idea of the jury as peers go back through several centuries. In 1682 William Penn, acting under the Charter for the Province of Pennsylvania granted to him the previous year by King Charles II of England, set out his Frame of Government of Pennsylvania. He specified certain "Laws Agreed upon in England," including: "That all trials shall be by twelve men, and as near as may be, peers or equals, and of the neighborhood." A century later we find in the Declaration and Resolves of the First Continental Congress: "That the respective colonies are entitled to the common law of England, and more especially to the great and inestimable privilege of being tried by their peers of the vicinage, according to the course of that law."[2]

The Supreme Court explained in the important 1879 case of *Strauder v West Virginia*: "The very idea of a jury is a body of men composed of the peers or equals of the person whose rights it is selected or summoned to determine; that is, of his neighbors, fellows, associates, persons having the same legal status in society as that which he holds." This was then as apt a statement of the doctrine of trial by a jury of one's peers as it would have been one or two centuries earlier. It is still an apt statement of that doctrine, as a current federal government publication declares that "a panel of one's fellow citizens—one's peers—are best qualified to judge guilt or innocence."[3]

These declarations by authority figures clearly describe the doctrine of the jury as peers. But the crucial question is whether this doctrine really describes the composition and role of the jury or is merely a myth without substantive evidence to support it. Certainly, in much earlier times this doctrine was no mere myth. As mentioned in chapter 1, the jury in medieval England was composed of the neighbors, fellows, and associates of the defendant, and this was essential to its role of determining whether he could be reabsorbed into the community. Possibly this was still the composition of the jury in parts of America when the Court decided *Strauder v West Virginia*. But in any event, this description of the jury is utterly divorced from present-day America.

A jury today will not include any "fellows" or "associates" of the defendant, because the prosecution would challenge for cause any prospective juror too closely acquainted with the defendant. Nor will the jury necessarily even include "neighbors" of the defendant. A criminal case is normally tried in the local jurisdiction where the crime was committed (courts rarely permit a change of venue), and the jury will be chosen from that locality. So jurors are more likely to be neighbors of any victims of the crime than of the defendant.

A broader interpretation of the idea of the jury as the peers of the defendant is that the jurors are to be members of the defendant's social and cultural community. Then, arguably, the jury is indeed "best qualified to judge guilt or innocence" because it is better able to understand and empathize with the defendant than a socially and culturally remote judge would be. This in itself could be a reasonable argument, because people might understand members of their own cultural community more easily and fully than anyone from outside that community does.[4]

The problem is that in practice the jury is not very likely to be matched socially or culturally to the defendant. As a result of legal developments in recent years, in most American judicial districts the list of persons who can be summoned for jury duty is generally reasonably representative of the populace of the district as a whole (see chapter 7). However, as the legal scholar William Stuntz observes, the major judicial districts today are metropolitan counties that include vast suburbs together with city neighborhoods. In a criminal trial, the defendant is likely to be from the higher-crime city, but the jurors may come from the culturally very different suburbs.[5]

Also, American society is heterogeneous, so that a broad range of social classes, languages, ethnicities, and religions may be represented on a jury.[6] This is especially so in the large metropolitan jurisdictions where most jury trials take place. Because of this, even the most basic communications can cause difficulties. In fact, this is an old problem. The 1702 New York trial of Nicholas Bayard for high treason was conducted in English, but the jury was "principally composed of Dutchmen, extremely ignorant of the English language." Communication remains a recurrent problem today, requiring courts to order language assistance for jurors unable to understand the proceedings at all.[7]

The prosecution may actually try to avoid having a social or cultural match between the defendant and the jurors. A typical illustration is a 1980s New

York state trial of a Latino defendant in a district with a substantial Latino population. Some witnesses were to testify in Spanish, and a certified court translator was to provide simultaneous translation into English. By law, the English version alone would constitute evidence; the Spanish spoken by the witnesses, or by the defendant, would not. So Latino prospective jurors who could not speak English were challenged by the prosecution and not empanelled, as they could not have understood the translator. Latino prospective jurors who were bilingual in English and Spanish were also not empanelled if they could not persuade the prosecution that they would "accept the translator as the final arbiter of the witnesses' responses."[8] The result was that no Latino juror was empanelled.

Of course, there is no reason to suppose that a judge will be socially or culturally any closer to the defendant. The point, though, is that there is really no evidence to support a preference for a jury over a judge in terms of being a social or cultural match to a criminal defendant.

This also applies to civil cases, where authority figures still present the same argument for the jury system. A typical example is a 1990s case alleging workplace sexual harassment, where the federal district judge had dismissed the case on the ground that the alleged conduct did not constitute impermissible sexual harassment. The appellate court granted the plaintiff's request for a jury trial: "The line between the permissible and the impermissible in this case must be drawn by a jury of the appellant's [—that is, the plaintiff's—] peers." The court argued that "a federal judge . . . usually lives in a narrow segment of the enormously broad American socio-economic spectrum, generally lacking the current real-life experience required in interpreting subtle sexual dynamics of the workplace based on nuances, subtle perceptions, and implicit communications." A jury, in contrast, would be "made up of a cross-section of our heterogeneous communities."[9]

The problem with this court's argument is that each juror also "lives in a narrow segment of the enormously broad American socio-economic spectrum." A jury of no more than a dozen people could cover only a tiny range of narrow segments of the enormously broad American socioeconomic spectrum. Yet these jurors would have to comprehend and—despite being a heterogeneous group—reach agreement on interpreting the subtle sexual dynamics of the particular workplace culture of the plaintiff in the case. Regardless of the court's assurance, there is no evidence that such a jury would do a better job of this than would a judge.

So there is ultimately nothing to support the idea that the jury as the "peers" of the defendant or of a party to a case is (as the government publication declares) "best qualified to judge" the situation, in terms of the regular trial task of determining the facts and applying the law to them to reach a verdict. Insofar as there is value in the notion of the jury as peers achieving better trial outcomes, it does not concern what the jury might be "best qualified" to do. It lies in the fact that, as the Court said in *Strauder v West Virginia*, the jury is composed of "persons having the same legal status in society" as the person whose rights it is to determine. That is, crucially, jurors are private citizens rather than government. By virtue of being private citizens, they are the "peers" of the defendant; and as private citizens they are concerned for the justice of the trial decision.

Concern for the justice of the trial decision may even lead jurors on occasion to set aside the law in favor of what they perceive as justice to one of their fellow private citizens—their peers. The potential to act in this way in appropriate cases is crucial to the role of the jury, but it goes beyond the subject of this chapter, which deals only with the regular trial task of determining the facts and applying the law to them to reach a verdict. Rather, the concern of jurors for the justice of the trial decision, and the capacity to set aside the law in appropriate cases, entail the political roles of the jury, which is the subject of parts III, IV, and V.

COMMUNITY VALUES AND INTERESTS

Another repeated theme in arguments for the jury system is that it supports community values and interests. Plainly, this can only be an argument in favor of the jury system if it is first accepted that trial verdicts ought to support community values and interests. So there are two distinct points of argument here. The first point is that how the law is interpreted or enforced should reflect community values and interests. The second point is that a jury is better able than a judge to take this into account, in terms of the regular trial task of determining the facts and applying the law to them to reach a verdict.

An illustration for this first point of argument comes from the criminal law regarding distribution of obscene materials. Written materials are generally protected from government regulation by the guarantee of freedom of speech in the First Amendment to the federal Constitution. The First Amendment is directly applicable to the federal government, and the Supreme Court has interpreted the Fourteenth Amendment to the federal Constitution to mean that the states must also comply with this First Amendment guarantee.[10] However, the Court has also held that obscene materials fall outside First Amendment protection. The question then is what standards are to determine whether material is deemed obscene. In 1973, the Court held in *Miller v California* that it was appropriate for a state court to determine this by local state standards rather than national standards: "It is neither realistic nor constitutionally sound to read the First Amendment as requiring that the people of Maine or Mississippi accept public depiction of conduct found tolerable in Las Vegas, or New York City."[11]

The second point of argument now becomes relevant to the comparison between jury and judge that is the present issue. That is, in a case such as *Miller v California*, the question here is whether a jury or a judge is better able to determine whether the materials at issue are obscene by local state standards. In general, the present question is whether, in a case where the substantive law requires community values and interests to be invoked, a judge or a jury is better able to identify those values and interests and apply the law accordingly.

In any such case, community values and interests must, of course, be identified in the only way acceptable in a court of law: on the basis of the evidence presented at trial. So, for example, in *Miller v California* the prosecution put its "expert on community standards"[12] on the witness stand to testify as to California values regarding obscenity. Whoever has the task of deciding the facts—whether judge or jury—must assess the testimony of such experts, along with any other evidence presented, as to what community values and interests are. This is just as is done with the evidence in every trial.

The question then is whether a jury is likely to be more competent than a judge in assessing evidence as to what community values and interests are, and applying the law accordingly. But this is just a particular instance of the general question of whether a jury is likely to be overall more competent than a judge in assessing evidence and applying the law accordingly. The relative competence of judge and jury is the next topic for discussion in this chapter, and the conclusion is that there is no serious evidence that a jury is likely to be overall more competent than a judge. There is no reason to suppose that cases requiring community values and interests to be identified are in any way exceptional. Even though a number of courts and commentators seem to assume, without giving any reasons, that a jury will be better at this task,[13] there is really no evidence to support this.

Yet, as mentioned earlier, concern for justice may lead jurors to set aside the law. They may do so on occasion in favor of community values and interests that they consider more significant than the letter of the law. This kind of jury behavior in appropriate cases is fundamentally important, but it goes beyond the subject of this chapter, which deals only with the regular trial task of determining the facts and applying the law to them to reach a verdict. Rather, this behavior entails the political roles of the jury, which is the subject of parts III, IV, and V.

JURY COMPETENCE

It is often claimed in support of the jury system that a jury is likely to be overall more competent than a judge, particularly in terms of deciding the facts in a case. So, for example, Jonakait broadly, and typically, asserts that "the data, evidence, history and logic have shown . . . that juries are better finders of fact than judges."[14] But none of the arguments presented in support of assertions such as this have any foundation in fact.

One argument rests on the idea that a jury is a better finder of fact than a judge simply because there are a number of jurors but only one judge. The source of this idea is an eighteenth-century work by the French philosopher and mathematician Condorcet on the application of probability theory to decision-making processes. This work was impressive in its time, and was an important precursor of the nineteenth-century trend to apply mathematical reasoning to the newly developing social sciences.[15]

This *Condorcet jury theorem* applies to group decision making in narrowly defined situations: the question to be decided must have just one correct answer and one incorrect answer, and each member of the group deciding the question must be more likely than not to choose the correct answer. Then straightforward mathematics shows that the larger the group, the greater is the probability of a correct majority decision.[16]

There is a vast literature on the Condorcet jury theorem that deals with its application to group decisions in many contexts, including trial decision making.[17] Yet despite this, it is not at all relevant to jury decisions in a present-day trial in a court of law. The theorem deals with the probability of a *majority* decision being correct, not the probability of a correct unanimous (or near-unanimous) decision as required of a trial jury. Also, the theorem presupposes that each member of the group decides independently of the others, but the members of a jury are expected to deliberate together to reach a joint decision in which each of them may have influenced and been influenced by the others. It is not possible to adapt Condorcet's theory mathematically to take account of these crucial differences.[18]

This does, though, raise the question whether groups that deliberate together reach better decisions than individuals deciding alone. A number of writers believe so, but the evidence is scanty. Studies on juries, mock juries, and other deliberative groups generally conclude that a group decision may be better or may be worse than any individual decision, depending greatly on the makeup of the group. Worse decisions may particularly result from "groupthink" that presses participants in a group towards conformity and uniformity in decision. Jury decisions are vulnerable to this; there are reported instances of jurors subjecting other jurors to extreme personal pressure to conform, even to the point of physical threats and attacks.[19]

Yet it is still frequently claimed that a jury, by virtue of how it is drawn from the community, is a group with special qualities, giving it increased competence in deciding the facts in a trial. An 1873 Supreme Court decision presents a typical version:

> Twelve men of the average of the community, comprising men of education and men of little education, men of learning and men whose learning consists only in what they have themselves seen and heard, the merchant, the mechanic, the farmer, the laborer; these sit together, consult, apply their separate experience of the affairs of life to the facts proven, and draw a unanimous conclusion. ... It is assumed that twelve men know more of the common affairs of life than does one man, that they can draw wiser and safer conclusions ... than can a single judge.[20]

This is in fact a typical expression of one of two sharply opposing views of the competence of the jury that dominate debate on the subject. It may be called the *levelheaded-jury view*. The opposing view expresses a low regard for the competence, and the expected behavior, of the people who sit on juries. It may be called the *unsound-jury view*.

The unsound-jury view is widespread and a staple of American popular humor. The humorist Dave Barry has declared: "The Sixth Amendment [to the Constitution] states that if you are accused of a crime, you have the right to a trial before a jury of people too stupid to get out of jury duty." This echoes Mark Twain's famous jibe: "We have a criminal jury system which is superior to any in the world; and its efficiency is only marred by the difficulty of finding twelve men every day who don't know anything and can't read." Similarly, in England the *Criminal Courts Review* notes that many of its contributors felt "that jury service is only for those not ... clever enough to get out of it."[21]

From time to time, incidents of jury behavior that can only support the unsound-jury view come to light. In a 1980s case, a juror made a sworn post-trial statement (supported by the statements of two other jurors) to the effect that during the trial several jurors drank as much as a quart of wine apiece during lunch recess, smoked marijuana regularly, and ingested cocaine, and that some of the jurors were falling asleep during the trial. A number of incidents of unsound-jury behavior occurring over the years have involved juror intoxication.[22]

A recent illustration of unsound-jury behavior comes from a Georgia case, noted in chapter 2, in which the jury imposed the death penalty on the defendant, and "either during or immediately following the penalty phase, some jury members gave the trial judge chocolate shaped as male genitalia and the bailiff chocolate shaped as female breasts."[23] Admittedly, these jurors may have reached a reasonably competent decision within the context of Georgia law even in the frame of mind that these gifts reveal. But to determine while in such a frame of mind that a human being should be put to death surely qualifies as unsound-jury behavior.

Other countries with a common-law jury system have also experienced unsound-jury behavior. An Australian trial had to be aborted after three months when it was discovered that five jurors, including the forewoman, had been playing the currently popular numbers game sudoku during the trial proceedings since the second week of the trial. The forewoman in fact "admitted to having spent more than half of her time in court playing the game." Notably, in the course of those weeks of trial "105 witnesses, including 20 police, had been in the witness box and not seen what was happening."[24]

In one English trial for murder, four jurors, including the foreman, set up a makeshift Ouija board during a break from formal deliberations in an attempt to make contact with the spirit of the murder victim. The spirit purportedly spelled out "Vote guilty tomorrow," which the jury unanimously did. The Court of Appeal ordered a retrial.[25]

When unsound-jury behavior is discovered during the course of a trial, it may lead to the trial being aborted and, usually, a retrial being ordered. But when such behavior comes to light only after the conclusion of a trial, courts will refuse to allow any inquiry—thus upholding the trial verdict—unless the circumstances are most exceptional. American courts have refused to inquire into allegations of juror intoxication, insanity, or mental incompetence, inability to understand English (the language of the trial proceedings), and having a hearing impairment that interfered with understanding the trial proceedings. The Supreme Court has explained that "the community's trust in a system that relies on the decisions of laypeople would . . . be undermined by a barrage of postverdict scrutiny of juror conduct."[26] This does rather suggest that the community's trust is maintained only by a refusal to inquire into unsound-jury behavior.

In any event, there is no substantial evidence as to how extensive unsound-jury behavior is. But there is also no substantial evidence as to how well juries live up to the very positive levelheaded-jury view. Both views have many supporters, yet there is really no evidence to determine which view comes closer to the reality of jury competence and behavior.

A topic that raises particular concerns about jury competence is that of complex cases, particularly those involving technical or scientific issues. Many people have doubted the capacity of juries to deal with cases in areas where jurors (and, for that matter, judges) are likely to be unqualified.[27] This often involves weighing the testimony of the experts that each side has put on the witness stand. Jonakait provides a helpful summary of the very limited research on whether a jury or a judge is likely to be more competent, and reasonably concludes that "we simply lack the information to decide which will be the better choice in a particular case."[28]

In sum, there is ultimately no basis for concluding that a jury is generally more competent, or less competent, than a judge in deciding the facts of a case and applying the law accordingly.

JUROR EXPERTISE

Another claim made in support of the jury system is that jurors bring a range of forms of expert knowledge into deliberations. This claim is closely related to the general claim of greater jury competence, but it is more convenient to treat it separately. Certainly, jurors do bring various forms of expert knowledge, or claims to possess expert knowledge, into jury deliberations. But it is questionable whether this is a benefit or a detriment of the jury system.

Certainly, some commentators argue that juror expert knowledge is a benefit of the jury system. So, for example, James Levine, dean of a New York college of criminal justice, served on a jury that had to decide whether an injury acquired in a public brawl was inflicted intentionally or accidentally. Levine reportedly approved of a fellow juror's claimed expertise: "I got educated by a guy who had an education in street fighting. He knew what blows you use to hurt and not hurt. He educated me, with all my degrees." Jonakait comments: "As a result, Levine rendered a more fully considered verdict than he would have had he been acting in isolation, as a judge in a bench trial would have."[29]

Among other commentators approving of juror expert knowledge, law professor Martha Minow criticizes the exclusion of a bilingual Latino juror in a case, discussed earlier, where evidence was given in Spanish: "This Spanish-proficient juror might base judgment on information unavailable to other jurors and this juror might claim special knowledge and authority in the course of the jury deliberations. Why are these worrisome instead of desirable traits for a juror?" Jonakait presents a similar argument regarding probabilistic data: "Most of us—judges included—are not competent to assess probabilistic data. With a jury, however, especially a twelve-person jury, there is a reasonable chance that at least one juror would know how to assess such information and be able to explain the approach to her colleagues on the jury."[30]

The problem, though, is that a juror who claims special knowledge and authority is essentially professing to function as an expert witness, but without having to establish his credentials and be open to cross-examination on them. So a juror may easily lay claim to special knowledge that he does not actually possess. It might be supposed that, on balance, the other jurors will weed out false claims to special knowledge and recognize valid claims to special knowledge. But it might equally well be supposed that, on balance, the other jurors will be taken in by false claims to special knowledge and fail to recognize valid claims to special knowledge. We simply do not know which is the case and have no way to find out.

Also, experts can disagree. It often happens in a trial that one fully qualified expert witness utterly contradicts another. It is the task of the trier of fact—the judge in a bench trial or the jury in a jury trial—to decide which expert, if any, should be believed. But when a juror makes a claim to special knowledge, even if that claim is valid, she will still be providing her fellow jurors with only one aspect of the possible range of expert opinions. There is no way to know whether, on balance, this constitutes a benefit of the jury system.

These concerns apply to the "guy who had an education in street fighting." Presumably, he exuded confidence and authority and appeared wholly convincing to his fellow jurors. But *every* expert (including self-styled experts) exudes confidence and authority and appears wholly convincing—until he is cross-examined by well-prepared counsel or rebutted by another equally confident, authoritative, and wholly convincing expert. They apply equally to the "Spanish-proficient juror" who supposedly possessed "information unavailable to other jurors." A juror who is not Spanish-proficient could not easily evaluate another person's claim to proficiency in a language that has rich variations by region and dialect and by the gender, class, and education of the speaker.

These concerns also apply to the juror who "would know how to assess [probabilistic data] . . . and be able to explain the approach to her colleagues on the jury." Even in seemingly simple cases there may be different ways to interpret probabilistic data, and a juror who is not proficient in probability theory could not easily evaluate another person's claim that her approach to the data is the correct one.

A 1999 English case illustrates these concerns and also shows how they raise questions of fairness. The defendant was prosecuted for an offense involving allegedly stolen tires. During deliberations, the jury sent the judge a note informing him that one of the jurors was a tire specialist who was able to interpret a code on one of the tires and so able to determine the date of manufacture of the tire (a potentially relevant fact). The jury asked whether it might take this into consideration, and the trial judge permitted this.

The appellate court allowed the defendant's appeal: "It was wrong that any juror should have been permitted, as it were, to introduce entirely new evidence into the case, let alone doing so at a time when neither party had been put on notice of it and given the opportunity to consider it and test it, and where the appellant in particular had not been given any opportunity to provide an explanation for it." A legal scholar makes a reasonable assessment: "Relying upon specialised knowledge in the jury room is indistinguishable from conducting and using the fruits of external research. Both violate the principle that no further evidence can be called after the retirement of the jury."[31]

In sum, there is no evidence to determine whether the expert knowledge, or claims of expert knowledge, that jurors bring to jury deliberations leads to better or worse decisions on the facts in trials.

JURY FAIRNESS

It is frequently claimed in support of the jury system that a jury is likely to be fairer than a judge to the parties in a case, and particularly to the defendant in a criminal trial. The discussion here focuses on the relative fairness of judge and jury, but only in terms of the regular trial task of determining the facts and applying the law to them to reach a verdict. It does not consider the jury's exercise of its political roles to achieve fairness.

One reason why, it is claimed, a jury is likely to be fairer than a judge is that a judge might be corrupt, or biased against a particular party or defendant, or against a class of defendants, but a jury is less likely to be any of these. This notion goes back at least as far as Thomas Jefferson, who preferred to entrust a case to "the common sense of twelve honest men" than "to refer it to a judge whose mind is warped by any motive whatever, in that particular case."[32]

However, there is no guarantee that a selection of twelve jurors will be honest. In England in earlier times there were repeated allegations of corruption of jurors, especially by bribes. One statute after another was enacted, from the thirteenth to the eighteenth centuries, purportedly to curb the bribery of jurors. This suggests prevalent jury corruption. But there is also evidence that these statutes were devised to facilitate judicial control of juries, so it is not clear how much bribery actually occurred.[33]

Yet certainly bribery of jurors has occurred and still does occur. A juror in a 1987 New York trial for racketeering and murder was convicted five years later for receiving a bribe in return for voting for acquittal. Bribery of judges also occurs. In 2010, a Texas state judge was convicted of bribery in a federal prosecution.[34] Of course, successful prosecutions for bribery may not be a good measure of how frequent bribery is, and there is no evidence as to whether bribery of jurors or of judges is the more frequent.

Both judges and jurors can also be corrupted by threats and fear of retaliation. In one case, a federal district trial judge learned that the FBI was investigating allegations that the defendant had threatened to kill him or members of his family. The judge advanced the sentencing hearing to an earlier date, declaring that he "wanted to get [the defendant] . . . into the penitentiary system as quickly as possible, and . . . refused to grant a continuance of the sentencing hearing even though defendant's counsel had been appointed only two days before the sentencing date." The appellate court found that these actions taken in the context of the alleged threats "could have contributed to an appearance that the trial court was prejudiced against" the defendant, and held that the judge should have removed himself from the case.[35]

At the same time, concern has been growing over threats against jurors and their families to influence the verdict, especially in cases involving violent crime. There is evidence throughout America of a "growing crisis of juror dread" of retaliation in such cases that has increasingly led courts to conceal the names and contact information of jurors from public, press, and defendants alike.[36] But not all courts are willing to conceal the identities of jurors, and even in the courts that do so it is questionable whether this sufficiently combats the danger.

In England, following several instances of juror intimidation, a 2003 statute now allows for a criminal trial to be conducted by a judge alone, against the wishes of the defendant, in any case where "there is evidence of a real and present danger that jury tampering would take place ... [and] notwithstanding any steps (including the provision of police protection) which might reasonably be taken to prevent jury tampering, the likelihood that it would take place would be so substantial as to make it necessary in the interests of justice for the trial to be conducted without a jury." The Court of Appeal recently authorized the first use of this provision in a prosecution for armed robbery, where a previous trial had been aborted because of juror intimidation. The court accepted that if there were a jury in the case, all jurors as well as their families would need constant police protection, and that this would require more police resources than could reasonably be provided.[37]

Bias is another source of unfairness. Both judges and jurors can be biased, but there is no substantial evidence as to which is more likely to render a biased verdict in a case. It has been argued that a judge with an entrenched bias is a greater danger than a jury with an entrenched bias, because the jury can decide only the case or cases that it hears while it is empanelled, but the judge will decide many cases. This argument is valid in terms of comparing one judge with one jury. However, there may be many juries with entrenched biases, especially if some form of prejudice pervades a community. This would, for example, be likely when a largely racist populace has elected racist judges. "Juries can never be expected to be much better, or worse, than the society that produces them. A society that is pervasively racist or otherwise corrupt is unlikely to produce fair juries." Overall, it is not clear whether judge or jury presents the greater danger in this respect.[38]

It is another matter when bias pervades an entire judicial system. This is a concern in the many states where judges in trial courts, appellate courts, and the highest court of the state are elected. It is estimated that over 80 percent of state judges, in thirty-nine states, are elected. Election campaigns are very expensive, and judges who need to finance a campaign every few years commonly rely on lavish contributions from advocacy groups and interested parties.[39]

This results in undue influence on judges. As Robert Gammage, a former member of the supreme court of Texas, observes: "People don't go pour money into [judicial election] campaigns because they want fair and impartial treatment. They pump money into campaigns because they want things to go their way. Why else would the contributors be there? They have interests to pursue. They have agendas to pursue. In some cases, they have ideologies to pursue. They're not just bland, benign philosophies. They want results."[40]

The overall impression is one of pervasive bias in many state judicial systems, as a number of jurists—including Sandra Day O'Connor, a former member of the Supreme Court—and others who are pressing for reform have recognized. A few states are undertaking some limited reforms.[41]

It might seem that the presence of pervasive judicial bias would furnish an argument in support of the jury system. But matters are not so straightforward. In fact, it is difficult for juries to deliver fair verdicts in a system with a biased judiciary as long as the jury merely performs the regular trial task of determining the facts and applying the law to them to reach a verdict. The reason is that in a common-law system the judiciary has tremendous power to shape the law. If a biased judiciary shapes the law to incorporate its biases, a jury that simply applies that law will not be able to deliver a fair verdict.

It follows that in a judicial system where bias has shaped the law, a jury can deliver a fair verdict *only* insofar as it is ready to apply its own view of how the case should be justly decided, even if this does not comport with how the judge has instructed it on the law. This kind of jury behavior in appropriate cases is crucially important, but it goes beyond the subject of this chapter, which deals only with the regular trial task of determining the facts and applying the law to them to reach a verdict. Rather, this behavior entails the political roles of the jury, which is the subject of parts III, IV, and V.

As a final topic regarding fairness, it is sometimes argued that in criminal cases juries are likely to be fairer than judges because judges are more inclined toward conviction than juries. It does seem to be true that judges are more inclined toward conviction than juries. Evidence of this comes from the study by Kalven and Zeisel discussed earlier. In the great majority of the cases where the judge disagreed with the jury verdict, the jury acquitted where the judge would have convicted. Only a very small minority of cases of disagreement showed the jury convicting where the judge would have acquitted. A more recent study by law professor Theodore Eisenberg and others also showed that when the judge disagreed with the jury's verdict in a criminal trial, most often the judge would have convicted when the jury acquitted.[42]

The judges in the Kalven and Zeisel study believed that in most of the cases where the jury acquitted but the judge would have convicted, "the jury set the standard of proof of guilt at a higher level of probability than" the judge used. The Eisenberg study reached a similar conclusion.[43] The question here is whether this difference in assessing the evidence indicates that the jury is fairer.

In terms of the regular trial task of determining the facts and applying the law to them to reach a verdict, a fair verdict is simply a verdict reached honestly and without bias that accords with what actually happened. The problem, of course, is that we do not know what actually happened; we know only what the judge thought happened and what the jury thought happened. If juries are generally right in assessing the evidence, then it must follow that judges would convict substantial numbers of innocent defendants. But if judges are generally right in assessing the evidence, then juries are unwittingly acquitting substantial numbers of guilty defendants. Possibly the truth lies somewhere in between; but no one knows where in between, and there is no way to find out. So the difference between judge and jury in how they respectively assess the evidence does not in any way indicate that the jury, or the judge, is fairer.

The judges in the Kalven and Zeisel study believed that in a few of the cases where the jury acquitted but the judge would have convicted, "sympathy for the defendant influenced the jury." It is sometimes claimed that judges in criminal cases become "case-hardened," so that convicting and punishing become routine. According to the early-twentieth-century English writer G. K. Chesterton, based on his own experience as a juror, "legal officials . . . do not see the prisoner in the dock; all they see is the usual man in the usual place. They do not see the awful court of judgment; they only see their own workshop."[44] This may be so, but to acquit on the basis of sympathy for the defendant goes beyond the regular trial task of determining the facts and applying the law to them to reach a verdict. It is an aspect of the political roles of the jury, which are discussed in parts III, IV, and V.

The judges in the Kalven and Zeisel study also believed that in a very small number of the cases where the jury acquitted but the judge would have convicted, "the jury just disagreed with the law."[45] Again, this kind of jury behavior, which is crucially important in appropriate cases, entails the political roles of the jury, discussed in parts III, IV, and V.

Putting the political roles of the jury aside until later, the conclusion is that there is no evidence as to how the fairness or unfairness of judges compares overall to the fairness or unfairness of juries, in terms of the regular trial task of determining the facts and applying the law to them to reach a verdict.

CONSISTENCY

It is worth only briefly dealing with a claim by a few writers in support of the jury system that "juries . . . produce less variable verdicts than judges."[46] There is in fact no evidence for this.

The claim relies entirely on a small 1990s study by the academics Neil Vidmar and Jeffrey Rice. The participants in the study were members of the public acting as "jurors" and some professional arbitrators. They were presented individually with a hypothetical civil case with a single disputed issue of monetary damages. The individual-juror damages awards showed much greater variation than the arbitrator awards.

The authors of the study then pooled these individual-juror awards together in random groups of twelve and noted the median award value in each group of twelve. These group-of-twelve median awards showed much less variation than the arbitrator awards.

The authors then referred to another small study, by the academics Shari Diamond and Jonathan Casper. This study had found that when a group of individuals were asked to award damages in a hypothetical civil case, there was a positive correlation (with correlation coefficient 0.62) between the median of the awards that they rendered as individuals (the median award of the group members) and the joint award that they agreed on when asked to deliberate as a group (the jury award of the group).

Vidmar and Rice relied on this for their conclusion that jury awards are likely to show less variation than judge awards. In effect, they assumed that *because* jury awards of groups are positively correlated (0.62) with median awards of group members, *therefore* a low level of variation in median awards of group members must imply a low level of variation in jury awards of groups.

However, this assumption is false and in fact results from a mathematical error. If all we know about two variables is that they are positively correlated (in this case, with correlation coefficient 0.62), we can only deduce that as one variable increases, the other variable will *overall* have an increasing *trend*. The trend will not necessarily be uniform, and the fact that the range of variation in one variable is low does not imply that the range of variation in the other variable is also low. In fact, it is easy to construct a counter-example, showing a low range of variation in one variable but a high range of variation in the other.[47]

So the Diamond-Casper study shows only that if we have a number of median awards of group members listed in increasing order, then the corresponding jury awards of the group will overall have an increasing trend. It does not show that if the range of variation in median awards is low, then the range of variation in jury awards will also be low. This wholly undermines the reasoning of Vidmar and Rice.

In reality, there is good reason why we might not expect a low level of variation in jury awards to accompany a low level of variation in median awards. The median award of a group largely ignores any extreme positions of a minority, but these positions might well influence jury deliberations and the eventual jury award. In any event, we simply have no evidence as to whether juries do or do not produce less variable verdicts than judges.

CONCLUSION

The conclusion of this chapter is that there is no substantial support for any of the often-heard arguments that a jury is likely in any way to achieve a better trial outcome than a judge, in terms of the regular trial task of determining the facts and applying the law to them to reach a verdict.

This chapter has not dealt with the political roles of the jury. It has noted only that these roles can markedly affect the outcome of trials, particularly in the contexts of the jury as the peers of the defendant, the jury upholding community values and interests, and jury fairness. The political roles of the jury form the subject of parts III, IV, and V of this book.

Chapter 5

The Myth of Promoting Democratic Citizenship

Chapter 4 showed that there is no substantial evidence that juries achieve better trial outcomes than judges, in terms of the regular trial task of determining the facts and applying the law to them to reach a verdict. This chapter looks beyond the outcomes of trials, and asks whether the jury system serves any broader social function that can justify its costs to society.

Authority figures have made a range of claims in this respect, all being variations on the general idea that the jury system promotes democratic citizenship. One of the claims is that the jury system provides an education in citizenship. Another claim is that it engenders citizen participation in the system of government. Yet others are that it fosters social community and that it maintains regard for the justice system.

This chapter assesses these claims and finds that there is insufficient evidence to support any of them as justification for the jury system, as long as the inquiry is confined to the regular trial task of the jury in determining the facts and applying the law to them to reach a verdict. However, parts III, IV, and V will take up this topic in terms of the political roles of the jury, where the fundamental importance of the jury system in promoting democratic citizenship will be evident.

THE COST OF USING THE JURY SYSTEM TO PROMOTE DEMOCRATIC CITIZENSHIP

The issues for this chapter are not simply whether the jury system provides an education in citizenship, engenders citizen participation in the system of government, fosters social community, and maintains regard for the justice system. Rather, the issue is whether it does so well enough to justify its cost to society.

Insofar as the jury system fulfills any of these functions, it does so only in regard to the individuals who actually perform jury duty. Essentially, the claims that authority figures make are that jurors emerge from their experience as better-educated citizens who have participated in government in a way that benefits society, who have an enhanced sense of social community, and who more fully appreciate the justice system.

Certainly, the jury system offers no significant benefit in promoting democratic citizenship to the millions of Americans who each year are summoned for jury duty, found to be qualified and available, but are then subjected to "boredom and irritation with endless waiting at court without being selected to serve on a jury."[1] Of course, if an individual does benefit from jury duty in terms of democratic citizenship, she may well subsequently exercise a good influence on other members of her society. Yet it is still she, and not the persons she influences, who has received the benefit.

Chapter 2 conservatively assessed the cost of the American jury system at over $2 billion per year and the average length of a jury trial as two days. On this basis, the societal cost of using the jury system to promote democratic citizenship is, on average, more than $600 per juror per day.[2] This is the average taken across America as a whole, and obviously the cost will vary from one state or local jurisdiction to another.

Recall also that this cost estimate of the American jury system excludes a range of costs that are not readily quantifiable. If a reasonable estimate of these costs were included, a realistic average assessment of the societal cost of using the jury system to promote democratic citizenship might well be several times more than $600 per juror per day.

JURY DUTY AS EDUCATION IN CITIZENSHIP

Alexis de Tocqueville, the French social and political theorist whose book on democracy in America is still influential nearly two centuries after its first publication, claimed that the jury system provides the populace with an education in citizenship. Authority figures and commentators since then have seized on the idea. So Dwyer declares: "What Tocqueville said ... about jury service being a great educator is still true." In England, the *Criminal Courts Review* cites to Tocqueville to describe the jury system as "a peerless teacher of citizenship."[3]

Tocqueville saw jury duty as bringing jurors into daily communication with what he described as the most learned and enlightened members of the higher classes of society—these being the lawyers and judges. Judges in particular were the educators in Tocqueville's view of the jury system. He saw jurors as viewing the judge with confidence, listening to him with respect, letting his intelligence rule theirs entirely, and being subject to his virtually unlimited influence in reaching their verdict.[4]

Just possibly this did at the time describe the relationship between jurors and some members of the judiciary. Consistent with this, the jurist Akhil Reed Amar claims that in trials of the time "judges often seized the occasion to educate the jurors about legal and political values, ranging well beyond the narrow issues before them." Yet, even at that time, surely by no means all judges merited, or enjoyed, the level of respect that Tocqueville regarded as their due. In fact, Jefferson had already written that it was better to entrust cases to a jury than to "a judge whose mind is warped."[5] Contrary to Tocqueville's view, with such a judge on the bench the value of a jury was precisely that it did *not* allow the judge virtually unlimited influence over the verdict.

In any event, Tocqueville's elevated view of the American judiciary, its reputation, and its relation to the populace has certainly been divorced from reality for many years. As long ago as the early twentieth century, an American law professor who had spent "more than five years as a member of the professional staff of the District Attorney of New York County" complained of "the judicial scolds, blatant bullies and third-rate politicians who preside over criminal trials in many jurisdictions in the United States, especially in the larger centers of population where judicial nominations are frequently controlled by corrupt political machines."[6]

More recently, the *Economist* and ABA surveys on American justice show the American populace having a generally low level of trust in the judiciary (see chapter 3). Recall also that there is widespread concern that expensive judicial election campaigns have resulted in pervasive bias in many state judicial systems (see chapter 4).

Also, as Dwyer observes, in many trials, jurors "are passive listeners treated more like sheep than decision-making citizens." Commentators complain that jurors "are simply told to sit down, shut up, and take orders" and are "never . . . more than passive receivers of information."[7] Even if jurors viewed judges with the level of confidence and respect that Tocqueville supposed, this high level of passivity demanded of them indicates that they cannot expect much of educational value from their interaction with the trial judge.

So in assessing the jury system as providing an education in citizenship, Tocqueville's arguments are frankly of no value today. Also, any argument that the jury system provides an education in citizenship needs to take into account that this system spends more than $600 per day on each of the jurors who are supposedly the "students" in the system.

This cost should be compared with that of the only other form of government-controlled education in America: the public school system for students between approximately six and seventeen years of age. The comparison is appropriate, because, as the leading educator Paul Houston points out: "If you look back in history, you will find that the core mission of public education in America was to create places of civic virtue for our children and for our society. As education undergoes the rigors of re-examination and the need for reinvention, it is crucial to remember that the key role of public schools is to preserve democracy and . . . our mission is central to the future of this country."[8]

The National Education Association provides data on the expenditure of the American public school system. The current national average expenditure per student in the public school system (including elementary and secondary schools) is $11,144. According to state statutes, American public schools devote at least 170 days per school year to training and instruction of their students.[9] Examination of some of the public school calendars that are posted online is consistent with this.

So the total average annual expenditure of $11,144 per student is spread over at least 170 days of training and instruction. This amounts to well under $70 per student per day. This is less than one-eighth of the level of expenditure on the education that the jury system supposedly provides, at more than $600 per juror per day.

Expenditure at this higher level needs to be supported by clear evidence of what the jury system actually provides as education in citizenship. But the extraordinary fact is that no evidence of any kind is available, nor has there been any serious attempt to garner evidence, as to what the "educational" benefit of the jury system really is. To understand why this is extraordinary, consider the environment in which educational institutions operate nowadays. Anyone who has ever been involved in any kind of educational institution—as faculty, administrator, or student—must be aware that all such institutions nowadays operate in an environment of constant reevaluation of educational goals and assessment of educational content, performance, and cost in light of the stated goals.

Institutions establish policies and guidelines for evaluating teacher performance and student attainment. On the basis of these policies and guidelines, teachers test and grade students; students give—and publish on the web— candid evaluations of teachers and their courses; committees assess the slightest expenditure in terms of its actual or potential educative value. All of this is considered vital to ensure that educational institutions understand what their functions are and perform them effectively and efficiently.

All of this is utterly lacking in the context of the jury system. There are no stated goals regarding what knowledge of or skills in citizenship jurors are expected to attain. There are no policies and guidelines to evaluate whether and to what extent jurors have acquired knowledge of or skills in citizenship as a result of their service. There is no testing of jurors to evaluate their attainment resulting from their jury duty. Certainly, jurors are neither invited nor encouraged to evaluate the performance of the court in furthering their "education" in citizenship—and any juror who published a candid evaluation on the web would risk being cited for contempt of court.

Also, when a person has had experience of jury duty, society does not appear to value the education in citizenship that he has supposedly acquired. Although many jobs are better performed by persons well educated in citizenship, search committees do not include "experience of jury duty" among their requirements, or even desires, in a candidate. No candidate for any position includes this in her curriculum vitae. Candidates for public office—especially for elected office—might have been particularly expected to draw attention in their campaigns to the educational benefit that jury duty has given them, but they do not do so.

All of this shows that there is no sufficient basis for the notion of jury duty as an education in citizenship, at least insofar as the jury is performing the regular trial task of determining the facts and applying the law to them to reach a verdict.

However, there is another dimension. In a recent text, the attorney and academic Robert Burns applauds Tocqueville for a quite different kind of argument that relates to the educative value of jury duty. This argument, in Burns's words, is that the jury trial confers on jurors "the burden of making public decisions affecting real people for which one is responsible." He elucidates: "The availability and shape of the trial . . . determine the range of opportunities for a certain *kind* of knowledge that responsible participation brings, a kind of understanding that has been thought to be an essential element of citizenship." He goes on to contrast "responsible participation" with the "passivity" that "deference to authority" entails, and views the educative value of jury duty in terms of finding the appropriate balance between these two contrasting modes.[10]

This argument interweaves two ideas about jury duty. One of the ideas is that of jury duty as participation in the system of government, which is discussed next. The other idea is that of jury duty as developing an appropriate sense of individual responsibility regarding when to defer and when not to defer to authority. This is indeed a crucially important kind of education in citizenship, but it goes beyond the regular trial task of determining the facts and applying the law to them to reach a verdict. Rather, it entails the political roles of the jury, which is the subject of parts III, IV, and V.

JURY DUTY AS PARTICIPATION IN THE SYSTEM OF GOVERNMENT

Jury duty is, obviously, a form of participation in the system of government, and authority figures have argued in favor of the jury system on this basis. A typical example appears in a Department of State publication: "As society grows more complex, many people worry that the average citizen is growing disconnected from the government, that he or she is losing a sense of participation in the daily processes of democracy. Jury service, almost alone of everything a person does as a citizen, continues to provide that sense of both responsibility and participation."[11]

Certainly, responsible citizen participation in the system of government is vitally important in a democracy. A fine explanation comes from the Illinois Citizen Participation Act:

> Pursuant to the fundamental philosophy of the American constitutional form of government, it is declared to be the public policy of the State of Illinois that the constitutional rights of citizens and organizations to be involved and participate freely in the process of government must be encouraged and safeguarded with great diligence. The information, reports, opinions, claims, arguments, and other expressions provided by citizens are vital to effective law enforcement, the operation of government, the making of public policy and decisions, and the continuation of representative democracy.[12]

As Lincoln declared, American government is to be "government of the people, by the people, for the people." This would become empty rhetoric without the participation of a responsible citizenry in the processes of government, as the Illinois statute insists. But for responsible citizen participation to be possible, the citizenry must possess certain qualities. One necessary quality is a constructive attitude to society that can be summed up as a sense of *civic responsibility*. This is best defined as "responsibility for the civic realm, responsibility not just to other people but for what we and others share—for the goods we have in common, for the quality of our life together, for the creation of a just social order."[13]

Another necessary quality, as the Illinois statute makes clear, is the actual capacity to gather information, assemble it into reports, form opinions, make claims, and present arguments. In short, responsible citizen participation requires citizens to possess the capacity to provide constructive input into the policy-making processes of government. This at the very least calls for citizens to maintain their independence of mind and judgment in relation to government.

Also, it is not enough for the citizenry simply to *possess* these qualities. As the Illinois statute stipulates, citizens must have full opportunity to *employ* these qualities in relation to government.

Consider now the role of jury duty as participation in the system of government. As throughout this chapter, the focus is on the jury performing the regular trial task of determining the facts and applying the law to them to reach a verdict. But this is a constrained role. The jury is presented with evidence and tasked with reaching a verdict in the individual case. It is not given any explicit opportunity to provide constructive input into the policy-making processes of government. On the contrary, as quoted previously, jurors are told to sit down, shut up, and take orders, and are often treated more like sheep than decision-making citizens.

Insofar as jurors are confined to such a constrained role and subjected to such repressive, disempowering treatment, they are offered no opportunity to employ their independence of mind and judgment in relation to government. The conclusion must be that jury duty does not fulfill the basic requirements for the kind of responsible participation in the system of government that is needed to promote democratic citizenship, in terms of the regular trial task of determining the facts and applying the law to them to reach a verdict.

Yet despite this, it remains possible for jurors to provide constructive input into the policy-making processes of the justice system, exercising their independence of mind and judgment in relation to government in the process. They can do so by taking political and moral issues into account in rendering their verdict in appropriate cases. This is a crucial aspect of the role of the jury, but it goes beyond the subject of this chapter. Rather, it entails the political roles of the jury, which is the subject of parts III, IV, and V.

A further issue in assessing the role of jury duty as participation in the system of government is whether, as the Department of State publication claims, jury duty is almost alone in providing citizens with the opportunity to participate in the system of government. In fact, this claim is completely false.

At the state and local level throughout America, a great deal of core government work wholly relies on volunteer citizens. A commentator explains: "Most town government in Massachusetts costs taxpayers nothing. There are paid positions to be sure. But the committees that run the budget, the schools and zoning are staffed by volunteers. In fact, if these positions were to be filled by paid appointees, it would bankrupt most towns." As another example, in 2000 Boulder County, Colorado "embarked on a project to redefine and strengthen volunteer participation in local government programs." It declared its philosophy as: "Boulder County government is a joint venture between its citizens and the individuals and departments that are charged with the responsibility of carrying out the functions of local government . . . [and will] assure that citizens have opportunities for meaningful and effective engagement in local government operations . . . [including] opportunity for input and suggestions regarding programs."[14]

The need to have volunteers undertake government work is so well recognized that states have enacted statutes establishing and closely regulating the right of government departments (state as well as local) to use the services of volunteers.[15] Throughout America, there is in many cases little to distinguish the many volunteers from regular government officials, other than the lack of a salary.

This pervasive need for volunteer services provides endless opportunities for responsible citizen participation in the system of government. In fact, the demand is greater than the supply. For example, the Massachusetts commentator complains regarding his own town: "we are coming up on town elections and no one has bothered to run for open seats on the Finance Committee, Library Trustee, Park Commission and Planning Board. . . . This may not be the most exciting way to spend time, but it is vital for the future."[16]

So jury duty is far from being the only opportunity for citizens to participate responsibly in the system of government. On the contrary, jury duty is in competition with the great range of volunteer opportunities for responsible participation in the system of government—the resource for which they are competing being the limited amount of time that the citizenry is able or willing to make available. And although volunteers are not absolutely free to society, as human resource personnel are needed to interview, hire, train, and supervise them,[17] a volunteer unquestionably costs much less than the more than $600 per day that each juror costs our society.

JURY DUTY AS FOSTERING SOCIAL COMMUNITY

Another of the claims made by authority figures is that jury duty brings together people from different walks of life that might otherwise not come into contact with one another and fosters a sense of social community among them, thereby promoting democratic citizenship. For example, a jurist refers to "the unifying effect of shared social responsibility" that supposedly results from jury duty.[18]

There is really no worthwhile evidence to support this. There are no relevant studies or surveys of American jurors, but at best only a few personal reminiscences, impressions, and anecdotes. For example, Dwyer recalls post-trial discussions with the members of a jury "who had bonded into a cheerful group, as jurors often do." A Los Angeles rabbi describes in glowing terms his experience of service on a racially mixed jury.[19] But the sum total of these accounts does not provide significant evidence of the general jury experience.

In fact, there is more persuasive evidence against this idea. To the extent that jury duty does bring together people from different walks of life, the evidence casts doubt on whether this fosters a sense of social community among them. Rather, it seems that bringing them together may reinforce any preexisting sense of social division and exacerbate tensions:

> New Yorkers who have deliberated on several recent juries say they have emerged feeling personally attacked, outraged and disillusioned. Court officers mention fistfights they broke up, chairs hurled out windows and jurors who screamed so loudly they were heard on other floors. . . . One Manhattan judge said that as more educated professionals are required to sit on juries and can no longer get exemptions, the social and political views in the jury room have become more varied and the rancor during deliberations has increased accordingly.[20]

There are many such reported incidents of extreme tensions among jury members, including physical threats and attacks. These do not support the idea that jury duty provides valuable training in democratic citizenship by bringing together people from different walks of life.[21]

Also, as previously discussed, many volunteer activities are available, and these may equally well be supposed to bring together people from different walks of life. An activity in which people from different walks of life participate voluntarily may be more likely to foster a sense of social community than an activity to which people are summoned under penalty of law, and in which they are compelled to remain together regardless of tensions among them. In any event, without evidence that jury duty does foster social community, the idea must be dismissed as speculative.

JURY DUTY AS MAINTAINING REGARD FOR THE JUSTICE SYSTEM

It is reasonable to suppose that serving on a jury would have some effect on a person's regard for the justice system. But in fact there is only very limited information from surveys as to what the effect actually is.

The ABA survey discussed in chapter 3 includes a summary of respondents' answers to questions about their changes in attitudes following "experience with the justice system." Unfortunately, this summary lumps together the answers of the various respondents who had been in court in any kind of "active" role. What the summary means by an "active" role includes: "going to traffic court, being a witness, a juror (either being called to serve or actually serving), a plaintiff, a defendant, or a victim." The answers of the respondents who had actually fulfilled jury duty are not broken out separately. The best that can be done with this is to make the rough, and questionable, assumption that the changes in attitude to the justice system resulting from the experience of being a juror are likely to be much the same as those resulting from other "active" role court experiences. Then it turns out that about 70 percent of respondents have no change in their opinions about the justice system resulting from the experience of being a juror. Of the remaining 30 percent, two-thirds have a lower opinion and one-third a higher opinion.[22]

A later survey by the American Bar Association on the specific topic of attitudes to jury duty could do no more than conclude: "In general, those who have served as a juror . . . feel as confident in the justice system as they did before they served."[23]

However, an important conference on the state of the judiciary held at Georgetown University School of Law in 2006 reports a more negative view. Under the heading "The Performance of the Courts Must Be Improved," the conference report declares:

> For the courts to continue to command the respect of those who use the system, improvements in judicial process are needed. A survey performed in preparation for the Conference by the Annenberg Center for Public Policy at the University of Pennsylvania found that Americans who have performed jury service within the past five years, or who had a family member in court in the last five years, were much more likely than those with little or no exposure to the courts to strongly agree that the courts favor the wealthy or the "connected."[24]

Many American courts request jurors who have completed their service to fill out an "exit questionnaire" regarding their experience. The questions, though, are generally confined to such matters as the courtesy of court officials, the physical comforts of juror accommodation, and the quality of parking and eating facilities. Jurors are rarely asked their views on the justice system. In any event, the information from these questionnaires should be assessed cautiously, since it is usually court personnel who provide the questionnaire and collate the responses, and also because there is no reason to suppose that those jurors who are willing to complete a questionnaire have views representative of the group of jurors as a whole.[25]

The best conclusion that can reasonably be drawn from all this is that the two ABA surveys suggest that, for around two-thirds of the American populace, serving on a jury has no effect whatsoever on their opinion of the justice system. For the remaining one-third, there is no significant evidence of any overall positive effect on their view of the justice system.[26]

CONCLUSION

The conclusion of this chapter is that there is no substantial support for any of the arguments that the jury system promotes democratic citizenship to a sufficient extent to justify its costs to society, in terms of the regular trial task of determining the facts and applying the law to them to reach a verdict.

This conclusion does not apply to the political roles of the jury. Within the political roles of the jury, jury duty provides an education in citizenship by developing an appropriate sense of individual responsibility regarding when to defer and when not to defer to authority. Also within the political roles of the jury, jury duty provides responsible participation in the system of government in the form of constructive input into the policy-making processes of the justice system, permitting citizens to exercise their independence of mind and judgment. These crucial political roles of the jury form the subject of parts III, IV, and V of this book.

Part III

The Jury as Political Institution

Chapter 6

The Long History of the Nullification Power

When the jury in a criminal trial delivers a verdict of not guilty, the verdict is final for that trial. The judge cannot alter the verdict, and the prosecution cannot appeal against it. This has been accepted without question for many centuries.

It is also true that the government has no recourse against the members of a jury that delivers a verdict of not guilty. This also seems obvious now, but it required a political struggle to establish it as a secure principle. A key turning point in the struggle was a landmark seventeenth-century English law case that many American courts and commentators continue to refer to, through to the present day.

In 1670, the Quakers William Penn and William Mead were on trial at the Court of Sessions in London, England, for preaching in a public street, the charge being that they "unlawfully and tumultuously did assemble and congregate themselves together, to the disturbance of the Peace of . . . the King." The jury brought in a verdict of not guilty on this charge. The court was openly enraged and demanded that the jury reconsider and bring in a guilty verdict. To press the jurors into changing their verdict, the court repeatedly berated them and treated them harshly. Despite this, they insisted on their verdict of not guilty. The court ultimately had no choice but to accept this acquittal. But the court then declared to the jury: "I am sorry, Gentlemen, you have followed your own judgments and Opinions, rather than the good and wholesome advice, which was given you; . . . but for this the Court fines you forty Marks a man; and imprisonment till paid."[1]

Jurors of that time were, of course, well aware that courts had powers of this kind, and because of this would often comply when the court clearly desired a conviction. But the times were changing. One juror, Edward Bushell, refused to pay the fine and challenged his imprisonment by a writ of habeas corpus in the Court of Common Pleas. Chief Justice Vaughan, allowing the writ and ordering Bushell released, held that a judge could not fine or imprison a juror for delivering a verdict contrary to the wishes or instructions of the judge.[2] This plainly denied the government any recourse whatsoever against a jury for delivering a verdict of not guilty. This effective result of *Bushell's Case* has come to be accepted in England, America, and every country with a common-law jury system.

It follows that a jury has the power to acquit a criminal defendant who is actually guilty of the offense as charged, even when the evidence of the defendant's guilt is overwhelming, and even if the jury itself is convinced beyond a doubt that he has committed the act as charged. In blunt terms, a jury has the power to acquit regardless of the law and of the evidence. If a jury does so, the government can do nothing about it. It cannot appeal the acquittal, and it has no recourse against the jury. The power of the jury to reach a verdict regardless of the law and of the evidence is its *nullification power*.

A jury is never required to explain or justify its verdict, so when a jury exercises the nullification power, it does not declare that it has done so. It simply delivers its verdict without comment.

Various terms are used to describe this power. The "nullification power" terminology is the most usual. In America it has been the most widely used terminology for some time, and is now increasingly recognized in England and elsewhere. The idea of this terminology is that the jury is deemed to be "nullifying" the applicable law.[3] It is not really doing this, but in any event the terminology is well established.

Another term is the "dispensing power" of the jury. The original idea of this terminology was that the jury was deemed to be "dispensing" mercy to the defendant. This terminology is most common in England, although it is also found in America.[4]

Neither of these terms is "neutral." As later chapters will discuss, the nullification power has long been controversial, and each term brings its particular historical and political overtones of controversy. In particular, the "nullification" terminology has become politically divisive, being often applied pejoratively and dismissively by those opposed to the jury's exercise of this power but aggressively and antagonistically by those in favor of it.[5]

As a result, a number of writers have introduced yet more terminology. For example, a fine history of jury "verdict according to conscience" shifts within a few pages from "nullification" to "jury discretion" and then "jury-based mitigation." Dwyer begins by talking of "jury nullification" but soon shifts to "jury mercy" and then "jury discretion." An English high school text refers to "jury equity." Also in England, the *Criminal Courts Review* adopts a relatively recent, obviously pejorative usage, describing an exercise of the nullification power as a "perverse verdict."[6]

In any event, there is no "neutral" terminology, so it makes sense simply to use the most usual form. Accordingly, this book refers throughout to the "nullification power," and as far as possible avoids other terms.

The nullification power of the jury is sometimes confused with another matter that has also long been controversial. This is whether the legal system tasks the jury with deciding the law as well as deciding the facts.[7] These two issues concerning the jury—on the one hand, as possessing the power to acquit regardless of the law and of the evidence, and on the other hand, as tasked with deciding the law—have been confused at least since the English trial of John Lilburne for treason in 1649. Lilburne, a prominent member of the radical Leveller Movement, argued to the jury that it was the judge of law as well as of fact, basing this contention on political history rather than legal theory or precedent. The jury did acquit him, and the case is sometimes referred to as an exercise of the jury's nullification power. But in fact the proceedings were too convoluted for the reason for the jury's action to be certain.[8]

Although these two issues are sometimes confused, they are quite distinct. Dwyer makes this clear in that he recognizes one but not the other: "While the jury no longer can define the law, it has the right to acquit regardless of the law." The stream of cases of jury nullification over the centuries discussed in this chapter entail the jury acquitting regardless of the law, rather than defining or deciding the law.[9]

It is not always clear whether a jury has actually exercised the nullification power. Even if it appears from press reports or the trial transcript that the prosecution established beyond any doubt that the defendant violated the law, the jury might still have acquitted without exercising the nullification power. The jury might simply not have believed the prosecution's witnesses, or its experts, or its forensic evidence. All such possibilities must be excluded before it can be certain that the jury exercised the nullification power. Yet despite this there are a number of cases in which it is sufficiently clear that a jury has exercised its nullification power.

In practice, juries generally exercise the nullification power in response to some form of perceived injustice in the law. As Dwyer explains, juries exercise the nullification power "when the government has gone too far, when a guilty verdict for whatever reason would do violence to fairness, common sense, and conscience."[10]

The cases where juries have exercised the nullification power divide into two roughly separate categories. One category comprises cases where the jury has considered it unjust to treat the conduct of the defendant as a crime at all. This may be because the jurors viewed the relevant law as altogether unjust, or, more particularly, unjust as applied to the defendant in the circumstances of the case. This category is considered next.

The other category comprises cases where the jury has likely accepted that the conduct of the defendant should be regarded as a crime, but has considered the penalty for the crime to be unjust. This category is considered later in this chapter.

EXERCISE OF THE NULLIFICATION POWER REGARDING UNJUST LAWS

In many cases, the sense of injustice that prompts juries to exercise the nullification power is one that is already pervasive in society at large.[11] So there has been more use of the nullification power during periods of intense political and social turmoil, and much less in times of relative political and social calm.

One of the earliest periods of activity in the exercise of the nullification power that is relatively well documented begins with two trials of Lilburne in England: the trial for treason in 1649 and a further trial in 1653. This period of activity, and the social agitation that it accompanied, extended through the decision in *Bushell's Case* in 1670 and more than a decade afterwards.

It is not certain that Lilburne's acquittal in 1649 was an exercise of the nullification power. But the jury certainly exercised the nullification power in Lilburne's later trial for flouting an order of banishment imposed on him by the House of Commons. The sole fact for the trial jury to determine was whether the defendant was actually the person named in the act of banishment—which he clearly was. However, Lilburne's supporters distributed pamphlets urging the jurors "that their duty as a jury was to distinguish real acts of Parliament from those against law and, therefore, counterfeit." So, the pamphlets argued, they should refuse to accept the order of banishment (which had been imposed without any formal charge or hearing) as valid law. In a clear rebuke to the government, the jury acquitted Lilburne.[12]

Juries exercised the nullification power against laws perceived as unjust in the American colonies prior to independence[13] and continued to do so in postindependence America. A notable and important postindependence instance arose out of a provision of the federal Fugitive Slave Act of 1850, which made it a criminal offense to assist the escape of a fugitive slave. A group of abolitionists in Boston burst into the courtroom where summary proceedings to return Shadrach, an escaped slave, to slavery in Virginia were in progress. The group hurried Shadrach from the courtroom and escorted him away through a cheering crowd; he eventually reached safety in Canada. In *US v Morris*, members of the liberating group were prosecuted for this all-too-clear violation of the plain terms of the act.

In an extraordinary interchange between defense counsel and the judge at the trial of these individuals, counsel told the jury that they could reject the Fugitive Slave Act as unconstitutional. He further told them that they could ignore any instructions that the judge might give to the contrary. The judge interrupted counsel and instructed the jury that they could do nothing of the kind. Despite this, the jury acquitted the defendants.[14]

Juries of the time in nonslavery states frequently refused to convict under the Fugitive Slave Act in cases where, as in *US v Morris*, there could be no doubt as to the facts and the involvement of the defendant. It became so notoriously difficult to obtain convictions that some federal district courts developed an alternative approach. The owner of the slave would seek a writ of habeas corpus against the person who had assisted the escape, demanding that he produce the slave. If he failed to cooperate, the court—a judge, sitting alone without a jury—could then imprison him for contempt of court.[15]

There was another period of activity in jury exercise of the nullification power in late-nineteenth-century America, coinciding with social shifts that extended jury duty to a somewhat broader range of social classes and also stimulated the labor movement.[16] Government had frequently suppressed union organization with prosecutions for conspiracy in restraint of trade, but it became harder to obtain convictions from juries that were more likely to perceive those prosecutions as unjust. Again, the government responded by developing an alternative approach: the use of civil injunction instead of criminal prosecution against organized labor. A judge sitting alone, without a jury, would hear the application for a civil injunction. In many cases, the injunction was granted against the defendant labor organizers without notice to them or opportunity for them to be heard. If a defendant then violated the injunction, the same court would then imprison him for contempt of court.[17]

In an 1898 case, an appellate federal court upheld a contempt conviction deriving from a civil injunction that had been based on claims that the defendants had conspired to organize a boycott, allegedly threatening injury to the business of the applicant for the injunction. In a passionate dissent, one judge referred extensively to the trial of Penn and Mead and to *Bushell's Case*. He concluded: "No American jury could be found who would say these defendants were guilty of a 'conspiracy,' or of making 'threats' to injure any one."[18] This clearly recognized that juries had been checking prosecutions of organized labor by exercising the nullification power, to such an extent as to induce government to evade any form of jury trial in its endeavors to suppress the labor movement.

During the period of Prohibition, juries frequently exercised the nullification power to thwart prosecutions under federal liquor laws in parts of America where those laws were largely viewed as unjust. Dwyer wryly observes: "During Prohibition, bootleggers were hard to convict in areas where the prevailing sentiment was wet. The 1929–30 acquittal rate in federal liquor law prosecutions was 13 percent for cases tried in Kansas, Oklahoma, and Nebraska, 48 percent in New England, and 60 percent in New York. There is no reason to believe that the indictments were any less accurate in the East."[19]

In these cases, the jury was exercising the nullification power to implement community values and uphold community interests, as discussed in chapter 4. Dwyer explains: "Jurors make judgments, and they do so by using not just the law laid out for them by the judge, but their own sense of justice as well. In this way they keep the law legitimately attuned to community values."[20]

This support of community values and interests was also apparent during a further period of activity in the exercise of the nullification power, not long after the Prohibition era. In the Pennsylvania coalfields during the Depression, many unemployed miners eked out a subsistence living by stealing coal. Juries in coal counties plainly considered these thefts justifiable and consistently refused to convict those accused of them.[21] As Jonakait notes, "the consequences of prosecutorial or judicial actions fall most heavily on the communities where the judges and prosecutors have power. If those officials need to be checked, the local community [as represented by local jurors] is in the best position to rein them in."[22]

The next quarter of a century or so was relatively quiet regarding the exercise of the nullification power. Then a further, very extended period of activity began around the 1970s, in both America and England. In America, a number of prosecutions were brought against persons protesting against the Vietnam War. The prosecutions were, of course, not for protesting in itself but for recognizably criminal offenses committed in the course of protesting, such as trespass, obstructing public officials, creating a public nuisance, destruction of government property (particularly draft-related documents), and resisting arrest. In many cases, the jury acquitted the defendants despite the clearest evidence that they had committed the acts of which they were accused.[23]

A well-known instance was the 1973 trial of the so-called Camden 28, a group of twenty-eight antiwar activists prosecuted for destroying draft-related records in a federal government office. There was no doubt that the defendants had committed the acts of which they were accused. However, evidence at the trial showed that the FBI, through an informant within the group, had supplied the group with tools and information. The trial judge, Clarkson Fisher, gave the jury in his instructions strong encouragement to exercise its nullification power: "if you find that the overreaching participation by Government agents or informers in the activities as you have heard them was so fundamentally unfair to be offensive to the basic standards of decency, and shocking to the universal sense of justice, then you may acquit any defendant to whom this defense applies."[24] The jury acquitted all the defendants.

Opposition to government policy was also at issue in England. In 1985, Clive Ponting, a senior civil servant (a government official), was tried for violating the Official Secrets Act by passing classified documents to a member of Parliament. Ponting admitted passing the documents, which showed that government ministers had substantially misled Parliament about an incident in the Falklands War. So he clearly admitted that he had violated the plain terms of the act.

Under the Official Secrets Act there was a defense available to Ponting that he had acted in the interests of the state. Accordingly, he argued at trial that his duty to make the information public superseded his obligation to comply with the act. However, the judge ruled that the "interests of the state" defense had to be interpreted narrowly as meaning the "interests of the government of the day." This interpretation, which was extreme in its antipathy to the defense, set a standard that Ponting could not meet. Despite this, the jury acquitted him.[25]

In the Ponting case, the jury likely did not consider the Official Secrets Act unjust in itself but did consider it unjust to prosecute Ponting under the particular circumstances. There are other cases of this kind, not all concerning high politics. A well-known English case was the 1991 trial of Stephen Owen for attempted murder. Owen's twelve-year-old child had been killed by a truck driven recklessly, under appalling circumstances. The driver—a violent career criminal who had never held a driver's license—served one year in prison. After his release, Owen sought him out and shot and wounded him at close range.

In summing up, the judge said: "Any person who does not feel for these parents in their agony and anguish must be made of stone." But he added: "If it should be that the prosecution has proved his guilt do not let the understandable emotions and sympathies distract you from performing the duty you swore in your oath of returning a true verdict according to the facts." Yet despite overwhelming evidence, the jury acquitted Owen. "Some describe the acquittal as a classic example of 'jury equity.' Hundreds cheered wildly at the verdict outside the court."[26]

The extension of jury duty to the great majority of the citizenry has likely led to a continuing increased use of the nullification power. Until relatively recently, American jurors were in practice drawn from a very limited range of the populace. For example, in the late 1940s the population of New York County was about 1.8 million, but the list from which jurors were drawn numbered only about sixty thousand. Many jurisdictions required jurors to possess a prescribed level of property. In addition, according to a typical state statute, they had to be "intelligent, of sound mind and good character, well-informed, able to read and write the English language understandingly." In some jurisdictions, particularly in the South, officials applied criteria of these kinds in ways that resulted in persons of color being severely underrepresented on juries, almost to the point of total exclusion.[27]

It was also possible in a number of jurisdictions to limit the list of prospective jurors further with the system of so-called blue ribbon or special juries used in certain cases. Officials selected people individually for the list of prospective special jurors, often after a personal interview. In the late 1940s, the list of prospective special jurors in New York County numbered only about three thousand out of the general jury list of about sixty thousand. The subjective criteria by which people were selected for the list of special jurors arguably enabled "jury officials to formulate whatever standards they desire[d]" for jurors. This could, for example, result in professional and managerial workers being proportionately overrepresented and manual workers being wholly excluded.[28]

The federal courts abandoned such forms of jury selection throughout the country in the 1960s, but many states did not do so until well into the 1970s and even later.[29] The subsequent extension of jury duty to include manual workers, persons of color, and so forth has resulted in less predictable juries that are arguably more likely to exercise the nullification power against perceived injustice in the law.

EXERCISE OF THE NULLIFICATION POWER REGARDING UNJUST PUNISHMENTS

In the development of the nullification power through to the present day, arguably its most consistent and important use has been in cases where the jury likely accepts that the defendant ought to be found guilty under the relevant law and punished, but is concerned that the judge may impose an unjust punishment.[30] In some situations, this concern may lead the jury to acquit the defendant entirely. In others, the jury may (if the case allows) convict of a less serious offense, on the assumption that this will result in a less severe sentence. In either situation—to adapt Dwyer's words, quoted previously—the jury will say no to the sentence that the law prescribes when the government has gone too far, when the prescribed sentence for whatever reason would do violence to fairness, common sense, and conscience.

Juries have repeatedly taken this kind of action for many centuries, with some evidence of it in England even as early as the thirteenth century.[31] The eighteenth-century English jurist William Blackstone focused attention on this kind of jury behavior, and as a result the English history of jury nullification to avoid unjust punishments is well documented.

Blackstone himself focused particularly on prosecutions for theft. At the time, certain convictions for theft incurred the death penalty when the value of what was stolen was at or above a certain amount. Referring to thefts where the amount specified for imposition of the death penalty was one shilling (twelve pence), Blackstone noted "that the mercy of juries will often make them strain a point, and bring in larceny to be under the value of twelvepence, when it is really of much greater value."[32] That is, the jury would avoid the death penalty by assessing the value of the stolen goods at under the fatal amount—even if the actual value was plainly more than this—and delivering the verdict accordingly.

This exercise of the nullification power in theft cases was sometimes remarkably blatant. In one 1733 case of theft, in which the fatal amount was five shillings (5s.), two men "in company together at the same time, stole the same goods privately in a shop, and the jury found one guilty to the amount of 4s. 10d. [four shillings and ten pence] and the other to the amount of 5s. That is, that the same goods were at one and the same moment of different values." The man who was found guilty of theft in the higher amount was, inevitably, sentenced to death. This man "had been tried before at the same sessions for a similar offence, and had been convicted of stealing to the amount only of 4s. 10d. The jury seem to have thought, that having had the benefit of their indulgence once, he was not entitled to it a second time."[33]

Blackstone used the expression "pious perjury" for what is now called the exercise of the nullification power on the part of the jury in these cases.[34] His assessment of this as perjury is based on the idea that the jury violates its oath in delivering such a verdict. But it is in fact not clear that this does violate the oath, and so not clear that it is appropriate to regard it as any form of perjury (see chapter 12).

Juries in English trials for theft continued to mitigate the offense in this way through to at least the early nineteenth century. Since the eighteenth century, the fatal amount in certain cases had been forty shillings (two pounds sterling). In one recorded eighteenth-century case, which was certainly typical of many, a defendant was charged with stealing a watch valued at forty shillings and also more than twenty guineas (twenty-one pounds sterling) in cash. The judge essentially cajoled the jury into exercising its nullification power, with his own report of the case being as follows: "The jury found him guilty to the value of 39s., which they did after I told them that 40s. was necessary to make him guilty of felony" that would carry the death penalty.[35]

The penalty for theft of less than the fatal amount was at that time transportation to a penal colony, normally in Australia. The period of transportation was seven years, but of course many remained in Australia at the end of their sentence. An Australian judge notes with delicious irony: "Countries like Australia which began as penal colonies and settlements, owe much to the English jury. Many a worthy life was spared by a jury, flying in the face of the evidence, reaching a decision which carried the punishment of transportation rather than the sentence of death."[36]

A great range of crimes besides theft carried the death penalty at that time. However, many of them did not give a jury any ready means to mitigate the offense to ensure a lesser penalty, in the way that prosecutions for theft allowed. For example, in a prosecution for forgery, which carried the death penalty, the jury could convict or it could acquit; there was no way to mitigate. As a result, juries persistently simply acquitted, even when evidence of guilt was overwhelming. This occurred to the point that in 1830 bankers throughout England petitioned Parliament to abolish capital punishment for forgery, on the ground that the prospect of this penalty prevented convictions "and thus endangers the property which it is intended to protect."[37]

Although the jury could not mitigate the offense in a crime such as forgery, if it convicted it could still recommend mercy. In fact, on any offense it could convict and recommend mercy, but of course there was no guarantee that the court would act on this recommendation. The problem for the jury of relying for the dispensation of mercy on a judge who might or might not choose to be merciful remains to the present day. Moreover, judges today are in many cases constrained by sentencing guidelines (see chapter 10), and so may have relatively little capacity to dispense mercy.

In many criminal prosecutions, several closely related charges are brought against the defendant with a view to increasing the overall penalty, as well as possibly increasing the likelihood of a conviction. The jury can attempt to mitigate the punishment by refusing to convict on some of the charges.

For example, in federal liquor law prosecutions during Prohibition, it was usual to charge the defendant with unlawful possession of intoxicating liquor intended for sale and also with maintaining a "common nuisance" in the form of premises where intoxicating liquor was unlawfully kept. The charges were based on the same evidence, so that it was logical for the jury to convict on both charges if it believed the evidence, or to acquit on both charges if it did not. Yet in one case the jury convicted on the charge of maintaining a common nuisance, but acquitted on the charge of unlawful possession. In another, the jury acquitted on the charge of maintaining a common nuisance but convicted on the charge of unlawful possession. As the court observed in the latter case: "There is a plain inconsistency in saying that the liquors were kept for sale, and in saying that the shop in which they were was not one in which the same liquors were kept for sale."[38] These appear to have been exercises of the nullification power, with a view to limiting the penalty.

This kind of jury action is also applicable to the common situation in which several charges are brought against the defendant, with some being lesser-included charges of others. For example, a defendant might be accused of reckless driving, and also of the lesser-included offense of careless driving, regarding the same incident.[39] The jury will reasonably believe that conviction on the careless-driving charge alone will likely incur a lower penalty than on the reckless-driving charge, and may be inclined to determine its verdict with this in mind.

Currently there is a particular tendency for juries to exercise the nullification power in drug prosecutions because of concern about the sentence. Dwyer observes "a spreading realization that prison terms for drug-dealing, especially in the federal system, are harsh beyond the expectations of nearly all jurors. Acquittals on these bases are another episode in the long history of jury discretion."[40]

There is a similar tendency in England. For example, Frances Crook, director of the long-established and prestigious Howard League for Penal Reform, indicates that a jury on which she served exercised its nullification power:

> I sat on one case that was completed, and obviously I can't talk about the details, but I can say that the interesting and representative group took the whole process extremely seriously. We found the chap not guilty of intent to supply, cannabis. Topical now of course, and I think a lesson for the Government. It is no good increasing the possible penalties for cannabis when juries won't convict, it just wastes everyone's time and money. Thank goodness for the jury system, it really is a bulwark of freedom, if a little time consuming and ponderous.[41]

THE NULLIFICATION POWER IN CIVIL CASES

It is difficult to assess how far juries exercise the nullification power in civil cases. There is some evidence of it in tort cases in the few states that still apply a doctrine (known as contributory negligence) that causes a plaintiff to lose her case *entirely* if her own negligence contributed *to any extent* to the harm she suffered. In cases where this would yield a very harsh outcome, some juries have reached a compromise verdict, deciding for the plaintiff but awarding her damages at a reduced level to take account of her negligence. Although courts in civil cases have powers to set aside the verdict or alter the terms of the jury's award of damages, they have substantially accepted the right of juries to do this.[42]

There is also some evidence that juries are inclined not to follow the law in order to decide in favor of an injured plaintiff bringing suit against a corporate manufacturer. In fact, it is often claimed that in civil actions juries tend to disfavor corporations generally, and particularly corporations from another state.[43]

Chapter 7

The Jury as Safeguard against Government

American juries, like English juries, have been exercising the nullification power for centuries. It would go too far to say that juries have routinely exercised the nullification power in routine situations. But it is true that juries through all this time have routinely exercised the nullification power in a range of situations that are by no means exceptional.

There has been a great deal of controversy as to what the source of this power of the jury might be. Much of the debate has centered on whether the legal system itself grants the jury the right to exercise the nullification power. This question has been long and often passionately disputed, and has generated a vast literature.

In both American and English jurisprudence, a focus of this debate has been whether *Bushell's Case* declared that juries have a legal right to exercise the nullification power. In favor of this, one recent article in the *Yale Law Journal* declares that "the landmark decision in *Bushell's Case* established the right of juries under English common law to nullify on the basis of an objection to the law the defendant had violated." But against this, another recent article in the *Yale Law Journal* insists that Chief Justice Vaughan, the judge in that case, "did not defend nullification: His opinion nowhere speaks of a juror's right to disregard the law."[1]

Determining the precise holding of *Bushell's Case* may greatly interest legal historians. Yet although Chief Justice Vaughan was an eminent judge, what he might or might not have decided in London in 1670 does not have much value today *as legal precedent* that courts would feel obliged to comply with. In any event, an English legal decision does not generally bind American courts—and certainly not after more than three centuries. Rather, the importance of *Bushell's Case* is that it marks a political watershed, as will be explained shortly.

As well as referring back to *Bushell's Case*, American jurisprudence turns to the federal Constitution and the views of its Framers for considering the question of the jury having a legal right to exercise the nullification power. A particular focus is the role of the jury at the time when the Sixth Amendment to the Constitution was adopted, since this may be deemed to have informed the views of the Framers. This is a fertile ground of debate and dispute, supporting a proliferation of views.[2]

JUDICIAL AMBIVALENCE REGARDING THE NULLIFICATION POWER OF THE JURY

Toward the end of the nineteenth century the American judiciary began to focus on the question of the jury having a legal right to exercise the nullification power. In the 1895 Supreme Court case of *Sparf v US*, the majority opinion and the dissenting opinion respectively set out a clear account of the arguments against and for the existence of such a right. The majority view was that although jurors do "have the physical power to disregard the law, as laid down to them by the court," the law of the jurisdiction does not grant them any right to do so. Rather, the majority insisted, "it is the duty of the jury to follow the law as it is laid down by the court."[3]

This language of the majority opinion in *Sparf v US* has become the official declared position of the great majority of the American judiciary.[4] In line with this, a recent federal appellate court decision considered that "a juror who intends to nullify the applicable law" is comparable to "a juror who disregards the court's instructions due to an event or relationship that renders him biased or otherwise unable to render a fair and impartial verdict."[5]

Yet a powerful theme in important, leading cases directly contradicts this declared position. This theme shows the judiciary clearly accepting, and in fact relying on, the nullification power as essential to the role of the jury. A key case is the 1968 Supreme Court decision in *Duncan v Louisiana* (mentioned in the introduction). This case arose in a context of tension surrounding the racial integration of a high school. Gary Duncan, a young African American man, seeing two of his younger boy relatives who had recently transferred to the school engaged in a conversation with four white boys, encouraged his relatives to break off the encounter, and left with them in his car. He was accused of slapping one of the white boys on the elbow just before leaving, and prosecuted for simple battery.

Duncan requested trial by jury, but at the time Louisiana law granted jury trial only in capital cases or cases in which imprisonment at hard labor could be imposed. Simple battery was a misdemeanor punishable by a maximum of two years imprisonment and a fine, so Duncan's request was denied. He was convicted in a bench trial, sentenced to serve sixty days in the parish prison, and fined $150. He appealed unsuccessfully against the denial of a jury trial through the Louisiana courts and then took his case to the Supreme Court.[6]

The Sixth Amendment to the federal Constitution, guaranteeing a jury in criminal trials, on its face applies to the federal system but makes no mention of the states. The same is true of all of the first eight amendments to the Constitution, these being collectively dubbed the Bill of Rights in this context. However, starting from the end of the nineteenth century, the Supreme Court has applied a range of the provisions of the Bill of Rights to the states, in a process that has become known as the *incorporation doctrine*.[7]

The incorporation doctrine is by no means a wholesale application of the Bill of Rights to the states. Rather, for each individual provision of the Bill of Rights, the Court has carefully considered whether fundamental constitutional values require its application to the states. So it was a substantial step for the Court in *Duncan v Louisiana* to hold (by the large majority of seven votes to two) that the incorporation doctrine must extend to the Sixth Amendment. That is, the guarantee of a jury in criminal trials must apply to trials in state court just as it does in federal court.[8]

To justify this step, the Court needed to give serious consideration to the values that the jury system serves. This was not an occasion for carelessly presented claims, sloppily reasoned and unsupported by evidence, of the kind that part II of this book scrutinized and rejected. Rather, the Court declared:

> A right to jury trial is granted to criminal defendants in order to prevent oppression by the Government. Those who wrote our constitutions knew from history and experience that it was necessary to protect against unfounded criminal charges brought to eliminate enemies and against judges too responsive to the voice of higher authority. The framers of the constitutions strove to create an independent judiciary, but insisted upon further protection against arbitrary action. Providing an accused with the right to be tried by a jury of his peers gave him an inestimable safeguard against the corrupt or overzealous prosecutor and against the compliant, biased, or eccentric judge.[9]

The crux here is that there is only one way for the jury to safeguard against the various dangers of prosecutorial and judicial misbehavior that the Court catalogs: by exercising its nullification power. This is plain in the particular case against Duncan. Although Duncan denied that he had slapped the white boy, he did admit that he had touched the white boy on the elbow, and this admission would have been enough to make him guilty as charged. The reason is that the criminal offense of simple battery has a very broad scope in law. Intentionally touching a person on the elbow without his consent can be enough to meet the legal definition of simple battery.

So the only way in which a jury could make a difference in the case against Duncan would be by exercising its nullification power to acquit, regardless of the law and the evidence. The Supreme Court in *Duncan v Louisiana* understood this and relied on it. The Court not only acknowledges the nullification power, but also fully recognizes that the exercise of this power is fundamental to the value of the jury system.

Driving the point home, the Court, referring to the Kalven and Zeisel study discussed in chapter 4, declares that "the most recent and exhaustive study of the jury in criminal cases concluded that . . . when juries differ with the result at which the judge would have arrived, it is usually because they are serving some of the very purposes for which they were created and for which they are now employed."[10]

In the case against Duncan, the relevant purpose of the jury was, in the words of the Court, to act as a safeguard against a corrupt or overzealous prosecutor and a compliant or biased judge. An overzealous prosecutor is one who brings charges that may have some basis in the strict letter of the law, but that for any of a range of reasons it makes no sense to prosecute (see chapter 11). But a prosecutor who wishes to harass a particular individual or group may well prosecute precisely when it otherwise makes no sense to do so.

Duncan v Louisiana itself was plainly a case of corrupt or overzealous prosecution to harass African Americans. As a federal appellate court observed in later proceedings in the same case, even if Duncan had indeed slapped the white boy on the arm—again, committing a simple battery according to the strict letter of the law—it was "clear beyond dispute that any violation that may have occurred was so slight and technical as to be generally reserved for law school hypotheticals rather than criminal prosecutions." These later proceedings in fact revealed a pattern of harassment. Following the Supreme Court opinion in *Duncan v Louisiana*, the Louisiana legislature reduced the maximum sentence for simple battery to a level where Duncan could, consistently with the Court's holding, be once more tried without a jury. Duncan returned to the federal courts and obtained a permanent injunction against further prosecution, on the ground that the state prosecution was "instituted in bad faith and for purposes of harassment."[11]

More recently, in a 2000 case, the Supreme Court reaffirmed its commitment to its holding in *Duncan v Louisiana*, and to the principles underlying that holding, as the core of a centuries-long commitment. Citing to an authoritative nineteenth-century constitutional text, the Court declared that trial by jury is required "to guard against a spirit of oppression and tyranny on the part of rulers, and as the great bulwark of our civil and political liberties."[12]

So the holding in *Duncan v Louisiana* remains the law. A jury is guaranteed in state criminal trials just as in federal criminal trials. The reasons remain those declared by the Court, based squarely on the nullification power of the jury.

Other cases reflect the approach of *Duncan v Louisiana*. Chapter 6 noted the 1973 federal trial of the Camden 28, in which the judge strongly encouraged the jury to exercise its nullification power in response to government over-reaching. In the important 1975 case of *Taylor v Louisiana*, the Supreme Court relied on congressional legislative committee reports as having "recognized that the jury plays a political function in the administration of the law," and having specifically recognized that "the jury is designed not only to understand the case, but also to reflect the community's sense of justice in deciding it." More recently, the highly respected federal district judge Jack Weinstein, in his long and passionately argued opinion in the 2008 case of *US v Polizzi*, declares that the jury is "expected to limit . . . governmental overreaching."[13]

A good summary comes from federal district judge Dwyer:

This ability of the jury to acquit—to extend unarticulated mercy—has saved us from our official selves many times. . . . By defeating unjust prosecutions, by protecting the weak against overzealous officialdom, by fending off oppressive uses of the law, jurors have strengthened not just liberty but the rule of law itself—and they still do. . . . Jury mercy . . . is one part of the discretion jurors must use in deciding an endless variety of questions. . . . Jurors make judgments, and they do so by using not just the law laid out for them by the judge, but their own sense of justice as well.[14]

How, though, can *Sparf v US* (and its progeny) be put together with *Duncan v Louisiana* (and its progeny) to yield a coherent legal framework? It is simply impossible to do so. These cases are inherently in conflict. A federal appellate court explicitly recognized this conflict in an important 1972 case:

The pages of history shine on instances of the jury's exercise of its prerogative to disregard uncontradicted evidence and instructions of the judge. . . . The existence of an unreviewable and unreversible power in the jury, to acquit in disregard of the instructions on the law given by the trial judge, has for many years co-existed with legal practice and precedent upholding instructions to the jury that they are required to follow the instructions of the court on all matters of law.[15]

That is, on the one hand, judges decry the nullification power and reject it as lawless. On the other hand, it is impossible to read certain key cases in any other way than as judicial recognition that the nullification power is fundamental to the role of the jury in preventing oppression by the government.

THE POLITICAL PRINCIPLE OF BUSHELL'S CASE

Because of the inherent conflict between the judicial views that *Sparf v US* and *Duncan v Louisiana* represent, it is best not to try to understand the nullification power of the jury in terms of a legally granted right, but rather to view it as a political power. As such, it forms part of the framework within which the legal system operates in the political order of society.

The nullification power of the jury developed as part of this framework in the second half of the seventeenth century in England. This was an era of political turmoil and flux, with major shifts in the relationships between the branches of government and in the relationship between the government and the populace. The political structure that survives to the present day in England and that strongly influenced the American political system was in the process of formation, and the unquestionable power of the jury to acquit in a criminal case was in the process of becoming part of this political structure.

Given the tensions among the various court systems that tussled over jurisdictional issues in England's legal landscape at the time, there can be no certainty that every judge in England at once accepted *Bushell's Case* as binding precedent. So it may well be that some judge rendered a jury compliant by threats, or even by punishments, at some point after 1670. Records of that time are incomplete, so it cannot now be known for certain whether this occurred. But this is not of great importance in assessing the present-day role of the jury.

The crucial point is that from around the late seventeenth century it has become accepted that a jury's decision to acquit a criminal defendant is final in that trial and unquestionable after the trial. Since then, no government in any country with a common-law jury system has seriously attempted to compel a jury to convict a criminal defendant. Another way of putting this is that there has been no open assault by government against the nullification power of the jury.

As a result, after many centuries of use and development of the nullification power, the societal meaning of the jury entails this power as an essential aspect. It is fundamental to the very concept of the jury system that a jury's decision to acquit a criminal defendant is final in that trial and unquestionable after the trial. *Bushell's Case* conveniently symbolizes this, but it does so more as a political symbol than as a legal precedent.

If, on the contrary, *Bushell's Case* were a mere legal precedent, it could simply be overturned by judicial decision. We might imagine that in a clear case of jury nullification—say, an acquittal despite overwhelming and uncontradicted prosecution evidence—the trial judge, outraged, punishes the jurors. We might, for example, suppose that the judge declares the jurors to be in contempt of court and sentences each and every one of them accordingly. Contemplation of this as a possibility already strains the imagination—although on rare occasions judges have approached this point in regard to one or two individual jurors (see chapter 9). In any event, the jurors would doubtless appeal to a higher court against their punishment. So in order to contemplate *Bushell's Case* being overturned as judicial precedent, we must further imagine that the appellate courts, through to the highest court having jurisdiction, uphold the position of the trial court. This has never occurred in the past three centuries, and it strains the imagination beyond the breaking point to suppose that it might.

Yet there is nothing *in the law* to preclude judicial action of this kind. The reason why it would not occur, and indeed could not occur, is because it would transgress the boundaries of the action of legal processes within the political system. The courts are perfectly aware, and have long been so, that they lack the political authority to punish jurors for acquitting a criminal defendant regardless of the law and the evidence. In sum, although *Bushell's Case* was a legal opinion, the principle that it represents is an established political principle. This principle is so deeply established that it is doubtful whether even legislation could now overturn it.

So the conclusion is that the nullification power of the jury is more appropriately viewed as a political power than in terms of a legally granted right. That is, the jury is *empowered* within the political structure of society to acquit the defendant in a criminal case, regardless of the law and the evidence.

THE JURY AS "THE PEOPLE" IN THE SYSTEM OF CHECKS AND BALANCES

The political view of the jury positions it squarely within the system of checks and balances of the American constitutional system. Recognition of this goes back to the foundation of the American republic. Adams wrote regarding the jury: "As the constitution requires that the popular branch of the legislature should have an absolute check, so as to put a peremptory negative upon every act of the government, it requires that the common people, should have as complete a control, as decisive a negative, in every judgment of a court of judicature."[16]

It is crucial to this political view that a jury should not be perceived as merely a collection of a dozen or so individuals. Rather, this view of the jury is founded on perceiving it as a single body of citizens that *represents the people* as a whole.

This view of the jury harks back to its medieval origins. An authoritative legal history text informs that in thirteenth-century England "the voice of the twelve men [of the jury] is deemed to be the voice of the country-side, often the voice of some . . . district which is more than a district, which is a community." This view of the jury persisted through the centuries. In the late eighteenth century, the great English champion of civil liberties Charles Pratt, Lord Camden, forthrightly declared: "The jury are the people of England."[17]

In America today, we see this view of the jury espoused in regard to the grand jury as well as the trial jury. So a federal government publication declares: "The principle that only *the people as a whole through their represen-tatives* should have the power to institute criminal prosecutions is embodied in the Fifth Amendment of the Constitution, which guarantees the institution of the grand jury. Most state constitutions have similar provisions."[18]

The notion of a "representative" encompasses a number of different mean-ings. A person might be a representative of some group of people in the sense of being a *delegate* from that group tasked with furthering the desires that the members of the group have expressed to him. As another meaning, a person might be a representative of a group in the sense of being a *trustee* of that group tasked with furthering what he believes to be the interests of that group. As yet another example, a person might be a representative of a group in the sense of being *descriptive*, or typical, of that group in certain specified qualities.[19]

Declarations to the effect that the jury "is deemed to be the voice of the . . . community" suggest a view of the jury as a combination of "delegate" and "trustee." But there is also some factual basis for the notion of the American jury as representative of the people in a "descriptive" sense. This results from a series of federal court decisions regarding the process of jury selection. These decisions have required that the list from which juries are drawn must be like the community as a whole in certain key respects.

This jurisprudence originated in struggles against the continuing efforts by a number of states, particularly but not exclusively in the South, to empanel all-white juries. In 1940 the Supreme Court unanimously declared: "It is part of the established tradition in the use of juries as instruments of public justice that the jury be a body truly representative of the community. For racial dis-crimination to result in the exclusion from jury service of otherwise qualified groups not only violates our Constitution and the laws enacted under it, but is at war with our basic concepts of a democratic society and a representative government."[20]

In *Taylor v Louisiana*, the Court enunciated the principle underlying this declaration in the form of the so-called *fair cross section* requirement. This requirement, applicable in federal and state courts, is essentially that a range of "large, distinctive groups" must be included in the list from which jurors are drawn, in numbers that broadly reflect their proportion in the community. The fair cross section requirement does not give any clear rule for determining which large, distinctive groups must be included in this way. The federal courts have indicated that women, African Americans, Hispanics, and Jews constitute such groups. The courts have not set any clear standard as to how closely the proportion of members of a nonexcludable group in the list from which juries are drawn must match the proportion in the community.[21]

The fair cross section requirement applies to the list from which jurors are drawn, not to the particular jury in any given trial. The Court in *Taylor v Louisiana* insists that it "impose[s] no requirement that petit juries [that is, trial juries] actually chosen must mirror the community and reflect the various distinctive groups in the population. Defendants are not entitled to a jury of any particular composition." In an earlier case, the Court explains that "a defendant may not, for example, challenge the makeup of a jury merely because no members of his race are on the jury, but must prove that his race has been systematically excluded."[22]

This accords with the discussion in chapter 4 regarding jurors as the "peers" of the defendant. As explained there, the particular jurors in a trial might not be the peers of the defendant in terms of any close social or cultural match. Rather, they are the peers of the defendant in the broader sense of being his fellow private citizens rather than government. As such, they can fulfill their political role as safeguard against government, as long as they are selected fairly from the citizenry. Another way of putting this is that for the jury to fulfill its political role as safeguard against government, it must be representative of the people.

The fair cross section requirement attempts to deal with one of the preconditions for this: a range of "large, distinctive groups" must be included overall in a reasonable way. So for the jury to be able to fulfill its political role as safeguard against government, it is plainly necessary that the fair cross section requirement be properly implemented.

Consequently, it is a matter of concern regarding this political role of the jury that some state justice systems still try to avoid the fair cross section requirement, and that the federal courts now give them leeway to do so. A person convicted in state court who claims that the state system violated the fair cross section requirement must first pursue his claim through the state judicial system. He can then raise it in habeas corpus proceedings in federal district court. However, by a unanimous 2010 decision of the Supreme Court, federal courts must grant considerable respect to the determination of the state courts regarding how closely the list from which jurors are drawn should mirror the community and how closely it does mirror the community.[23]

Courts are also able to finesse the fair cross section requirement at the point of jury selection for individual trials, by permitting prosecutors to exercise their peremptory challenges to exclude members of particular groups. This was particularly used to ensure all-white juries for criminal trials of persons of color. In the 1986 case of *Batson v Kentucky*, the Supreme Court declared this practice to be unconstitutional. But, as a number of commentators have pointed out, any reasonably skilled prosecutor can avoid the restriction of *Batson v Kentucky* by finding pretexts to justify peremptory challenges against members of a particular group. In fact, chapter 4 noted a trial of a Latino defendant in which the prosecution successfully challenged every prospective Latino juror.[24]

In sum, although the fair cross section requirement does attempt to deal with an important precondition for juries to be reasonably regarded as representative of the people, some concerns remain as to how effectively it is implemented. Also, the inclusion of "large, distinctive groups" in a reasonable way is not the only precondition for the jury to be regarded as representative of the people; chapter 9 will consider another important precondition.

Note, though, that the view taken by government, as expressed in judicial opinions, endorses the fair cross section requirement. According to government, this requirement, as it is currently implemented, is sufficient to ensure that the jury is representative of the people. This is in fact very doubtful, as the discussion in this chapter has made clear and the discussion in chapter 9 will further make clear. Nonetheless it is fair to hold government to the standard that it has set and implemented. So when the jury exercises its nullification power to check the power of government, then government must surely accept that it is not merely a group of a dozen or so individuals but, rather, the representative of the people as a whole that has checked its power. Chapter 8 considers this further.

THE JURY SYSTEM AS LEGITIMATION OF GOVERNMENT

Government in a democracy can function only on the basis of being *legitimate*, enabling it to promulgate laws and expect the populace to conform to them.[25] The jury system has long fulfilled the political role of contributing to government legitimacy.

An illustration comes from the dispute, discussed in chapter 1, over the measurement of fishing nets in fourteenth-century London, where the mayor passed responsibility for the decision to a jury of fishmongers. By doing so, "the mayor increased the likelihood that the offending fishermen ... [as well as] other fishermen who did not have a direct stake in the matter would treat the decision as legitimate."[26] It was crucial for this that the sworn fishmongers should be respected in the community of fishermen. By taking responsibility for the outcome of the adjudication, the fishmongers then provided a public perception of fairness that gave legitimacy.

The modern jury, by taking its share of responsibility for the outcome of the trial, likewise provides a public perception of fairness that gives legitimacy.

Recall the ABA survey discussed in chapter 3. When presented with the statement, "The jury system is the most fair way to determine the guilt or innocence of a person accused of a crime," 78 percent of respondents expressed some level of agreement.[27] They perceived the justice system as being fairer with the jury system than it would be without the jury system. The justice system gains legitimacy from this public perception, regardless of whether it actually is fairer with the jury system.

As Dwyer explains: "The result in a given case may be debatable, but it is greatly legitimized if it comes from a jury." Similarly, William O. Douglas, as a member of the Supreme Court, observed: "Since [the jury] . . . is of and from the community, it gives the law an acceptance which verdicts of judges cannot do."[28]

In this vein, the Supreme Court has declared that "the essential feature of a jury obviously lies in the interposition between the accused and his accuser of the commonsense judgment of a group of laymen, and in *the community participation and shared responsibility* that results from that group's determination of guilt or innocence."[29] Of course, a jury decision can only be viewed as community participation if the jury is chosen in such a way as to fairly represent the people.

The jury, in delivering its verdict, may authorize government to take action. It does so whenever it delivers a verdict of guilty in a criminal trial or a verdict that may result in a judgment requiring enforcement in a civil trial. The entire train of government actions, from entry of judgment through to all forms of enforcement, ultimately depends wholly on the authorization that the jury's verdict has conferred. This authorization provides government with legitimacy for the action it takes in accordance with the jury's verdict.

The jury gives legitimacy to the action that government takes only because it is composed of individuals with the capacity to decide whether to authorize the government to act or whether not to do so. It follows that in a criminal trial a guilty verdict from the jury can potentially confer legitimacy only if the jury was able to deliver a verdict of not guilty, free of any control by government. Another way of putting this is that *the jury's political role of contributing to government legitimacy depends on the jury's possession of the nullification power.*

A court has occasionally recognized this. In a 1949 federal criminal prosecution of an association of fishermen for price-fixing, the association argued that the price-fixing protected them from hardship. The appellate court, affirming the conviction, stated: "in flagrant instances, the jury has always exercised the pardoning power, notwithstanding the law, which is their actual prerogative. This feature is of more importance here, since the jury, notwithstanding the arguments regarding economic oppression, did not see fit to acquit appellants."[30] That is, the fact that the jury refrained from exercising its nullification power gave legitimacy to the conviction.

So in a criminal case a jury has the capacity to safeguard against government by exercising the nullification power, thereby declaring that government has attempted to overreach. But it also has the capacity to legitimate government by refraining from exercising the nullification power, thereby declaring that government's intended action is appropriate to the situation. In this way, the political role of the jury in contributing to government legitimacy is a counterpart of the political role of the jury as safeguard against government. These roles are counterparts by virtue of the nullification power of the jury.

Chapter 8

The Worth of the Jury System

This chapter assesses whether the jury system is worth the considerable costs that it imposes on society. In making this assessment, the first step is to establish that whatever worth the jury system may have lies in its political roles, which in turn depend on the jury's possession of the nullification power.

Recall that part II (chapters 4 and 5) considered the various claims that have been made regarding the worth of the jury system. The conclusion there was that none of these claims have any merit except in certain particular situations. These situations can now be reexamined in terms of the political roles of the jury.

Chapter 4 dealt with the range of claims that a jury is likely to achieve a better result in a trial than a judge. It dismissed those claims as unpersuasive and lacking any evidentiary basis, with three possible exceptions. The first of these exceptions is that the jury, as the "peers" of the defendant, might set aside the law in favor of what it perceives as justice to a fellow private citizen. The second is that a jury might set aside the law in favor of community values and community interests that it considers more significant than the letter of the law. The third is that a jury might check pervasive judicial bias insofar as it is ready to apply its own view of how the case should be justly decided, even if this does not comport with how the judge has instructed it on the law.

All of these forms of jury action fit within the political role of the jury as safeguard against government. They all depend on the capacity of the jury to exercise the nullification power to reach a verdict regardless of the law and the evidence.

Also, if the jury does not exercise its nullification power, it is effectively declaring that the law should take precedence over any issues of citizen fellowship, community values and interests, or pervasive judicial bias. That is, in refraining from exercising its nullification power, the jury is fulfilling its political role as legitimation of government.

Chapter 5 dealt with a range of claims that the jury system promotes and maintains democratic citizenship. It dismissed those claims as unpersuasive and lacking any evidentiary basis, with two possible exceptions. One exception is that jury duty may serve as an education in citizenship insofar as it develops in jurors an appropriate sense of individual responsibility regarding when to defer and when not to defer to the authority of government. The other is that jury duty as participation in the system of government may promote democratic citizenship insofar as it enables jurors to provide constructive input into the policy-making processes of the justice system, which they can do by taking political and moral issues into account in rendering their verdict in appropriate cases.

A jury that decides not to defer to the authority of government will do so when it determines that government has acted or intends to act inappropriately. That is, the jury will act within its political role as safeguard against government. A jury that decides to provide constructive input into the policy-making processes of the justice system will do so by interposing its own judgment against that of government regarding what policy ought to be. So this form of jury action also fits within the political role of the jury as safeguard against government. Both these forms of jury action depend on the capacity of the jury to exercise the nullification power to reach a verdict regardless of the law and the evidence.

Also, if the jury does not exercise its nullification power, it is effectively declaring that, in the case it has been empanelled to decide, it should defer to the authority of government and does not need to provide input into the policy-making processes of the justice system. That is, in refraining from exercising its nullification power, the jury is fulfilling its political role as legitimation of government.

In sum, none of the various claims regarding the worth of the jury system that were examined in part II have any merit except insofar as they entail the political roles of the jury as safeguard against government and legitimation of government. The conclusion is that any worth that the jury system may have lies in its political roles. The jury expresses these roles in the particular situations noted in part II, as well as in the range of situations discussed in chapters 6 and 7.

THE NEED FOR AN ONGOING SAFEGUARD
AGAINST GOVERNMENT

American citizens are bound to differ as to whether our society needs any form at all of ongoing safeguard against government. Some might prefer to place total trust in government throughout its tenure in office, and in judges throughout their judicial tenure, to shoulder the responsibilities of running American society for all citizens. But it does not seem very likely that the majority would take this view. The populace overall has a very low level of trust in every branch of government (see chapter 3), which certainly suggests that most people would likely prefer not to place total, continuing trust in government, including the judiciary. Also, it is most likely that for anyone who considers that a safeguard against government is needed, the $2 billion a year that the jury system costs (see chapter 2), or even several times that amount, would seem a small price to pay for a satisfactory safeguard.

The question, though, is whether the jury system does satisfactorily meet the needs of American society for an ongoing safeguard against government. Note that the pertinent question is not whether the jury system is ideal in this respect. Rather, the question is whether the jury system is better than no ongoing safeguard at all, and better than any other ongoing safeguard that has been thought of and is at all likely to be implemented. This must be taken into account in assessing the various criticisms that have been leveled against the jury system in its role as an ongoing safeguard against government, through its exercise of the nullification power. These criticisms are the subject of the remainder of this chapter.

ARE THE POLITICAL ROLES OF THE JURY REDUNDANT
IN A MODERN DEMOCRACY?

Some judges claim that although the role of the jury as an ongoing safeguard against government may have been important in former times, it is no longer so. For example, the two members of the Supreme Court who dissented in *Duncan v Louisiana* recognized "that the principal original virtue of the jury trial [was] the limitations a jury imposes on a tyrannous judiciary," but insisted that this justification for the jury "has largely disappeared." As a reason for this, they stated that present-day trial judges are subject to review by higher courts, including the Supreme Court itself.[1]

The dissenters here evaded the most blatant aspect of the actual case before them: the only prospect for getting justice for Duncan was to interpose a jury between him and the Louisiana judiciary. Although Duncan had clearly been prosecuted solely for purposes of racial harassment, the prosecution was in accordance with the strict letter of the law. There is no constitutional provision to check such a prosecution.[2] Similar issues arise wherever there is pervasive bias in a judicial system, as discussed in chapter 4.

The dissenters continued: "We no longer live in a medieval or colonial society." This is characteristic of a theme in American jurisprudence that links the nullification power to the preindependence colonial era. This theme appears in a 1972 federal appellate court opinion opposing the exercise of the nullification power. The court argued that after independence "the judges in the courts were not the colonial appointees projecting royalist patronage and influence but were themselves part and parcel of the nation's intellectual mainstream, subject to the checks of the common law tradition and professional opinion and capable ... of providing 'true judicial justice' standing in contrast with the colonial experience."[3]

These arguments are unpersuasive, because they casually ignore the range of postcolonial American cases (a number of which were surveyed in chapter 6) in which juries have exercised the nullification power to prevent injustice. The judges who heard these cases did not project royal patronage and were as much "part and parcel of the nation's intellectual mainstream" as they are today. Again, these arguments also ignore the issues of pervasive judicial bias discussed in chapter 4.

The dissenters in *Duncan v Louisiana* argued further that the structure of modern government makes the jury's political role as a safeguard against government superfluous: "Judges enforce laws enacted by democratic decision. ... They are elected by the people or appointed by the people's elected representatives." Similarly in England, the *Criminal Courts Review* finds "it unreal to regard the random selection, not election, of 12 jurors from one small area as an exercise in democracy ... to set against the national will. ... They are not there to substitute their view of the propriety of the law for that of Parliament or its enforcement for that of its appointed Executive."[4]

In characterizing the jury as the random selection of twelve persons from one small area, the *Review* rejects the defining idea of the jury as representative of the people. This is unacceptable. As chapter 7 explained, government cannot be permitted to celebrate the jury as "the people" at one moment and derogate it as twelve random individuals at another moment, according to its own convenience.

Of course, in the great majority of cases the jury does exactly as the *Review* desires. That is, the jury finds the facts and applies the law to them, and finds nothing of concern regarding the propriety of the law or the manner of enforcement of it. However, for several centuries, in America as much as in England, the jury has been there precisely so that in particular cases it *can* substitute its view of the propriety of the law for that of the legislature or its enforcement for that of the executive. As one legal scholar points out, "trials in which juries sit are long, expensive, prone to unseemly forensics, and sometimes productive of decisions that are probably at odds with the substantive rules that the judge instructs the jury to apply. But the . . . inconveniences of jury trial were accepted precisely because in important instances, through its ability to disregard substantive rules of law, the jury would reach a result that the judge either could not or would not reach."[5]

It is also misleading to claim that a jury that exercises the nullification power is "set against the national will." The jury may well be set against the will of the current government, but the will of the current government cannot simply be equated with the national will.[6] In fact, in terms of the specific outcome of a particular case, it would generally be difficult to determine what the "national will" is, or even whether there is such a thing as a "national will" at all. It is true to say that "on most issues there is no uniform will or opinion of the people or the majority of the people. There are several mutually inconsistent opinions of different groups of people, and a mass of largely uninterested persons."[7] But the key point is that the continuing institution over several centuries of juries endowed with the nullification power is powerful evidence that insofar as there is a "national will" on any matter, there is a "national will" that juries should be endowed with the nullification power. So it is fair to say that when a jury acts contrary to the will of the current government in an appropriate case, it is doing precisely what the national will has established it to do.

IS THE NULLIFICATION POWER OF THE JURY AN UNWIELDY AND INCONSISTENT INSTRUMENT?

The legal scholar Andrew Leipold makes this criticism:

[J]ury nullification is far better equipped for doing individual justice than for carrying out a conscious political campaign. Indeed, it is hard to imagine a more unwieldy instrument for legal reform. At the heart of any successful reform effort is the ability to convey a clear message, but because general verdicts in criminal cases are opaque, any message that the jurors hoped to send can easily be lost. Moreover, juries are independent actors, so verdicts in similar cases on the same laws will differ, which not only further blurs the political message, but also means that huge numbers of acquittals are required to catch the legislature's attention.[8]

Of course, there is some truth to this. Yet despite this, juries in a range of situations have managed to send a message clear enough to catch the attention of the political establishment and the general populace. In an important federal appellate case, Chief Judge Bazelon explained:

> The noble uses of the [nullification] power—the uses that "enhance the over-all normative effect of the rule of law"—also provide an important input to our evaluation of the substantive standards of the criminal law. The reluctance of juries to hold defendants responsible for unmistakable violations of the prohibition laws told us much about the morality of those laws and about the "criminality" of the conduct they proscribed. And the same can be said of the acquittals returned under the fugitive slave law as well as contemporary gaming and liquor laws.[9]

Other illustrations of the political effectiveness of the exercise of the nullification power of the jury through the centuries are among the cases surveyed in chapter 6. In eighteenth-century England there was general awareness that juries would exercise the nullification power to avoid the death penalty in theft cases; because of this, Blackstone was able to give the practice a name—pious perjury—that became widely recognized. Half a century later, the refusal of juries to convict in capital cases led to petitions to reduce the number of capital offenses and ultimately strongly influenced the eventual passage of the desired legislation.

In sum, it is true that juries that exercise the nullification power can convey blurred messages. Yet even so, these messages have on many occasions conveyed a public mood well enough to induce government to take notice.

Of course, a clear message conveying a public mood would be yet more likely than a blurred message to lead to reform. But the point made earlier applies here. That is, the crucial issue is not whether the jury system is the ideal way of conveying a public mood regarding legal reform, but whether there is any better way that is at all likely to be implemented. None has been suggested so far. And again, criticism of the nullification power of the jury as an unwieldy and inconsistent instrument must face up to the fact that whatever worth the jury system may have lies in its political roles, which in turn depend on the jury's possession of the nullification power.

IS THE EXERCISE OF THE NULLIFICATION POWER A PATH TO ANARCHY?

A 2001 decision of the California Supreme Court provides a typical expression of the criticism considered here. In regard to jurors who are prepared to exercise the nullification power, the court declares:

> In addition to refusing to follow laws they view as unjust, such jurors could choose to disregard instructions mandated by the Legislature not

to read media accounts of the trial, not to discuss the case with others, or not to conduct their own investigation by visiting the crime scene. The jury might feel free to ignore the presumption of innocence or find the defendant guilty even though some jurors harbor a reasonable doubt. A jury might disregard an instruction not to draw an inference from the exercise of a privilege and assume the defendant must be guilty if he or she chooses not to testify. In a capital case, a juror could vote to impose the death penalty without considering mitigating evidence. Some jurors might decide not to view a defendant's confession with caution or not require corroboration of the testimony of an accomplice. A jury even might determine that deliberations are too difficult and decide the defendant's guilt by the flip of a coin.[10]

Presumably, a jury might do any of these things. In fact, as chapter 4 discussed under the rubric of unsound-jury behavior, juries have actually done some of them. Certainly, unjust verdicts—both acquittals and convictions—can result.

However, the crucial question is whether jurors who are prepared to exercise the nullification power are more likely to engage in the various improper forms of behavior that the California Supreme Court catalogs than jurors who are not prepared to do so. The court does not state candidly that this is the case, but plainly wishes to imply that it is; otherwise, the court's outburst is pointless. The problem is that there is not a shred of evidence to support any such accusation. The court had several centuries of well-documented instances of the exercise of the nullification power in America, England, and elsewhere at its disposal. Yet it failed to cite to any case or any study that even suggests that the exercise of the nullification power has been in the slightest degree associated with any of the frightful eventualities that it catalogs.

As a federal appellate court has acknowledged, the idea that "avowal of the jury's [nullification] prerogative runs the risk of anarchy ... contains an element of hyperbole." In fact, chapter 6 reviewed many cases in which juries showed serious and commendable commitment to the burdensome responsibilities of their political roles, in exercising the nullification power to prevent grave injustice. Some of them—beginning with the jurors in *Bushell's Case*—showed great courage in the face of judicial arrogance and hostility. "The pages of history shine" on these jurors.[11] In associating their behavior with the irresponsibility of jurors who "determine that deliberations are too difficult and decide the defendant's guilt by the flip of a coin," the California Supreme Court was gratuitously offensive.

Although the *Criminal Courts Review* in England refrains from such invidious comparisons, it takes a similar view of the nullification power as anarchical, describing it as "a blatant affront to the legal process and the main purpose of the criminal justice system—the control of crime."[12] The problem with this description is that the main purpose of the criminal justice system is not the control of crime unconditionally, but rather the control of crime *by legitimate means in a just society*. Juries have appropriately exercised the nullification power to acquit a defendant when a conviction would entail serious injustice. As federal district judge Nancy Gertner rhetorically asks: "if the system is not about justice, what is it about?"[13]

Also, the *Review* here forgets that jurors as well as judges wish to control crime. In fact, an average jury will quite possibly be composed of persons more exposed to the dangers of crime, and so even more directly interested in controlling it, than a judge. So a jury that exercises its nullification power may well have taken the need to control crime fully into account, but despite this has rejected the law as unjust.

Yet putting aside hyperbole, it is possible that a jury exercising its nullification power might be imbued with a responsible sense of imposing a justifiable political check on government, and might nonetheless overreach with damaging effects on society. Part V considers this further within the general context of conscientious fulfillment of jury duty, including conscientiousness in the exercise of the nullification power.

IS THE NULLIFICATION POWER A LICENSE
FOR UNJUST ACQUITTALS?

The nullification power permits a jury to deliver a verdict of not guilty, in disregard of the law and the evidence, according to its principles, sense of fairness and justice, and good conscience. But it likewise permits a jury to deliver a verdict of not guilty, in disregard of the law and the evidence, according to its eccentricities, prejudices (individual or popular), or perversities. A jury whose members have abhorrent attitudes possesses the nullification power just as much as does one whose members have admirable attitudes. In every case, the jury delivers its verdict without giving reasons or justifications, and the government has no recourse when the verdict is one of not guilty.

Among the most harrowing illustrations of the exercise of the nullification power to support injustice was the practice in some Southern states around the middle of the twentieth century. All-white juries there routinely acquitted any white person accused of lynching a black person, regardless of the evidence. Yet these cases do not amount to any devastating critique of the political role of the jury as a safeguard against government through the exercise of the nullification power. These juries were generally not acting to safeguard against government but were collaborating with government. As one legal scholar explains:

> Many southern state and local legal institutions through the civil rights era demonstrated themselves unable or unwilling to administer nonracist justice. Juries were only one manifestation of biased decisions arising from immoral local norms. Local judges, as well as law enforcement officials and prosecutors, demonstrated equally blatant racial bias. Judges violated the rule of law roughly as much as juries. Southern justice administration during that period demonstrates not that juries are a particularly bias-prone decisionmaker, but that the rule of law is contingent upon a political and moral culture, including popular culture, for its existence.[14]

Also, as long as juries possess the nullification power, the fact that one jury might use that power to do injustice is not *in itself* a reason for another jury to decline to use that power to do justice. As James Madison pointed out two centuries ago: "Some degree of abuse is inseparable from the proper use of every thing."[15]

Finally, there is some reason to hope that unjust acquittals based on prejudice may ultimately draw societal attention to the prejudice, and may thereby focus efforts on combating the prejudice. As Bazelon observed:

> One often-cited abuse of the nullification power is the acquittal by bigoted juries of whites who commit crimes (lynching, for example) against blacks. . . . But the revulsion and sense of shame fostered by that practice fueled the civil rights movement, which in turn made possible the enactment of major civil rights legislation. That same movement spurred on the revitalization of the equal protection clause and, in particular, the recognition of the right to be tried before a jury selected without bias. The lessons we learned from these abuses helped to create a climate in which such abuses could not so easily thrive.[16]

Part IV

Government Obstruction of the Jury

Chapter 9

Obstruction of the Jury in the Trial Process

Government is ambivalent toward juries. In a criminal case, a jury verdict of guilty gives legitimacy to the trial process and to the punishment that government then imposes on the convicted defendant. A jury verdict of not guilty also gives legitimacy to the trial process, but it frustrates the desire of government to impose punishment on the defendant. The frustration is particularly severe if the acquittal appears to be an exercise of the jury's nullification power to impose a check on government. As a result, government, including the judiciary, has developed a range of practices that obstruct the jury's exercise of the nullification power, and so hinder the jury in fulfilling its political roles.

JURY SELECTION THROUGH VOIR DIRE

A practice with a long history is that of selecting a jury that is unlikely to exercise the nullification power. This practice first developed in England, with one of the earliest documented cases involving the grand jury rather than the trial jury. In 1681, Stephen Colledge, an author of anti-Catholic ballads during the reign of a Catholic king, was accused of "ostentatiously displaying weapons and . . . speaking threateningly against the king." In a tense political context of continuing furor over the decision in *Bushell's Case*, a London grand jury frustrated the government by refusing to issue an indictment.

The government then transferred the case to Oxford, and the secretary of state wrote to the official entrusted with jury selection, requesting "a good, honest, substantial grand jury . . . consist[ing] of men rightly principled for the Church and the King." The grand jury selected in accordance with this request duly issued the indictment. Colledge was found guilty at the ensuing trial and hanged.[1]

The English government was keen to select amenable trial juries as well as grand juries. An important way of doing this was through the institution of the so-called special jury. The special jury had its origins in panels selected for particular knowledge or expertise. An early precursor was the jury of fishmongers convened in fourteenth-century London to decide a dispute over the measurement of fishing nets, discussed in chapters 1 and 7. But by the nineteenth century the special jury had become a jury selected from a secret list of persons acceptable to government, who were sometimes paid for their services. Two centuries ago, the English jurist Jeremy Bentham denounced the institution of the special jury: "[In] giving to a Board, secretly composed of commissioners, paid, placed, and displaceable by the servants of the crown, the respected and almost sacred name of *Jury* . . . [the government] thus contrived to transfer, to the counterfeit institution, all that attachment and confidence, so justly possessed by the genuine one which it supplants."[2]

Not surprisingly, once it became generally known that the special jury was such a "counterfeit institution," confidence in the jury diminished. The practice of selecting special juries eventually became more of a liability than a benefit to the English government, which finally abolished special juries in 1949.[3]

However, starting in 1948 the English government developed the practice of "jury vetting," whereby in certain cases the prosecution privately checked the jury list against police records, eliminating anyone that it considered unsatisfactory. The aim, as declared by the attorney general when the practice was eventually acknowledged, was to ensure that jurors were "well inclined towards their king's and country's service and interest." The echo of the terms used in 1681 is remarkable. The published official guidelines for jury vetting in England suggest that it is now quite limited in scope, although it is hard to be certain of what happens in practice.[4]

Although the American system of special or blue ribbon juries, noted in chapter 6, was not at all the same as the English system of special juries, it too could produce juries that were more inclined to favor government and, in particular, relatively unlikely to exercise the nullification power. But with the broad enlargement of the list from which jurors are drawn, as mandated by the Supreme Court (see chapter 7), government could no longer rely on this system.

Government in America has come to rely instead on *voir dire* scrutiny of prospective jurors to eliminate anyone who might be disposed to exercise the nullification power. In most state and federal courts, each prospective juror can expect to be asked whether he is willing to accept the law from the judge as she gives it in her instructions. Many courts also question prospective jurors as to whether they are aware of the existence of the nullification power, although without necessarily using the "nullification" terminology. No prospective juror will be allowed to serve unless he can sufficiently assure the judge that he will accept the law as she gives it in her instructions and will not under any circumstances exercise the nullification power.[5]

A number of courts go yet further and simply reject any prospective jurors who are at all aware of the nullification power, even if they have only heard of it through literature, radio shows, or discussion.[6] It is in fact surprising that there are enough people unaware of the nullification power of the jury to provide a sufficient supply of jurors for these courts. The jury system is a cornerstone of the American justice system, and juries have been exercising the nullification power since the foundation of the Republic, and did so in the colonies prior to independence. The key case on nullification, *Bushell's Case*, derived from the prosecution of William Penn, who, as the founder of Pennsylvania, is a famous, much studied figure in American history. In particular, the public schools are tasked with teaching the history and civic values of the nation; it is hard to comprehend how they are able to avoid mentioning the nullification power of the jury.

Insofar as prospective jurors may be unaware of the nullification power of the jury, a number of jurisdictions do their best to keep them unaware. They prevent people, particularly members of various organizations devoted to advocating the exercise of the nullification power, from providing prospective jurors at the courthouse with even the most general information and advocacy material on the nullification power. A few have even been prosecuted for jury tampering.[7]

There would be no difficulty in creating powerful advocacy material for the exercise of the nullification power of the jury composed entirely of passages drawn from Supreme Court and federal appellate court opinions and the writings of presidents of the United States. It is sobering to reflect that standing on the steps of a courthouse and distributing such material could feasibly result in being prosecuted and sentenced to a term of imprisonment.

However, the crucial point here is that excluding from the jury persons who might exercise the nullification power undermines the capacity of the jury to fulfill its political roles. The jury that results has been purposely selected to favor government, and so cannot reasonably be regarded as representative of the people in relation to government (see chapter 7). Such a jury is unlikely to fulfill its political role of acting as a safeguard against government by acquitting in cases of severe injustice. In addition, its decisions can provide no legitimacy for government. That is, such a jury has no capacity to fulfill its political role as legitimation of government. In Bentham's terms, a jury from which anyone who might exercise the nullification power has been purposely excluded is a mere "counterfeit institution."

Recall also that only the political roles of the jury, based on its nullification power, can justify the substantial costs that society bears for the jury system. A jury system that purposely excludes everyone who might exercise the nullification power is simply a waste of billions of dollars worth of society's valuable resources every year.

JURY SELECTION THROUGH ABOLITION OF EXEMPT CATEGORIES

Until a generation or two ago, the state of New York granted exemption from jury duty to the following classes of persons: "clergymen, physicians, dentists, pharmacists, embalmers, optometrists, attorneys, members of the Army, Navy or Marine Corps, or of the National Guard of Naval Militia, firemen, policemen, ship's officers, pilots, editors, editorial writers, sub-editors, reporters and copy readers." It also granted exemption to all women.[8]

It used to be typical of most jurisdictions to prescribe such a miscellany of so-called exempt categories of people who were granted the right to refuse to perform jury duty. In addition, various government officials, including judges, were generally ineligible for jury duty.

Over the years, there was a growing tendency to view these provisions overall as unfair. They excused a large segment of the populace from jury duty, which increased the burden on those who were not excused. In addition, many of those who were excused were in the professional, relatively privileged classes, which enhanced the sense of unfairness.[9]

During the last twenty years or so, virtually all of these excusals from jury duty on the basis of profession or occupation have been abolished throughout America,[10] as well as in England. This has made perfect sense regarding most of the professions and occupations whose members were formerly excused. There is, after all, no good reason why embalmers and editors should be excused from jury duty, and the same holds for most of the rest of the miscellany of formerly excused professions and occupations.

However, there was a good deal of controversy over making government officials, including judges, eligible for jury duty. Most of the criticisms that were leveled against this development concerned trial values, of the kind discussed in chapter 4. That is, the criticisms focused on how the inclusion of government officials on the jury might affect the jury's regular trial task of determining the facts and applying the law to them to reach a verdict.

For example, the critics were concerned that a government official serving on a jury might have excessive influence on other jurors. They were also concerned that a judge serving as a juror could apply her knowledge of the justice system to glean information that is supposed to be withheld from the jury. But throughout America, and also in England, many such concerns relating to trial values were swept aside in the interests of abolishing the range of categories of excusal from jury duty and enlarging the list from which jurors are drawn.[11]

Several American states, as well as a number of other countries with a common-law jury system, still do not allow police officers, prosecutors, and prison officers to serve on a jury, because "the possibility of bias . . . inevitably flows from the presence on a jury of persons professionally committed to one side only of an adversarial trial process."[12] However, England has abolished by statute all categories of ineligibility or excusal based on occupation, so police officers, prosecutors, and prison officers are officially allowed to serve, although they can still be challenged on an individual basis.[13]

Yet virtually no attention has been paid to the concern that is of central importance here: the inclusion of government officials on a jury undermines the jury's capacity to fulfill its political roles. As a matter of principle, if a government official serves on a jury, then that jury no longer represents the people in relation to government. As a matter of practice, a government official is in no position to act as a safeguard against government by exercising the nullification power in regard to a law enacted by the government of which he is an official.

So, for example, in the state of New York each of two successive mayors of the city of New York—Rudolph ("Rudy") Giuliani and Michael Bloomberg— appeared in state trial court in response to a summons for jury duty.[14] There was extensive press coverage and considerable fanfare in celebration of these events. Although the court was a state court and the mayor is a city government official, he is such a powerful official within the tightly woven web of relationships running throughout government at the federal, state, and local levels that it is difficult to view him as representing the people in relation to government. Certainly, it is difficult to imagine that the mayor would be willing to act as a safeguard against any level of government by exercising the nullification power of the jury.

Overall, the inclusion of government officials on the jury risks making a "counterfeit institution" of the jury. Also, this development, by focusing on the jury's regular trial task of determining the facts and applying the law to them to reach a verdict, has failed to recognize that only the political roles of the jury, based on its nullification power, can justify the substantial costs that society bears for the jury system.

There has also been controversy over making attorneys eligible for jury duty, which virtually all jurisdictions have now done. Again, most of the criticisms have focused on how having lawyers on the jury might affect the jury's regular trial task of determining the facts and applying the law to them to reach a verdict. A few criticisms have voiced a general disquiet. For example, an experienced English barrister comments: "I'm a great believer in the jury system and one of the reasons why people have had such confidence in it in the past is because lawyers weren't allowed. . . . The system worked on the basis that the lawyers ran the trial and a judge presided over it, but the ultimate decision-making was left to the layman. That's a very important feature that has been completely overlooked." As another experienced English barrister insists: "The whole point of having a jury system is that it is comprised of non-lawyers."[15]

However, the issue of central importance here is quite specific: that the inclusion of lawyers on a jury has the potential to undermine the jury's capacity to fulfill its political roles. The key point is that attorneys are members of the bar of their jurisdiction, and so are subject to control by the bar authorities. In some states, the bar authorities are the regular courts, which directly control the behavior of attorneys. In other states, the bar authorities are nominally separate from the regular courts, but they still effectively wield government power insofar as the regular courts will enforce their decisions as necessary. So, particularly, when the bar authorities suspend or disbar an attorney, she commits a criminal offense if she subsequently practices law, and is subject to prosecution in the regular courts.

A recent disciplinary proceeding against a California attorney shows the potential danger. The attorney, Fahy, was a juror in a civil trial in which the jury became deadlocked, with Fahy in the minority. After the judge urged the jury to continue to deliberate, Fahy changed his vote, explicitly telling his fellow jurors that he was doing so to bring the trial to a close and allow him to return to his law practice.

At the ensuing disciplinary proceeding, evidence was heard as to the jury deliberations, with the jury foreperson brought in to testify as to Fahy's jury-room statement.[16] On appeal, the Review Department of the California State Bar Court did not find it worrisome that the judge at the disciplinary hearing had scrutinized the jury deliberations. As to the substance of the appeal, the Review Department stated:

> With regard to the hearing judge's findings that respondent violated his duty as an attorney to comply with the law . . . by violating his duties as a civil trial juror, the conclusion is inescapable that he is culpable as charged. . . . [T]he harm to the parties and to the fair administration of justice is clear and serious when respondent [Fahy] disregarded his duty to vote as the facts and judge's instructions guided him, and instead voted as the convenience of his law practice swayed.[17]

There can surely be no sympathy whatsoever for Fahy's appalling behavior in voting "as the convenience of his law practice swayed." The problem is that this holding of the Review Department *uses a quite different ground* to set a strong precedent for future disciplinary proceedings against attorneys. The

holding of the Review Department was that Fahy, serving as a juror, was subject to discipline as an attorney because he "disregarded his duty to vote as
the facts and judge's instructions guided him." But any juror who acts as a
safeguard against government by exercising the nullification power does not
vote as the facts and judge's instructions guide him. His capacity to vote in
appropriate cases contrary to the facts and the judge's instructions is precisely
the basis of the political roles of the jury, which alone can justify the substantial costs that society bears for the jury system.

This holding of the Review Department is consistent with the position of
the California courts, which are generally hostile to the exercise of the nullification power of the jury. Their position is similar to that of *Sparf v US* (see
chapter 7). In fact, the California Supreme Court has specifically declared that
a juror who refuses to deliberate "according only to the evidence presented . . .
and to the instructions of the court" has shown himself "unable to perform his
duty" as a juror.[18]

In general, government has no recourse against a juror who exercises the
nullification power—unless, it now seems, that juror is an attorney. It is plain
from the Fahy case that any attorney serving as a juror who exercises the nullification power faces the danger of a disciplinary proceeding. A disciplinary
proceeding can result in disbarment, destroying the attorney's professional
life. This threat undermines the capacity of any attorney serving as a juror to
act as a safeguard against government by exercising the nullification power.

More than three centuries after *Bushell's Case*, it is hardly appropriate that
any individual, whatever her profession, should need to consider the possibility of severe penalties for her vote as a juror. As long as this threat remains, a
jury on which an attorney serves must be viewed as a mere "counterfeit
institution."

CONCEALMENT OF THE NULLIFICATION POWER
FROM THE JURY

The previous discussion showed many courts doing their best to select
jurors who are unaware of the nullification power of the jury. Most courts will
also take measures as necessary during the course of the trial to ensure that
jurors remain unaware. Sometimes the defense in a criminal trial tries to
argue to the jury that it should take into account issues extraneous to the law
and the evidence in reaching its verdict, but the judge will usually intervene
to prevent this.

For example, in a prosecution of protestors against the Vietnam War for
burglary of offices of the Dow Chemical Company, the defendants tried to
introduce arguments regarding the role of Dow in the war. The judge disal-
lowed this, and the appellate court affirmed, explicitly rejecting the defendants'

claim that they had a right to argue the issue of "nullification" to the jury. A more recent instance occurred in a federal prosecution for distributing marijuana to seriously ill patients on behalf of an official program of the city of Oakland in California. The trial judge prevented the defendant "from putting on a 'medical marijuana' defense, introducing evidence or argument aimed at jury nullification."[19]

A judge who conceals from the jury that it possesses the nullification power can effectively control the outcome of the case. In *US v Krzyske*, a federal prosecution of a tax protestor for failing to file tax returns:

> Krzyske mentioned the doctrine of jury nullification in his closing argument. During its deliberation the jury asked the court what the doctrine stood for. The court responded, "There is no such thing as valid jury nullification. Your obligation is to follow the instructions of the Court as to the law given to you. You would violate your oath and the law if you willfully brought in a verdict contrary to the law given you in this case."[20]

The judge here was being disingenuous. It is absolutely not true that the jury's exercise of the nullification power violates the law. There is no law whatsoever—whether statutory or judicially developed within the common law—that the exercise of the nullification power of the jury even arguably violates. Also, it is not at all clear that the jury's exercise of the nullification power violates the jurors' oath (see chapter 12).

The jury convicted the defendant Krzyske, and the appellate court affirmed. An application to the appellate court for reconsideration was denied, so that the conviction was upheld. In that application, the defendant submitted the sworn affidavit of one of the original trial jurors:

> On June 25, 1985 we jurors asked the trial judge, Charles W. Joiner, during the first day of deliberations and before any verdicts were returned, the following question:
> "WHAT IS JURY NULLIFICATION?"
> This question was in the form of a note to the judge, and it was asked because we were very inquisitive as to its meaning. When the trial judge responded by saying "There is no such thing as valid jury nullification," we were left very confused. After the trial was over, I learned what jury nullification was because I was still in doubt over its meaning as the trial was concluding. If we were told the truth about jury nullification a different outcome would have resulted in favor of the defendant, Kevin

Elwood Krzyske, because I (for one) would have voted for "acquittal" on all counts of the indictment.[21]

By securing a conviction in a case where the jury would have exercised its nullification power, the judge effectively obstructed the jury in the fulfillment of its political roles. This is a clear case of the judiciary making a mere "counterfeit institution" of the jury.

Among the minority of judges who support the nullification power of the jury, there is considerable debate as to whether the jury should be instructed on it. One federal appellate judge expresses concern that informing the jury of its nullification power "conveys an implied approval," and prefers rather "to structure instructions in such wise that the jury must feel strongly about the values involved in the case, so strongly that it must itself identify the case as establishing a call of high conscience, and must independently initiate and undertake an act in contravention of the established instructions." Similarly, Dwyer states: "What, then, should jurors in a criminal case be told about their right to acquit for the sake of conscience, regardless of the evidence? The best answer, in my view, is to say nothing. . . . Jurors . . . know that their sense of justice has a rightful place in court."[22]

These are frankly incoherent views. A more persuasive argument is that "a jury carefully instructed on its power and responsibility" would be most likely to exercise the nullification power appropriately.[23]

A closely connected issue is whether the jury should be informed of the possible sentence to be imposed on the defendant in the event of a conviction. Trial courts generally refuse to inform the jury, or allow the defense to inform the jury, of any matters relating to sentencing. The reason is plain from Blackstone's "pious perjury" theft cases: if the jury in such a case had not known what the fatal amount was, it would not have been able to assess the value of goods stolen at slightly less than this amount.

For this very reason, some judges who approve of the nullification power feel that information on sentencing should be made available to the jury. In a recent federal prosecution for receiving and possessing child pornography, defendant was a troubled individual who had himself suffered sexual abuse. Weinstein, the trial judge, plainly would have liked to make sentencing information available to the jury, but higher-court precedent prevented him from doing so. After the jury had rendered a verdict of guilty and was discharged, the judge requested its members to stay for a moment. He asked them: "Had you known that the penalty was . . . a minimum of five [years imprisonment] . . . would that have affected the verdict of any of you?" Several jurors declared that they would have found the defendant not guilty by reason of insanity.[24] Here, keeping the jury unaware of the consequences of its verdict effectively obstructed it in the fulfillment of its political roles.

PRESSURE ON THE JURY

Before the jury retires to consider its verdict, the judge instructs it as to its duties. Trial courts commonly use an admonitory form of jury instruction that effectively denies the existence of the nullification power of the jury. One standard instruction is: "If, based on your consideration of the evidence, in light of the law that applies, you are satisfied that the defendant's guilt has been proven beyond a reasonable doubt, then you *must* find him/her guilty." One writer—a retired judge—assesses this as a "strong and provocative . . . direction from the judge" that may well influence the jury not to exercise its nullification power.[25]

Another standard form, used in federal trial courts within the jurisdiction of the Eleventh Circuit Court of Appeals, is: "You *must* . . . follow the law as I explain it to you whether you agree with that law or not; and you *must* follow all of my instructions as a whole. You *may not* single out, or disregard, any of the Court's instructions on the law."[26]

Feelings on this matter run high. One commentator expresses his indignation at the Eleventh Circuit jury instruction, and any akin to it, in ringing tones: "Imagine a jury composed of Thomas Jefferson, Alexander Hamilton, John Adams, and James Wilson. They would not have stood silent in the face of such an instruction, and neither should their rightful heirs."[27]

The court may be able to maintain its pressure during jury deliberations. For example, a federal trial court dismissed a juror during deliberations after several other jurors reported to the judge that this juror intended to exercise the nullification power. The jury of the eleven remaining members convicted the defendant. The appellate court declared:

> We categorically reject the idea that, in a society committed to the rule of law, jury nullification is desirable or that courts may permit it to occur when it is within their authority to prevent. Accordingly, we conclude that a juror who intends to nullify the applicable law is no less subject to dismissal than is a juror who disregards the court's instructions due to an event or relationship that renders him biased or otherwise unable to render a fair and impartial verdict.[28]

The appellate court considered that there was some doubt about whether the juror actually did intend to exercise the nullification power. Because of this, it remanded for a new trial instead of simply upholding the conviction.[29] But the ultimate result was that the trial court thwarted any possibility of this juror exercising the nullification power.

A California trial court dismissed a juror during deliberations under similar circumstances, and the remaining jurors convicted the defendant. The California Supreme Court, upholding the conviction, declared: "The circumstance that, as a practical matter, the jury in a criminal case may have the ability to disregard the court's instructions in the defendant's favor without recourse by the prosecution does not diminish the trial court's authority to discharge a juror who, the court learns, is unable or unwilling to follow the court's instructions."[30]

Clearly, pressure of these various kinds can effectively obstruct the jury in the fulfillment of its political roles, and so undermine the value of the jury system to society.

THREAT AGAINST THE JURY

Since the time of *Bushell's Case*, it has become a generally accepted principle that the jury must be able to reach its verdict without being subjected to threat, coercion, or fear of retribution. So Dwyer wrote in 2002: "We are accustomed to juries doing their work without fear. Whatever their verdict may have been, today's jurors leave the courthouse immune to official reprisals and even to questions about how they reached their decision."[31]

Even a vague, indirect threat can be enough to invoke this principle. In a recent federal case, a juror had been told by an attorney friend that she "could get into trouble" if she failed to follow the judge's instructions. The appellate court said: "Jurors cannot fairly determine the outcome of a case if they believe they will face 'trouble' for a conclusion they reach as jurors. The threat of punishment works a coercive influence on the jury's independence, and a juror who genuinely fears retribution might change his or her determination of the issue for fear of being punished."[32]

In a 1960 English case, after the jury had been deliberating for two hours the trial judge called the jurors back and told them that unless they reached a verdict within ten minutes, he would keep them locked up overnight. Within six minutes, the jury reached a verdict of guilty. The Court of Appeal declared:

> It is a cardinal principle of our criminal law that in considering their verdict, concerning, as it does, the liberty of the subject, a jury shall deliberate in complete freedom, uninfluenced by any promise, unintimidated by any threat. They still stand between the Crown and the subject, and they are still one of the main defences of personal liberty. To say to such a tribunal in the course of its deliberations that it must reach a

conclusion within ten minutes or else undergo hours of personal incon-
venience and discomfort, is a disservice to the cause of justice.[33]

Unfortunately, practice can fall short of these fine standards. Certainly, it
falls short in regard to attorneys serving as jurors, as explained earlier.
Occasionally, practice falls short for others besides. A much-discussed case
arose out of a Colorado trial in which one juror, Laura Kriho, was the lone
holdout for acquittal. She was subsequently prosecuted for contempt of court
for failing to reveal during *voir dire* questioning that she might be inclined to
exercise the nullification power. It is accepted that a person who deliberately
conceals relevant information about herself, such as a relationship with a party
to the case, during *voir dire* in order to gain acceptance as a juror may be held
in contempt of court.[34] But it was extraordinary to extend this to a juror's dis-
position to exercise the nullification power in the case.

The evidence supporting Kriho's conviction for contempt of court included
the complaint of other jurors that she refused during deliberations to consider
the evidence in the case at trial. The conviction was eventually reversed on
appeal, on the ground that this evidence against the juror violated the secrecy
of jury deliberations, the remaining evidence against her being insufficient to
support a conviction.[35]

The Colorado state prosecutor was apparently averse to the principle that
"jurors leave the courthouse immune to official reprisals and even to questions
about how they reached their decision." Following Kriho's successful appeal,
the prosecutor petitioned the Colorado Court of Appeal for rehearing. When
this failed, the prosecutor took a further, unsuccessful appeal to the Colorado
Supreme Court. The whole process against the juror Kriho, including the trial
judge's investigation, took several years that were undoubtedly grueling for
Kriho.

Although this case entailed a threat against only a single individual juror, it
potentially has a chilling effect on any juror who wishes to avoid Kriho's experience. In the case of *US v Krzyske*, discussed earlier, the judge directly created
a threatening atmosphere against all the jurors by telling them: "You would
violate your oath and the law if you willfully brought in a verdict contrary to
the law given you in this case."[36] Jurors would surely hear this as a warning
of possible criminal penalties if they did not follow the judge's instructions
on the law. Clearly, such threats can effectively obstruct the jury in the fulfillment of its political roles, and so, again, undermine the value of the jury system to society.

Chapter 10

Obstruction of the Jury in the Sentencing Process

In federal and state jurisdictions in America, the judge can obstruct the jury by imposing punishment that is not in accordance with the jury's decision. Obviously, this can only occur if the jury finds the defendant guilty on some charge, because if the jury acquits the defendant on all charges, the court has no choice but to let him go free. But if the jury does find the defendant guilty on some charge—even a relatively minor charge—the practices that this chapter discusses allow the judge in a range of cases to impose a sentence far more severe than would accord with the jury's verdict. As will be seen, in this way the judge can prevent the jury from fulfilling its political roles.

To understand how this can occur requires close consideration of the process of sentencing. This is a complex area of the law, and even the limited account presented in this chapter, which is confined to the issues that are relevant here, will require several stages of analysis.

THE SENTENCING HEARING

Suppose then that the defendant has been charged with, and tried for, committing a criminal offense, and that the jury has found him guilty. The jury's role in the trial has now ended (with the exception of certain death-penalty cases that are not relevant here).

The statute that defines the criminal offense for which the defendant has been convicted will also state the penalty for violation of it. The statute will normally specify the penalty only within a certain range, and for most offenses the penalty range is very broad. For example, a federal statute dealing with so-called loan-sharking offenses declares the penalty as being "imprisoned not more than 20 years," but the statute does not in any way prescribe where the sentence should lie within the specified range.[1]

Broad sentencing ranges were not always common. In fact, up to around two centuries ago most offenses carried a fixed penalty. But during the nineteenth and a good part of the twentieth centuries, the criminal justice system shifted its penological goals toward rehabilitation and reform of the criminal. Broad sentencing ranges were seen as serving these goals, allowing the trial judge to fashion a penalty appropriate to the treatment of the individual offender.

According to this view, as Gertner explains, the role of the judge was "similar to that of a social worker or doctor exercising clinical judgment." The task of the judge was to treat the individual offender, which required the judge to know as much as possible about the offender as an individual. To this end, "the judge was encouraged to look at everything and use his 'judgment' to individualize the sentence. . . . As a corollary, sentencing procedures were informal; there were few rules, and, generally, no appeals [against the sentence]."[2]

The present-day result of this historical development is the *sentencing hearing* that follows a verdict of guilty. Commonly, prior to the sentencing hearing a probation officer will investigate the background both of the offense and of the offender, and then, with the help of both defense and prosecution, prepare a presentence report for submission to the judge.[3] The judge may also receive information of all kinds from other parties. In one recent case, the judge received and considered a "small flood" of letters sent on behalf of a convicted defendant by various family members and business associates, "uniformly praising his character and work ethic."[4]

In sum, the judge will receive and consider all kinds of information. This information is not restricted by any rules of evidence, and in particular may include hearsay without limitation.[5] The judge will also take into account her own assessment of the defendant from the trial, as discussed later in this chapter.

On the basis of all such information, the judge will make her findings of fact at the sentencing hearing. The appropriate evidentiary standard for her to apply is known as "preponderance of the evidence."[6] What this means is that if she considers an item of information that she has received to be more likely true than not true, she regards it as proved and adopts it as a finding of fact. This of course is a far weaker evidentiary standard than "proof beyond a reasonable doubt," which is the evidentiary standard for the trier of fact on any issue needed to support a verdict of guilty.

SENTENCING GUIDELINES

The judge must now determine the sentence. The framework in which she does this is the result of certain developments in governmental and more general societal attitudes that have taken place since the 1980s. The development from which all else has followed was a dramatic shift in the penological focus of American government, both state and federal, and to some extent of American society in general. This shift was away from rehabilitation and reform of the offender and toward retribution against the offender for committing the offense.[7]

It followed from this shift in viewpoint that the punishment should correspond closely to the offense. Consequently, there was a drive to reduce disparities in sentencing. There was less concern with fashioning a punishment appropriate to the treatment of the individual offender. But the prior criminal history of the offender was still regarded as relevant, under the reasoning that a person who continues to commit offenses deserves more severe retribution.

The obvious way to achieve a closer correspondence between offense and punishment would have been to enact statutes defining criminal offenses more specifically and narrowly. Then each offense could have a narrower statutory sentencing range, with sentence increases prescribed for offenders with prior criminal history.

However, this would have required a major reform of penal codes. Several attempts were made in Congress to reform the federal penal code, but all foundered. In place of such a reform, Congress established a mechanism to reduce sentencing disparities within the existing federal penal code structure. It was for this that it established the *United States Sentencing Commission*, an agency in the judicial branch of the federal government, to develop sentencing guidelines for the use of the federal judiciary. Each state also has its own sentencing guidelines, although their approaches vary somewhat.

The federal sentencing guidelines that the Commission has developed are specific and detailed, being currently set out in a 583-page manual. A basic idea of the guidelines is that generally two factors should determine the sentence to within a small range: the seriousness of the offense and the criminal history of the offender. To this end, the guidelines categorize each offense by its *level* of seriousness, and also categorize each offender by his *criminal history category*. Accompanying the manual is a *sentencing table*, with rows corresponding to the offense levels and columns corresponding to the criminal history categories.[8]

There are forty-three levels of criminal offenses in the federal guidelines classification system, numbered with arabic numerals, with level 1 being the least serious. Correspondingly, there are forty-three numbered rows in the sentencing table. There are six criminal history categories, numbered with roman numerals from I to VI, with level I denoting a nonexistent or minimal criminal history. Correspondingly, there are six columns in the sentencing table.

To determine the level of a criminal offense, the guidelines start from the *base level* that is specified in the guidelines for that offense. For each offense, the guidelines also list various factors, each of which is to increase or decrease the level of the offense by a specified number. The result of taking all the factors into account is the final level for the offense as committed by the particular defendant.

To see how this works, federal loan-sharking offenses give a convenient illustration because they are defined succinctly in a single statute that also specifies the penalty, and also because the guidelines list relatively few factors that affect the level of the offense.

The guidelines specify a base level of 20 for the loan-sharking offenses. But if in the commission of a loan-sharking offense a dangerous weapon (including a firearm) was *brandished* or *possessed*, there is an increase by 3 levels. If the weapon was actually *used*, the increase is 4 levels rather than 3, except that if the weapon was a firearm and it was *discharged*, the increase is 5 levels.

There is a further increase of up to 6 levels if any victim sustained bodily injury, with the amount of increase depending in a specified way on the seriousness of the injury. (If a victim was killed, provisions dealing with murder come into play.) But the weapon and injury provisions together are limited to a total increase of 9 levels.

In addition, if any person was *physically restrained* to facilitate commission of the offense or to facilitate escape, there is an increase by 2 levels. If the person was actually *abducted*, the increase goes up to 4 levels.

So, depending on these various factors, the level of a loan-sharking offense can rise from its base of 20 to as high as 33.

The guidelines determine the criminal history category of an offender on the basis of his total *criminal history points*. Points are specified for each prior sentence of imprisonment and for various other aspects of criminal history. Then criminal history category I is defined to be a total criminal history point count of 0 or 1; category II, a total point count of 2 or 3; category III, a total point count of 4, 5, or 6; and so forth. The highest category, category VI, is defined as a total point count of 13 or more.

As an illustration, consider a person who has one previous criminal conviction for which he was sentenced to eighteen months imprisonment (3 points), but who committed the offense for which he has now been convicted while on supervised release from that sentence (a further 2 points). He has 5 criminal history points and is therefore in criminal history category III. But suppose now that before all these events he had a further previous criminal conviction for which he was sentenced to six months imprisonment (2 points). He would then have a total of 7 criminal history points, and his criminal history category would be IV.

The entry in the federal sentencing table at the intersection of a given offense level and a given criminal history category specifies the corresponding guideline sentence. This is given as a range of months of imprisonment. Take as an example a base-level loan-sharking offense (level 20). Reading across the columns shows for criminal history category III a guideline sentence of 41–51 months imprisonment, but for criminal history category VI a guideline sentence of 70–87 months imprisonment.

As another example, consider a first offender (who is in criminal history category I) convicted of a loan-sharking offense. For a base-level offense (level 20) the guideline sentence is 33–41 months. But if the offense entailed firearms, serious injury, and abduction (level 33), the appropriate row shows a guideline sentence of 135–168 months.

Congress had intended the guidelines to be mandatory. However, the Supreme Court invalidated the statutory provision that purported to make them mandatory, so that they became effectively advisory.[9] But in practice they still exercise a great deal of control over sentencing. The Court requires the trial judge to "begin all sentencing proceedings by correctly calculating the applicable Guidelines range." Although the judge should also, apart from the guidelines, "make an individualized assessment [of the appropriate sentence] based on the facts presented," she "must give serious consideration to the extent of any departure from" the guidelines and explain any such departure "with sufficient justifications."[10]

It is possible for a convicted defendant, or the prosecution, to appeal against the sentence that the trial judge has imposed. In fact, the judge "must adequately explain the chosen sentence to allow for meaningful appellate review and to promote the perception of fair sentencing." Despite this, appeals against a criminal sentence are rarely successful. In the federal system, the Supreme Court has assured this by holding that a federal appellate court cannot reject the determination of the trial court on sentencing unless the trial judge has abused her discretion in determining the sentence. This very deferential standard of review applies whether or not the sentence is within the guidelines.[11]

In fact, very deferential appellate review is usual in regard to sentencing; this is true in the state systems as well as the federal system. The Colorado Court of Appeals expresses the view characteristic of appellate courts: "Sentencing is by its nature a discretionary function. Because the trial court is more familiar with the defendant and the circumstances of the case, it is accorded wide latitude in its sentencing decisions. Thus, a trial court's sentencing decision will not be disturbed absent a clear abuse of discretion. Only in truly exceptional situations will an appellate court substitute its judgment for that of the trial court as to an appropriate sentence."[12]

In any event, it is clear that in many cases the possible penalty is far higher than the jury appears to realize. This came to public attention in the recent federal prosecution of Wesley Snipes, a well-known actor, for tax-related offenses:

> [A] jury convicted Snipes on the misdemeanor charges, but he was acquitted of more serious felony charges of tax fraud and conspiracy. Jurors accepted his argument that he was innocently duped by errant tax advisers. . . . One juror, Frank Tuttle, gave "Larry King Live" [a television talk show] a written statement. . . . The jury's verdict was a compromise between those jurors who thought Snipes was guilty and those who didn't, Tuttle said in the statement. "That's when a deal was made to find him guilty on the failure to file taxes and not guilty on the federal tax evasion charges," Tuttle said in the statement. "We did not think he would go to jail."[13]

Snipes was in fact sentenced to three years imprisonment.

SENTENCING FACTOR OR ELEMENT OF THE OFFENSE?

In a jury trial, it is the task of the jury to decide the facts, but at the sentencing hearing the judge alone decides the facts. The actual division of fact-finding responsibilities depends on the distinction between an *element of the offense* for which the defendant has been tried and a *sentencing factor* that is taken into account in determining the sentence imposed on him.

Any criminal offense is defined in terms of some specified form of conduct, undertaken with some specified level of intent, and possibly some specified motive. The conduct and the intent (and possibly the motive) that together constitute the offense are defined to be the elements of that offense.[14] For example, in most jurisdictions crimes of theft have two elements: first, the taking of property from another person; second, doing so with intent to deprive the owner of that property.

To prove that someone committed a given criminal offense, every element of the offense must be proved beyond a reasonable doubt from the evidence presented at the trial. If the trial is a jury trial, it is the jury that must be convinced beyond a reasonable doubt regarding every element of the offense.[15]

The federal loan-sharking offenses again provide a convenient illustration. The elements of a loan-sharking offense are the making, financing, or collecting an extension of credit (as defined in the statute) and the intentional use of extortionate means (also as defined in the statute). In a jury trial, these must be charged against the defendant, and then proved to the jury beyond a reasonable doubt, to support a conviction for loan-sharking.

However, none of the factors listed in the guidelines as affecting the level of a loan-sharking offense constitutes an element of the offense. That is, nothing concerning a weapon, nothing concerning bodily injury to a victim, and nothing concerning restraint or abduction of any person constitutes an element of the loan-sharking offenses. In a trial, the jury may well hear evidence that includes reference to a weapon, or to bodily injury, or to restraint or abduction, but it is not called upon to *decide* anything at all about any of these issues. These are all sentencing factors, for the judge alone to decide at the sentencing hearing, using the "preponderance of the evidence" standard of proof.

The judge's fact-finding in regard to sentencing factors is effectively final. The highly deferential standard of appellate review applies fully to the judge's findings on sentencing factors. If the judge follows appropriate procedure and states that she has found certain facts constituting sentencing factors by a preponderance of the evidence, no appellate court will intervene unless the evidence is so weak that no reasonable person could be persuaded by it.

As we have seen, sentencing factors could increase the level of a loan-sharking offense from the base level of 20 to as much as 33. Suppose, for purposes of illustration, that the judge imposes a sentence around the middle of the guidelines range. Then for a first offender (criminal history category I) the facts proved to the jury beyond a reasonable doubt support a prison sentence of about three years. But facts that the judge alone finds by a preponderance of the evidence can add more than a further nine years to the sentence.

This use of sentencing factors can impinge on the capacity of the jury to fulfill its political roles. As federal district judge Gertner observes in a published public lecture: "Juries continue to pass on broad categories of offenses—'yes' or 'no' to money laundering, and 'yes' or 'no' to armed robbery, even while more and more issues that have a direct, unmediated impact on a defendant's liberty have been pushed into the sentencing sphere." She further points out that any justification for this that may arguably have existed under the former regime of rehabilitation and reform of the offender now no longer exists:

> The jury was the fact finder and the judge, a sentencing specialist. Specific facts did not have determinate consequences; the judge's discretion—his or her *judgment*—was pivotal. Indeed, with rehabilitation as the preeminent goal of sentencing, the judge, like a social worker, exercised something akin to a clinical judgment regarding the appropriate sentence. While one might disagree with the judge's decision (and that happened often enough), one did not believe that the judge was usurping a role that did not belong to him or her.

With detailed sentencing guidelines and congressional pressure to enforce them mechanistically, the judge is just another fact finder, finding facts with determinate consequences.... Concerns that a judge would usurp the jury's function are even more acute because the sentencing procedures remain as they were pre-Guidelines, having few evidentiary rules and a lower standard of proof. Procedures that had their genesis in an earlier indeterminate regime, although they may have made sense in that context, continue to apply.[16]

The combination of broad sentencing ranges with judicial determination of crucial sentencing factors sharply limits the capacity of the jury to fulfill its political roles. Admittedly, the jury can still act as a safeguard against government by acquitting a defendant of all charges. But this is a drastic step. The jury is deprived of its more nuanced capacity to safeguard by mitigating an offense. For example, it cannot mitigate a loan-sharking conviction by deciding, against the evidence, that the defendant was not guilty of carrying a weapon; the judge, not the jury, decides whether the defendant carried a weapon.

Also, under these circumstances the jury cannot effectively fulfill its political role as legitimation of government, because when a broad sentencing range is combined with judicial determination of crucial sentencing factors, the jury cannot be aware of what it is supposedly authorizing government to do. Of course, the view of the Supreme Court is that the jury by its verdict has authorized the judge to impose any sentence up to the statutory maximum, but from a political perspective this is frankly disingenuous.

FURTHER OFFENSES AS SENTENCING FACTORS

A defendant who is convicted of an offense can have his sentence increased on the basis of other offenses. These other, sentence-increasing offenses may be offenses with which the defendant was not charged at all and which he does not admit, but which the judge finds proved by a preponderance of the evidence at the sentencing hearing.

Many instances of this practice are based on a provision in the federal sentencing guidelines that stipulates a two-level increase for obstructing or impeding the administration of justice in regard to the offense for which the defendant has now been convicted.[17] A typical illustration is a 1993 federal prosecution for conspiracy to distribute cocaine, at which the defendant testified in her own defense. The jury delivered a verdict of guilty. In the sentencing hearing, the trial judge found regarding the defendant's testimony that "the defendant was untruthful at trial with respect to material matters in this case."[18] Based on this finding—explicitly, a finding that the defendant had committed perjury—the judge increased the offense level by two, increasing her sentence accordingly.

The Supreme Court unanimously upheld the increase in sentence: "It is rational for a sentencing authority to conclude that a defendant who commits a crime and then perjures herself in an unlawful attempt to avoid responsibility is more threatening to society and less deserving of leniency than a defendant who does not so defy the trial process." The Court did require that "if an accused challenges a sentence increase based on perjured testimony, the trial court must make findings to support all the elements of a perjury violation in the specific case."[19] Yet this is in effect the imposition of a penalty for perjury based on findings by a judge alone, requiring proof only by a preponderance of the evidence.

Another typical illustration is the recent prosecution of Wesley Snipes, noted earlier. The probation officer's presentence report recommended a two-level sentence increase on the ground that Snipes had obstructed justice by directing an employee to conceal evidence from a grand jury investigation. But only that employee's own testimony supported the accusation that Snipes had directed her to conceal evidence, and Snipes objected that she was unreliable. Despite this, the trial judge accepted the employee's testimony as true by a preponderance of the evidence at the sentencing hearing. The appellate court affirmed, declaring that it would invalidate "a district court's factual finding of obstruction of justice . . . [only in a case of] clear error."[20]

In such cases, it would certainly be open to the prosecution to bring a further charge against the defendant for perjury, or for obstruction of justice. This would generally require a further trial. Conviction of perjury or of obstruction of justice in a further trial would likely result in a sentence longer than the additional sentence resulting from a two-level increase in the original trial. But of course a jury in a further trial might not be persuaded beyond a reasonable doubt that the defendant had committed perjury or committed obstruction of justice—in which case there would be no conviction at all, and no penalty.

In addition, at a trial for perjury it would be open to the jury to decide that it was excessive to punish someone for lying in her own defense, and accordingly the jury might decide to exercise its nullification power. It would then be fulfilling its political role as a safeguard against government. Of course, a jury might well decide that this perjury should be punished just as much as any other perjury and therefore refrain from exercising its nullification power. It would then be fulfilling its political role as legitimation of government. Equivalent issues for the jury would also arise at a trial for obstruction of justice. By avoiding the possibility of laying the charge of perjury, or of obstruction of justice, before a jury, the courts in these cases undermine the capacity of the jury to fulfill its political roles.

Yet another typical illustration of increasing a sentence on the basis of offenses with which the defendant was not charged comes from the 1995 Supreme Court decision in *Witte v US*. Witte had first been indicted for conspiring and attempting to possess marijuana with intent to distribute it. After some negotiations with the prosecution, the conspiracy charge was dropped, and Witte pleaded guilty at trial to the charge of attempted possession.

Despite this, the trial judge at the sentencing hearing found that Witte had been part of a continuing conspiracy. Moreover, the judge found that this conspiracy involved not only the marijuana offense for which Witte had been convicted but also further marijuana offenses and, in addition, cocaine offenses. Witte had not been charged with any of these further offenses. Nevertheless, under the sentencing guidelines all of these further offenses constituted "relevant conduct" for purposes of determining the offense level of the marijuana offense for which he had been convicted. The trial judge therefore took all of these further offenses into account and increased Witte's sentence accordingly.[21]

Certainly, Witte could have been prosecuted separately for the cocaine offenses. Indeed, Witte *was* prosecuted separately for the cocaine offenses. Shortly after he had been sentenced for the marijuana offense for which he had been convicted—a sentence that had taken account of the cocaine offenses with which he had not been charged—Witte was indicted for these selfsame cocaine offenses. He sought to dismiss this new indictment on the ground "that punishment for the cocaine offenses would violate the prohibition against multiple punishments contained in the Double Jeopardy Clause of the Fifth Amendment."[22]

The Supreme Court rejected Witte's constitutional claim, declaring that "use of evidence of related criminal conduct to enhance a defendant's sentence for a separate crime within the authorized statutory limits does not constitute punishment for that conduct within the meaning of the Double Jeopardy Clause." Consequently, the Court declared, it was "impossible to conclude that taking account of petitioner's plans to import cocaine in fixing the sentence for the marijuana conviction constituted 'punishment' for the cocaine offenses." Since, according to the Court's reasoning, Witte had not been punished for the cocaine offenses, prosecution of him for these offenses could proceed.[23]

This kind of procedure undermines the capacity of the jury to fulfill its political roles. To see this, first suppose hypothetically that a jury were somehow to be directly faced with the situation of a first trial at which the judge increases the sentence based on the defendant having committed a further offense (beyond that for which he was convicted), followed by a second trial for that further offense. On the one hand, the jury might consider this to constitute double punishment for that further offense (contrary to the view of the Supreme Court). Consequently, the jury would likely view this as government overreaching and fulfill its political role as a safeguard against government by exercising its nullification power. On the other hand, the jury might consider this not to constitute double punishment (the same view as that of the Supreme Court). In this case, the jury would not exercise its nullification power. It would then still be fulfilling its political role, now as legitimation of government.

The problem is that no such hypothetical situation could occur. If there is a jury at the first trial (which in the case of Witte there was not), it has no way to know what offenses the judge might use to increase the defendant's sentence. If there is a jury at the second trial (for the further offense, which in the case of Witte included the cocaine offenses), it is not informed that the defendant has already suffered an increase in sentence at an earlier trial, based on the offense for which he is now being tried. As a result, no jury has an opportunity to act either on the view that this practice constitutes government overreaching or on the view that it does not. Plainly, this substantially diminishes the capacity of the jury to fulfill its political roles.

We have seen that in determining the level of an offense, further offenses that constitute "relevant conduct" can be taken into account. The notion of relevant conduct can extend quite far. In the 1949 case of *Williams v New York*, the defendant had been convicted of murder while engaged in a burglary. The jury convicted him but recommended a life sentence rather than the death penalty. The trial court was not obliged to accept this recommendation.

At the sentencing hearing, the judge referred to thirty other burglaries that had been committed in the vicinity where the murder had been committed. "The appellant had not been convicted of these burglaries, although the judge had information that he had confessed to some and had been identified as the perpetrator of some of the others. The judge also referred to certain activities of appellant as shown by the probation report that indicated appellant possessed 'a morbid sexuality,' and classified him as a 'menace to society.'"[24] None of this was established beyond a reasonable doubt. Nonetheless, the judge imposed the death penalty, and the Supreme Court rejected a constitutional challenge.

The reader may be reflecting that, after all, we are mainly dealing here with extremely unpleasant characters. It might be thought unlikely that a jury would be disposed to exercise its nullification power in any way to the benefit of loan sharks, drug dealers, tax dodgers, burglars, and murderers. But insofar as this is the case, it is precisely the crux of the present discussion. A jury that knowingly declines to exercise its nullification power is nonetheless fulfilling its political role as legitimation of government, as discussed in chapter 7.

Again, the crux is that the jury does not only fulfill its political roles when it chooses to exercise its nullification power. It also does so when it enjoys full capacity to exercise its nullification power and knows that it has that capacity, but chooses rather to authorize government to impose a penalty on the defendant. It is essential to keep in mind that the jury system serves as an ongoing safeguard against government in regard to the treatment of even the most unpleasant members of the populace. In fact, this constitutes a vital protection for all of us as members of society. As two deservedly respected judges wisely observed some eighty years ago, "the rights of the best of men are secure only as the rights of the vilest and most abhorrent are protected."[25]

ACQUITTED-CONDUCT SENTENCING

The previous discussion explained how the courts impose an increased sentence on the defendant based on offenses with which he was not charged. But the courts in fact go beyond this. In many cases, they have imposed an increased sentence on the defendant based on offenses with which he was indeed charged but for which the jury has acquitted him.

In the federal courts, this procedure was established in the 1997 case of *US v Watts*, where the Supreme Court consolidated for review two cases of drug-related offenses. The facts of the trial court case of *US v Watts* as the Court presented them in its review were as follows:

> In *Watts*, police discovered cocaine base in a kitchen cabinet and two loaded guns and ammunition hidden in a bedroom closet of Watts' house. A jury convicted Watts of possession of cocaine base with intent to distribute . . . but acquitted him of using a firearm in relation to a drug offense. . . . Despite Watts' acquittal on the firearms count, the District Court [—that is, the judge alone—] found by a preponderance of the evidence that Watts had possessed the guns in connection with the drug offense. In calculating Watts' sentence, the court therefore added two points to his base offense level [according to sentencing guidelines, resulting in an increased sentence].[26]

The facts of *US v Putra*, the case consolidated with *US v Watts*, as the Court presented them were as follows:

> The indictment charged Putra with . . . one count of aiding and abetting possession with intent to distribute five ounces of cocaine on May 8, 1992; and a second count of aiding and abetting possession with intent to distribute five ounces of cocaine on May 9, 1992. . . . The jury convicted Putra on the first count but acquitted her on the second. At sentencing, however, the District Court [—that is, the judge alone—] found by a preponderance of the evidence that Putra had indeed been involved in the May 9 transaction. The District Court explained that the

second sale was relevant conduct . . . and it therefore calculated Putra's base offense level [according to sentencing guidelines] . . . by aggregating the amounts of both sales [resulting in an increased sentence].[27]

By seven votes to two, the Court upheld this procedure against constitutional challenge, allowing the increased sentences to stand. The Court stressed that the sentencing judge may consider "information concerning the background, character, and conduct of a person convicted of an offense," without limitation. It then summarily dismissed an argument that the appellate court had accepted in these cases, that "a jury 'rejects' some facts when it returns a general verdict of not guilty." Rather, the Court declared, "it is impossible to know exactly why a jury found a defendant not guilty on a certain charge."[28]

Developments in certain Supreme Court cases in the next few years gave some reason to wonder whether the rationale of US v Watts would survive against constitutional challenge. Two constitutional provisions were relevant here. One is the double jeopardy provision of the Fifth Amendment. The case of US v Watts itself had rejected a challenge based on this provision. The Court reaffirmed this in 2005.[29]

The other relevant constitutional provision is the Sixth Amendment right to trial by jury. At the time of writing, the Supreme Court has not issued an opinion on whether increased sentencing based on acquitted conduct might violate this provision. But a number of federal appellate courts have considered, and have rejected, this Sixth Amendment challenge.[30] A key holding is US v White, a 2008 decision en banc of the Sixth Circuit Federal Court of Appeals. In this case, the appellate court was able to focus exclusively on "the single question . . . whether the district court violated White's Sixth Amendment right to trial by jury by relying on acquitted conduct for sentencing."[31] By nine votes to six, the court decided that it did not.

The Supreme Court declined to review the case. Although the Court routinely denies review of the great majority of cases, the denial is more significant in a case such as this: an authoritative en banc decision where the single key issue is cleanly presented, without any side issues to complicate review. So it is highly likely that a majority of present members of the Court would reject the Sixth Amendment argument against increased sentencing based on acquitted conduct. The holding in US v Watts remains valid: the trial judge has the power to increase the sentence on the basis of conduct of which the jury has acquitted, as long as he does not exceed the statutory maximum sentence.

The effects can be dramatic. In US v Hurn, "a jury acquitted Mark Hurn of possession of cocaine base with intent to distribute, but found him guilty of possession of powder cocaine with intent to distribute. At sentencing, the district court found that Hurn distributed cocaine base, notwithstanding the jury's acquittal on that count and ... sentenced him to 210 months imprisonment." The appellate court noted that if this acquitted conduct (distribution of cocaine base) had not been taken into account, the sentence "range would have been 27–33 months" imprisonment. The appellate court dismissed Hurn's appeal, despite its acknowledgement that the sentence in this case was "based almost entirely on acquitted conduct."[32]

In *US v White*, "White was convicted of bank robbery but acquitted of all counts charging him with the use of weapons in connection with the robbery. Despite the acquittal of the use-of-weapons charges, the sentencing judge increased the sentence as though the jury had found White guilty of these weapons charges." The dissent observed: "The two judicial upward adjustments for acquitted charges account for approximately 14 years of the 22-year sentence."[33]

Acquitted-conduct sentencing is accepted policy in some states as well as in the federal system. In an early North Carolina precedent nearly a century ago, the defendant was tried for carrying a concealed weapon and for assault with a deadly weapon. During the course of the trial he pleaded guilty to the former charge, and the jury acquitted him of the latter charge. He appealed against the high sentence that the trial judge imposed. The North Carolina Supreme Court noted that "the judge ... appeared to disapprove the verdict and asked the jury why they had rendered it," and effectively recognized that the judge had based the sentence on his finding of guilt on both charges. But it declared: "While the jury acquitted defendant of the other charge, because, as they explained to the judge, the evidence had not satisfied them of the defendant's guilt, the verdict did not estop the judge, or deprive him of the right, to form his own opinion of the defendant's guilt, and to consider it as a circumstance in estimating the degree of punishment he should impose for carrying the concealed weapon."[34]

Among more recent state court decisions, the Wisconsin Supreme Court has held: "A sentencing court may consider uncharged and unproven offenses and facts related to offenses for which the defendant has been acquitted." The Connecticut Supreme Court agreed that "a sentencing judge may consider ... evidence bearing on charges for which the defendant was acquitted." The Colorado Court of Appeals cited *US v Watts* with approval in upholding a sentence based on conduct of which defendant had been acquitted. However, New York courts have refused to implement acquitted-conduct sentencing.[35]

Plainly, acquitted-conduct sentencing thwarts any attempt by the jury to fulfill its political roles by exercising the nullification power to mitigate the punishment. As the distinguished federal appellate judge Gilbert Merritt, who disapproves of the practice, explains in dissent: "A jury cannot mitigate the harshness of a sentence it deems excessive if a sentencing judge may use acquitted conduct to sentence the defendant as though he had been convicted of the more severe offense."[36]

In fact, it is sometimes clear that a judge has based a sentence on acquitted conduct with the specific intent of thwarting the jury's exercise of the nullification power. In one case, the jury convicted the defendant of one gun charge but acquitted him of a second gun charge. At the sentencing hearing, the judge found by a preponderance of the evidence that the defendant was also guilty of the second gun charge and increased his sentence on the first gun charge accordingly. The defendant appealed against this increase in sentence.

The appellate court, affirming the increased sentence, declared:

> An inference that the jury found the defendant to be actually innocent of the [second] gun charge would be particularly far-fetched because there is no doubt that his accomplice brandished a gun during the attempted robbery in question. The judge thought the acquittal was due to the fact that the jury had learned from the cross-examination of one of the defendant's accomplices that to convict the defendant of a second gun charge would subject him to a 25-year mandatory minimum sentence.[37]

In another noteworthy case, undercover government agents had purchased cocaine from two defendants.[38] The two were tried together on the same charges: distributing cocaine, and carrying a firearm during and in relation to a drug trafficking offense. The jury convicted both defendants on the cocaine charges. On the firearm charge, it convicted one defendant but acquitted the other.

The judge imposed identical sentences of imprisonment on the two defendants, making it quite clear to defense counsel that he was purposely thwarting the jury's acquittal on the firearm charge:

THE COURT:	The jury could not have made—the jury could not have listened to the instructions.
MR. BARROSO:	Your Honor,—
THE COURT:	The testimony was so strong. The gun was even in the apartment. That's all they needed. There was no dispute of that fact. The mere fact that that gun was in the apartment, being used in association with—he didn't have to have it on his person.
MR. BARROSO:	They perhaps didn't believe it was being used in association with drug-related activity, your Honor.
THE COURT:	Well, I'll tell you something: I have been disappointed in jury verdicts before, but that's one of the most important ones, because what it did, it set up a disparity in result between the two defendants. Your client was consistently selling cocaine from his apartment and using a firearm. . . . It's all

	a pattern. This firearm was used. They [—the jurors—] had to absolutely disregard the testimony of a government agent for no reason—no reason.
MR. BARROSO:	Perhaps they considered the testimony of the other agent who testified that he couldn't be sure, your Honor.
THE COURT:	Well, you can take it up with an appellate court, because I've made my findings on the record.

The appellate court dismissed the appeal of the defendant who had been acquitted on the firearm charge, holding that it was within the trial court's discretion to determine the sentence on the basis that both defendants were guilty of the firearm charge.

Some jurists have expressed disquiet at acquitted-conduct sentencing. The eminent federal appellate judge Myron Bright protests:

[W]e have a sentencing regime that allows the Government to try its case not once but twice. The first time before a jury; the second before a judge.

Before the jury, the Government must prove its case beyond a reasonable doubt. But if it loses on some counts, that matters little. Free of the Federal Rules of Evidence, most constitutionally-imposed procedures, and the burden of proving any critical facts beyond a reasonable doubt, the Government gets the proverbial "second bite at the apple" during sentencing to essentially retry those counts on which it lost. With this second chance at success, the Government almost always wins by needing only to prove its (lost) case to a judge by a preponderance of the evidence. . . . Permitting a judge to impose a sentence that reflects conduct the jury expressly disavowed through a finding of "not guilty" amounts to more than mere second-guessing of the jury—it entirely trivializes its principal fact-finding function.[39]

A few federal appellate court opinions have considered whether the trial judge should be required to apply the moderately higher evidentiary standard of "clear and convincing evidence" at the sentencing hearing when the resulting increase in sentence is very great. But appellate review of a judge's assessment of the facts is so deferential that such a change would be entirely formal. Specifically, the judge would no longer state plainly that she had found by a preponderance of the evidence that defendant was guilty of the acquitted conduct. Rather, she would state plainly that she had found by clear and convincing evidence that defendant was guilty of the acquitted conduct. In virtually every case, it will not be possible to conclude from the record that a reasonable person could have been persuaded to the lower evidentiary standard but not to the higher.[40]

Some federal district judges have tried to resist acquitted-conduct sentencing. In one recent case, the defendant was charged with a range of drug distribution offenses and two money-laundering offenses. The jury acquitted him of all the drug distribution charges and one of the money-laundering charges. The charge of which he was convicted bore a sentence of 51–63 months imprisonment under the guidelines.

The presentence report of the probation office recommended a twenty-year sentence, based substantially on the entire range of drug distribution offenses of which the jury had acquitted the defendant. At the sentencing hearing, the judge considered only one of these charges at all believable, and consequently found by a preponderance of the evidence that the defendant had sold some amount of drugs. Under the guidelines, this would result in a sentence range of 151–188 months imprisonment. However, the trial judge, describing acquitted-conduct sentencing as "Kafkaesque," explicitly declined to take acquitted conduct into account in sentencing, and imposed a sentence of 55 months imprisonment.[41]

The prosecution appealed, with the result that this case in fact illustrates a wry exception to the general appellate deference to the decision of the trial judge on sentencing. The appellate court, relying on Supreme Court precedent, declared that the trial court had "committed significant procedural error by categorically excluding acquitted conduct from the information that it could consider in the sentencing process." Accordingly, the appellate court sent the case back to the trial court, *requiring* the judge to take acquitted conduct into account in sentencing.[42]

It remains possible that in any given case a trial judge opposed to acquitted-conduct sentencing might simply not allow herself to be persuaded, even by a preponderance of the evidence, that the defendant had committed the acquitted conduct in question. As we have seen, appellate review of a judge's assessment of the facts is normally extremely deferential. But it would probably not remain deferential for long if a judge resisted acquitted-conduct sentencing by *never* being persuadable regarding acquitted conduct.

A JUROR'S ASSESSMENT

In the recent case of *US v Antwuan Ball*, acquitted-conduct sentencing was invoked so vigorously that one juror took the remarkable step of expressing his concern in an open letter to the judge, which was published in the press.

The prosecution had presented the case as a major conspiracy in which, it claimed, defendants "were members of a crew that had engaged in a series of crimes, including crack cocaine dealing, armed robbery, attempted murder, and murder in the Congress Park neighborhood of Southeast Washington, DC for over a decade."[43] But the jury acquitted the defendants of all conspiracy and racketeering charges, convicting them only of a number of offenses of selling drugs, mostly in very small amounts. On learning subsequently that one of the defendants had been sentenced to sixteen years and another to fifteen years imprisonment—sentences based largely on the acquitted conduct—the juror wrote to the judge as follows:

> [A]fter 30 years of living in the District [of Columbia], I believe people selling small amounts of crack on the street usually end up with probation or only a year or two in prison if they have a previous offense.
>
> The District Attorney's press release states that "The government presented evidence that [these individuals] were members of a crew that had engaged in a series of crimes, including crack cocaine dealing, armed robbery, attempted murder, and murder . . . for over a decade." I don't feel that statement is accurate. There was really no evidence presented at all that these individuals operated as a "crew" which is why we, the jury, found them not guilty of the conspiracy and racketeering charges. . . .
>
> As you remember, Judge Roberts, we spent 8 months listening to the evidence, filling countless court-supplied notebooks, making summaries of those notes, and even creating card catalogues to keep track of all the witnesses and their statements. We deliberated for over 2 months, 4 days a week, 8 hours a day. We went over everything in detail. If any of our fellow jurors had a doubt, a question, an idea, or just wanted something repeated, we all stopped and made time. Conspiracy? A crew? With the evidence the prosecutor presented, not one among us could see it. Racketeering? We dismissed that even more quickly. . . .
>
> What does it say to our contribution as jurors when we see our verdicts, in my personal view, not given their proper weight. It appears to me that these defendants are being sentenced not on the charges for which they have been found guilty but on the charges for which the District Attorney's office would have liked them to have been found guilty.[44]

This juror's final assessment of the situation is an accurate description of acquitted-conduct sentencing. Defendants are indeed routinely sentenced not on the charges for which they are found guilty but on the charges for which the prosecution would have liked them to be found guilty.

AN ASSESSMENT OF GOVERNMENT OBSTRUCTION OF THE JURY

The various practices of government obstruction of the jury, as this part of the book has explored, are designed to frustrate any possibility of the jury exercising its nullification power effectively. This undermines the jury in the fulfillment of the political roles that constitute its value to society. A jury that cannot effectively exercise the nullification power cannot serve as a safeguard against government or as legitimation of government. The more government succeeds by its various practices in obstructing the jury, the more it renders the jury system worthless. Yet the considerable cost of the jury system, in billions of dollars each year, remains undiminished, for our society to bear.

This assessment applies to the various practices, discussed in chapter 9, that are aimed at preventing the exercise of the nullification power during the trial process. These practices are socially destructive. If government— and the general populace—cannot accept that jury verdicts may ignore or subvert the text of the law, there is no honest way to retain the jury system in its present form.[45] It is pointless to retain a jury system that has been rendered worthless but remains costly. It is disingenuous for the judiciary to pretend respect for a jury system while undermining its chief value to society.

This assessment applies equally to the judicial practices discussed in this chapter. These are practices that effectively circumvent the decision of the jury by failing to act in accordance with its decision in the sentencing process. These practices undermine the capacity of the jury to fulfill its political roles. A jury whose verdicts are not honored cannot serve as a safeguard against government or as legitimation of government. If government—and the general populace—cannot accept that the sentence should in every jury trial be based on the verdict of the jury rather than the opinion of the judge, there is no honest way to retain the jury system in its present form.

The judicial practices discussed in this chapter are disingenuous to the point of deceit. They show the judiciary treating the verdict of the jury as a mere impediment and devising unseemly stratagems to avoid it. In the football image, they show the judiciary doing an "end run" around the jury's verdict. But in this context the consequences are harsher than in football.

For the jury to be able to fulfill its political roles effectively, it should be fully informed as to the consequences of a guilty verdict. The information that the jury receives should include both the possible sentence range and the factors that the judge may take into account in determining the sentence.

As some judges have acknowledged, if juries were fully aware of all aspects of sentencing procedures, they might well be reluctant to convict in a number of cases. For example, if the jurors in the case of *US v Antwuan Ball* had known that sentences could be based on acquitted conduct, the trial would likely have resulted in a hung jury or an outright acquittal on all charges. However, this would simply be a matter of the jury fulfilling its political roles, and as such would represent the benefit rather than any detriment of the jury system.

Government obstruction drains the jury of the power that sustains its vital political roles. The judiciary should recognize this and accept responsibility for conducting trials and guiding juries in ways that foster the responsible exercise of the nullification power. In addition, citizens themselves need to become aware that the political roles of the jury, fulfilled through the responsible exercise of the nullification power, are the prerogative of each individual citizen. It is time for each individual citizen to reclaim the political power of these roles.

Part V

Jury Responsibility

Chapter 11

Discretion and Responsibility

The political roles of the jury empower the individual citizen as juror. But the possession of any power entails responsibility. Every juror is responsible for her political roles as safeguard against government and as legitimation of government. What this means is that every juror bears the responsibility of determining when it is appropriate and when it is not appropriate to exercise the nullification power.

A summons to jury duty draws people abruptly out of their accustomed social roles, with their familiar tasks, objectives, and responsibilities, and thrusts them into a role with quite different demands. An individual in his accustomed social roles develops a sense of judgment of which he may hardly be aware, combining common sense, a certain wisdom, and even shrewdness. This sense of judgment allows him to cope, more or less readily, with the demands of his accustomed social roles.

However, the social role of jury duty, with the political power and responsibility that it entails, is unfamiliar to most citizens—in part because of the practices of government obstruction of the jury criticized in part IV. Accordingly, the goal of this final part of the book is to construct a framework for citizens to familiarize themselves with the sense of judgment needed for responsible fulfillment of the political roles of jury duty.

This chapter begins with a brief survey of the idea of a role in society and the function of a sense of judgment in fulfilling a role. It then discusses some key roles within the justice system and the sense of judgment needed to fulfill those roles. This will serve as a foundation for examination of the role of the juror and its responsibilities in chapter 12.

SOCIAL ROLES

The fundamental concept of a social role is centered on the idea of fulfilling a function in society. It generally refers to what someone characteristically does or is socially expected to do by virtue of his or her situation in society.[1] Various kinds of situations in society can define a role. Some of these situations relate to a person's continuing status in society. For example, certain role behavior is characteristic of, or is socially expected of, a person whose continuing status is that of parent, or physician, or airline pilot, or student. But transitory situations can also define a role. As an extremely transitory example, during a pickup softball game certain role behavior is characteristic of, or is socially expected of, the players.

Other situations in society that can define a role may be not as stable as that of a physician yet not as transitory as that of a player in a pickup softball game. An illustration is the role of the juror.

Of course, a particular individual may occupy more than one role, at different times or at the same time. For example, a physician may be a parent who brings her child with her while she plays in a pickup softball game. A person may perform jury duty while being a student but may later cease being a student and become an airline pilot.

Roles can be defined both descriptively, in terms of what someone characteristically does in the role, and normatively, in terms of what someone is socially expected to do in the role. Plainly, opinions can differ as to what someone is socially expected to do in a role. Also, social expectations about a role can change. So social expectations and actual practice can diverge, at least for a time.

The changing role of the general-practice physician in America illustrates this.[2] At one time, physicians routinely made home visits to patients—known as "house calls"—and were socially expected to do so. That is, making house calls was part of the role of a physician, both descriptively and normatively. For a range of reasons, physicians became increasingly reluctant to make house calls, and almost all eventually ceased doing so entirely. But in recent years a number of physicians have revived the practice of routinely making house calls.

At first, physicians who refused to make house calls were widely viewed as falling short of social expectations regarding the role of a physician. General society maintained the normative definition of the role and viewed physicians who did not make house calls as deviating from their proper role. But as more physicians ceased making house calls, social expectations regarding the role of a physician gradually adapted to the general practice of physicians. The normative definition of the role shifted to fit the descriptive definition. At the present day, social expectations on this issue may again be in flux.

MEANS AND ENDS

Many roles in society can only function as part of a network of interdependence with other roles. For example, a physician who, as part of her role, writes a prescription is interdependent in society with the pharmacist who, as part of his role, is expected to fill the prescription. She is also interdependent with her patient who, as part of his role as "patient," is expected to follow her instructions regarding the prescribed medication.

A role thus exists to serve some function, or to achieve certain aims or objectives, within the network of social roles in society. At the same time, for any social role, certain behavior will be regarded as appropriate and certain other behavior regarded as inappropriate to the role. What then is the relationship between the behavior that is appropriate to a given role and the objectives of the role?

For some roles, the relationship is very weak or even nonexistent. Consider the role of witness in a court of law. It is reasonable to identify the objectives of the role as having a true account of the witness's knowledge relevant to the case placed before the court, to the extent that this will serve the ultimate objective of achieving a correct and just result in the case. But a person fulfilling the role is not permitted to decide for himself how to achieve these role objectives and then give his account accordingly. Rather, he is under the obligation to answer truthfully to specific questions and to do virtually nothing else. The person fulfilling the role of witness is strictly confined to carrying out the specific obligations of the role as the court instructs.

Consider, though, the role of trustee of what is known as a discretionary support trust. An example of this could be a trust set up by the parents of a severely disabled child to ensure his welfare after the parents' death. The law and the particular trust instrument together define the role of the trustee. Certainly, the law will impose some specific obligations on her, particularly with regard to how the funds in the trust are held, invested, and accounted for. But the law and the trust instrument will also explicitly recognize the objective of the role: ensuring the welfare of the beneficiary. The law and the trust instrument will then entrust the trustee with acting to further that objective, and will broadly respect her judgment in determining what constitutes the welfare of the beneficiary. So the person fulfilling the role determines how to fulfill it by direct consideration of role objectives.

The standard term for the freedom or authority within a role to make decisions based directly on the objectives that the role serves is *discretion*. The trustee of a discretionary support trust enjoys a high level of discretion; the witness in a court of law has virtually none.

DEVIATION FROM A ROLE

For the network of roles to function properly, everyone who fulfills a role must pay due respect to the range of roles with which his role interacts. Another way of putting this is that there are boundaries that differentiate each role from other roles. For example, consider a pharmacist who supplies a prescription-only medication without any physician's authorization, in a situation where there is no officially recognized emergency. In doing so, he has deviated from his role by straying beyond its boundaries into the zone that belongs to the role of the physician. Even if, under particular circumstances, there are good reasons for him to do so, he has nevertheless deviated from his role. However good the reasons are, if they do not amount to an officially recognized emergency, they are not reasons that are recognized within the role of pharmacist. A common terminology for reasons that are not recognized as appropriate to determine behavior within a role is that they are *excluded reasons* from the perspective of the role.[3]

For virtually any social role, there will be circumstances where excluded reasons are weighty enough to justify deviation from the role. These excluded reasons could be moral considerations, or issues of conscience, or political commitments, or some combination of these.

A person who is fulfilling a role is herself responsible for determining whether there are excluded reasons that justify deviating from the role. It is crucial to recognize that no one can be permitted to hide behind her role. Even if a person's role endorses her performing a certain action, even if her role commands her to perform that action, it is she—not her role, and not the institution that defines her role—that performs the action. This applies to all social roles, including those defined by powerful institutions such as the legal system.

A person fulfilling a role defined by the authority of an institution may be tempted to ascribe her actions to the institution. As the moral philosophers Justin Oakley and Dean Cocking explain, "there can be a strong temptation to withdraw one's conscience (or even one's sense of self) from the institutional role-based actions one carries out." This allows people to imagine that "whatever wrongs occur through . . . discharging their conventionally defined role are to be laid at the door . . . of the institution" in which they act. But pretenses of this kind are no more than "self-deception about the nature of one's involvement in such actions" and do not in any way excuse an individual's responsibility for acts that he performs in fulfilling his social role.[4]

As an illustration, consider a hypothetical situation of an individual called to testify in a case under the nineteenth-century Fugitive Slave Act. Chapter 6 described how, because juries refused to convict under this act, some federal district courts developed a procedure whereby the owner of the slave would seek a writ of habeas corpus against the person who had assisted the escape, demanding that he produce the slave. But it was, of course, still necessary to prove to the court that the accused person had in fact assisted the escape.

Suppose then that the individual called to testify is someone who saw the escape take place. Plainly, there are good reasons for her to resist enforcement of the Fugitive Slave Act by not informing the court as to who assisted the escape. These might be categorized as moral reasons, or issues of conscience, or political reasons. But however they are categorized, they are excluded reasons as far as the role of witness in a court of law is concerned. If the individual decides to act on the basis of the excluded reasons, she has no choice but to deviate from her role as a witness. Specifically, she can refuse to testify, or she can testify falsely, in either case risking punishment for her failure to fulfill the role obligations of a witness. But it remains her responsibility to determine whether, taking everything into account, she should deviate from the role of witness. She cannot absolve herself from this responsibility by simply claiming that she must obey the orders of the court.

In determining whether excluded reasons justify deviating from a social role, a person fulfilling that role must conscientiously balance between restraint and vigilance. Restraint is needed in invoking excluded reasons, because social roles have value. A person's commitment to society entails his commitment to coherent fulfillment of his social roles. It would be socially damaging if people were to permit every slightest nuance of their moral or political sensibilities, or every least twinge of conscience, to control whether they fulfill their social roles. Yet because virtually no social role can rightly command an absolute commitment, every individual fulfilling a role needs to remain vigilantly aware of excluded reasons that might justify deviation from the role.

Kadish and Kadish introduce the constructive idea of a *surcharge* (or *extra burden*) that represents the value to society of coherent fulfillment of a social role. When a person fulfilling a social role is faced with a conflict between excluded reasons and the demands of the role, he should not merely assess the one against the other and deviate from the role whenever the excluded reasons prevail over the demands of the role. Rather, he should assess the excluded reasons against the demands of the role *plus* the surcharge that represents the value to society of coherent fulfillment of the role. Because social roles have value, it is fair to stipulate that a person should conform to the specific prescriptions of his role unless he has not merely a reason but a powerful or *weighty* reason—or, as Kadish and Kadish forthrightly declare, a "damn good reason"—to deviate from them.[5]

It still remains the responsibility of the person fulfilling the role to determine whether there is in fact a weighty reason to deviate from it. If he determines that there is a weighty reason to deviate from the role, it still remains his responsibility to determine how to act. These responsibilities impose on the person fulfilling the role the obligation to exercise reasonable judgment, taking all the circumstances into account.

RECOURSE ROLES

The witness in the hypothetical illustration discussed previously is in a difficult and stressful situation. If she deviates from her role, she risks punishment that may blight her life and the lives of others who depend on her. In general, conflicts between role obligations and excluded reasons of any kind can give rise to stresses in individuals and in society as a whole. Because of this, some important social roles have developed to incorporate a degree of flexibility.

The term for a role incorporating this flexibility is a *recourse role* in society. What characterizes a recourse role is a certain kind of divergence between the official or other authoritative definition of the role and the accepted practice of the role. The role as officially defined is narrowly constrained by specific obligations, apparently allowing very little discretion. But the role as socially, legally, and politically accepted in practice incorporates a degree of flexibility. As a result, the person fulfilling the role is able to bypass the specific obligations without any loss of effectiveness in fulfillment of the role, and generally without suffering any penalty.[6]

As Kadish and Kadish explain, this flexibility in a recourse role permits the person fulfilling the role "to incorporate into his decision what would ordinarily be excluded reasons, or to put the matter differently, to convert excluded reasons for an action into role reasons."[7] This can allow him to take direct account of the objectives of the role. As a result, recourse roles incorporate a degree of discretion in practice, even where they are officially defined as having little or no discretion.

Kadish and Kadish give an example: "Central to the physician's role is the requirement that he preserve the life of his patient, but he may, when the costs in pain are great enough, and long before meeting the problem of euthanasia, act to reduce pain in a way that in some measure increases the danger to his patient's life. Few would say in such circumstances that he had failed to act as a physician."[8]

So the physician's role in regard to the patient suffering intolerable pain is a recourse role. The witness's role in regard to opposing the Fugitive Slave Act is not. The physician is able to relieve the suffering of her patient while remaining within her role, but the witness is unable to oppose the Fugitive Slave Act while remaining within her role. As Kadish and Kadish conclude, the development and acceptance of a societal role as a recourse role is "the finesse that introduces flexibility into role behavior and reduces the instances in which people simply step out of their roles in order to do what must be done."[9]

Although a person fulfilling a recourse role in society is able to convert excluded reasons for an action into role reasons, it does not by any means follow that she should do so lightly. Coherent fulfillment of all social roles, whether recourse roles or not, is important for the proper functioning of society, so the idea of a surcharge that represents the value to society of coherent fulfillment of a social role is as much applicable to recourse roles as to other roles. It follows that a person fulfilling a recourse role should still conform to the specific prescriptions of his role unless she has a *weighty* reason not to do so.[10] The reason could consist of moral considerations, or issues of conscience, or political commitments, or some combination of these.

A person fulfilling a recourse role bears the responsibility to determine whether there is in fact a weighty reason to bypass specific obligations of the role. If she determines that there is a weighty reason to do so, it still remains her responsibility to determine how to act. As with any role, these responsibilities impose the obligation to exercise reasonable judgment, taking all the circumstances into account.

THE RECOURSE ROLE OF THE POLICE

There are a number of recourse roles in the justice system. One example is the role of the police officer, as Kadish and Kadish explain:

> By and large, American statutes and municipal ordinances do not explicitly grant the police discretion to decide which laws they should enforce, under what circumstances they should enforce the laws, or whom they should enforce the laws against. . . . It is well known, however, that . . . the police in fact exercise a broad power of choice in deciding whether to arrest, even in cases where probable cause is manifest. . . . Instances include the deliberate nonenforcement of gambling laws against social gamblers, even though the laws make no such exception, . . . the nonenforcement of legislation prohibiting extramarital or deviant sexual behavior between adults . . . and the nonenforcement of laws considered obsolete.[11]

In fact, the police exercise this broad power of choice not only at the level of the higher police echelons deciding policy with regard to various categories of crimes. They also exercise it at the level of the individual officer deciding whether to intervene or arrest in a particular situation. Former federal prosecutor Butler explains:

> Before cases came to me [as a federal prosecutor], law enforcement officers—police and FBI agents—often decided not to arrest people they knew were guilty. Maybe a cop thought a dime bag of marijuana wasn't worth saddling a kid with a criminal record. Perhaps an FBI agent thought a charge against a popular official right before an election would be seen as political, or be so divisive that it would do more harm than good. Such extrajudicial acts of excusing criminal conduct seldom upset most people.[12]

When the police decide not to enforce a particular law, or not to enforce a law against a particular person or entity, in most cases there is no review or control of their decision. In general, nothing will then happen to people or entities that have broken the law in question. Even if in theory someone might be prosecuted later, "in the overwhelming majority of cases a police decision not to invoke the criminal process is, as a practical matter, dispositive."[13]

In this way, the role of the police officer fits the definition of a recourse role. It follows that the police should not excuse criminal conduct unless there is a weighty reason to do so. The police themselves, whether at the level of policy or at the level of individual decision, bear the responsibility to exercise reasonable judgment to determine whether there is in fact a weighty reason not to enforce a law. Of course, this does not mean that everyone need agree with any particular police decision not to enforce a law—even if, as Butler claims, in practice most people are not upset by police decisions not to enforce a law.

THE RECOURSE ROLE OF THE PROSECUTOR

In many states, the legal system formally requires the prosecutor to prosecute all criminal offenses within her jurisdiction, without exception, as long as she has sufficient evidence to sustain a prosecution. But in practice "the prosecutor's self-determined power not to prosecute . . . is nonetheless substantially uncontrolled."[14] There is in general no authority to compel the prosecutor to change her decision, and usually there is no other party to bring a prosecution.[15] Much the same is true in the federal system, as the Supreme Court has recognized: "so long as the prosecutor has probable cause to believe that the accused committed an offense defined by statute, the decision whether or not to prosecute, and what charge to file or bring . . . generally rests entirely in his discretion."[16]

Within any prosecutorial system, some of these discretionary decisions are made at the level of general policy. In particular, government enforcement priorities are likely to be set at this level. There is often dispute within prosecutorial systems as to how much discretion local prosecutors should have. For example, in the drive that began in the 1980s to reduce disparities in sentencing, discussed in chapter 10, the federal Department of Justice declared a new policy to limit the discretion of individual federal prosecutors. In fact, it has proved impossible for the Department of Justice to enforce this policy effectively, so that local prosecutors continue to exercise a good deal of discretionary power.[17] But in any event, the power to decide whether or not to prosecute, as well as what charges to bring, lies within the prosecutorial system as a whole.

A supposed limitation on this power is that, as the Supreme Court has declared, a decision whether to prosecute must not be "deliberately based upon an unjustifiable standard such as race, religion, or other arbitrary classification."[18] However, this limitation is more apparent than real. In practice, it is largely ineffective against prosecutorial systems that choose to discriminate on the basis of race or other classification.[19]

In sum, the prosecutor is legally obliged to prosecute when there are sufficient legal grounds to do so, but despite this has broad discretion not to prosecute. So the role of the prosecutor fits the definition of a recourse role. It follows that the prosecutor should prosecute when there are sufficient legal grounds to do so, unless there is a weighty reason not to prosecute. The prosecutor bears the responsibility to exercise reasonable judgment to determine whether there is in fact a weighty reason not to prosecute.

There are several potential sources of weighty reasons why a prosecutor— and particularly, a fair and just prosecutor—might exercise her discretion not to prosecute. These reasons could be moral considerations, or issues of conscience, or political commitments, or some combination of these. In fact, these are not separate and distinct sources of weighty reasons. Moral considerations, or issues of conscience, must be an integral part of political commitments in regard to the role of the prosecutor. This is because it is in the interests of society to have law that is just and right rather than law that is unjust and wrong. Because the prosecutor fulfills a recourse role, it is part of her role to exercise reasonable judgment to determine what is just and right in the law.

In this vein, George Fisher, a former Massachusetts assistant attorney general and assistant district attorney, and currently a faculty codirector of the criminal prosecution clinic at Stanford Law School, insists: "Prosecution work is all about using power morally. There is a strict ethical code that prosecutors must follow.... They are supposed to serve justice."[20]

In effect, the role of the prosecutor includes incorporating moral reasons (or reasons of conscience) into the determination of political reasons as a basis for the exercise of discretion not to prosecute. The legal system accepts this, and the public expects it.

There are many situations where prosecutors do not prosecute because a prosecution would, quite simply, be of no benefit to society. The catchall expression for this is that prosecution would not be "in the public interest."[21]

So, for example, in many cases prosecutors would consider it to be not in the public interest to prosecute very trivial violations of the law. To illustrate, even in a jurisdiction with a "theft by finding" law, a person who picks up and pockets a single penny in the street would very likely not be prosecuted, despite having transgressed the strict letter of the law. In fact, if a prosecutor did prosecute in this and other situations where it makes no sense to prosecute, she would likely be criticized as overzealous.

A prosecutor may also find it to be not in the public interest to prosecute for violation of laws widely considered obsolete, and may be sensitive in prosecuting under poorly written laws that do not make clear sense. A good deal of legislation, both federal and state, is poorly written, and a substantial amount of obsolete legislation remains on statute books.[22] The prosecutor can at least mitigate any problems by exercising her discretion not to prosecute in appropriate cases.

The public interest can shift as social attitudes change. During periods when public opinion is in flux regarding acts that have been treated as criminal, prosecutors have sometimes concluded that it is not in the public interest to prosecute. For example, attempted suicide had long been a criminal offense in England, until in 1961, after several years of fluctuating public opinion and debate, the offense was abolished. During those immediately preceding years, attempted suicides were generally not prosecuted.[23]

Prosecutors are supposed to serve justice. But, as discussed in chapter 6, some laws are unjust and some punishments under the law are unjust. In particular, the prospect of an unjust punishment has led some prosecutors to exercise their discretion.

This occurs with certain drug-related offenses. Bright had been a federal appellate judge for over twenty-seven years when, in 1995, he wrote: "These unwise sentencing policies which put men and women in prison for years, not only ruin lives of prisoners and often their family members, but also drain the American taxpayers. . . . The public needs to know that unnecessary, harsh and unreasonable drug sentences serve to waste billions of dollars without doing much good for society. We have an unreasonable system." A number of prosecutors, federal and state, share this view. As a result, when someone has sold only a small quantity of a prohibited drug, some prosecutors routinely downgrade the charge from "selling" to "illegal possession."[24]

Some prosecutors have also exercised their discretion with regard to certain special statutes applying to repeat offenders. About half of the states have enacted repeat-offender statutes, which typically impose a very long prison sentence for a third criminal offense of a specified level of seriousness. These statutes are generally known as "three strikes and you're out," or simply "three strikes" laws, with the reference being to the game of baseball.

The California enactment has received particular attention.[25] It applies to anyone who has been convicted at least twice previously of a felony that California defines as "serious" or as "violent." A further felony *of any kind* then triggers the three-strikes law. If the person is charged with any further felony, the charging document must allege the two prior convictions, and the defendant has a right to a jury determination that the prosecution has proved the prior convictions beyond a reasonable doubt. If the person is convicted, he receives a mandatory life sentence. He first becomes eligible for parole after at least twenty-five years.

The California enactment is especially harsh because of how it defines a felony for the third offense. Under California law, certain offenses may be classified as either felonies or misdemeanors. These crimes are known as "wobblers." Some crimes that are normally misdemeanors become wobblers because of the defendant's prior record. For example, petty theft, a misdemeanor, becomes a wobbler when the defendant has previously served a prison term for committing specified theft-related crimes. Other crimes, such as grand theft, are wobblers regardless of the defendant's prior record.

A wobbler offense is treated as a felony unless the prosecutor exercises discretion to treat it as a misdemeanor. California trial courts also have a very limited discretion, derived in part from the statute and in part from decisions of the California Supreme Court, to reduce a wobbler that was charged as a felony to a misdemeanor, in order to avoid imposing a three-strikes life sentence. California trial courts also have a limited, similarly derived discretion to vacate (that is, essentially, to ignore) allegations of prior serious or violent felony convictions, either at the request of the prosecution or on its own initiative, likewise in order to avoid imposing a three-strikes life sentence.

The California trial courts have only rarely exercised this discretion. In consequence, some of the third offenses that have resulted in sentences of life imprisonment have been relatively minor. They include "stealing a floor jack from a tow truck" and "stealing a dollar in change from the coin box of a parked car."[26]

One offender with a substantial prior criminal record shoplifted on two occasions two weeks apart, for a total of nine videotapes with a retail value of less than $160 in all. Each shoplifting offense was a wobbler petty theft, and at his trial for both offenses together, each was treated as a felony. Under a simultaneous twofold application of the three-strikes law, the defendant received two consecutive life sentences. He is due to become eligible for parole after imprisonment for fifty years in 2047, when he is eighty-seven years old.[27]

Such cases led Los Angeles District Attorney Steve Cooley to develop a policy attempting to limit application of the three-strikes law:

> The 63-year-old Republican prosecutor ... joined the D.A.'s office straight out of law school. His office notched more death sentences last year than the state of Texas, and his lunchmates include Pete Wilson, the former governor who signed three strikes into law. Yet despite his conservative bona fides, Cooley shares the conviction that some number of third-strike offenders ... don't belong in prison for life.
>
> After three strikes became law, Cooley watched one of his colleagues in the D.A.'s office prosecute Gregory Taylor, a homeless man who at dawn one morning in 1997 went to a church where he'd often gotten meals and pried open the door to its food pantry. The priest later testified on his behalf. Taylor's first crime was a purse-snatching; his second was attempting to steal a wallet. He didn't hurt anyone. Taylor was sentenced to life. "It was almost one-upmanship, almost a game—bye-bye for life," Cooley says, remembering the attitude in the office.
>
> Three years later, Cooley ran for D.A. on a platform of restrained three-strikes enforcement, calling the law "a necessary weapon, one that must be used with precision and not in a scatter-gun fashion." In office, he turned his critique into policy. ... The presumption is that prosecutors ask for a life sentence only if a third-strike crime is violent or serious. ... During Cooley's first year in office, three-strikes convictions in Los Angeles County triggering life sentences dropped 39 percent. No other prosecutor's office in California has a written policy like Cooley's, though a couple of D.A.'s informally exercise similar discretion.[28]

Chapter 12

Conscientious Fulfillment of Jury Duty

A case within the criminal justice system normally begins with some form of police action, such as an arrest. The prosecutor takes over to continue the case through to trial. If the trial is a jury trial, the jury will deliver the verdict. Each of these roles fulfilled in sequence—police, prosecutor, and jury—possesses an effective power to absolve the accused person from criminal responsibility. Law professors Alan Scheflin and Jon Van Dyke explain: "Police officers investigating criminal matters have discretion whether or not to make an arrest. Prosecutors have discretion whether or not to bring criminal charges to court. ... Jurors, who also act on behalf of the public, have discretion in deciding whether or not to convict the accused."[1] Chapter 11 discussed these discretionary powers of police and prosecutor. This chapter considers the discretionary powers of the jury.

JURY DUTY AS A RECOURSE ROLE

Just as the role of the police officer and the prosecutor are recourse roles, so also the role of the juror is a recourse role in society. As Kadish and Kadish explain, this role fits the definition of a recourse role in every respect.[2] The key point is that the official definition of the role diverges from the accepted practice of the role in the way that is characteristic of recourse roles. As discussed in chapter 7, the official definition of the role of the juror is as the Supreme Court declared it in *Sparf v US*. This is, that the role is narrowly constrained by specific obligations to apply the law as the judge sets it out.

However, the accepted practice of the role, as the Court recognized it in *Duncan v Louisiana*, is that in appropriate cases the juror is to exercise the nullification power to achieve justice regardless of the law. The nullification power allows the juror to bypass the specific obligations of the role, and in this way incorporates into the role the flexibility that is characteristic of recourse roles. This flexibility allows the juror to incorporate into his verdict what would, according to the official definition, be excluded reasons from the perspective of the role of juror. As generally with a recourse role, these excluded reasons could be moral considerations, or issues of conscience, or political commitments, or some combination of these.

By incorporating excluded reasons, the juror is able to take direct account of the objective of achieving justice. In this way, through the exercise of the nullification power in appropriate cases, the jury can fulfill its political role of acting as safeguard against government.

As with any recourse role, the person fulfilling the role should comply with the specific obligations of the role unless there is a weighty reason not to do so. Specifically for the role of the juror, the juror should apply the law as the judge sets it out, unless there is a weighty reason that justifies exercising the nullification power.

Kadish and Kadish summarize:

> [H]ow is the conscientious juror to understand his role? The duty of the jury is indeed to find the facts on the basis of the evidence presented and to return a general verdict by applying those facts to the law as given by the judge. This is the rule, and it imposes an obligation to comply. But the obligation is not absolute. Sometimes considerations of common sense, or considerations of fairness to the defendant, or the jury's appraisal of the law in contrast to the judge's statement of it may weigh so heavily that the jury may justifiably depart from the rule requiring it to defer to the judge's instructions.[3]

MORALITY AND CONSCIENCE

It has long been recognized as an important aspect of the role of the jury that it can incorporate moral considerations, or issues of conscience, into its verdict. In 1771, Adams wrote: "[T]he jury have a power of deciding an issue upon a general verdict. And, if they have, is it not an absurdity to suppose that the law would oblige them to find a verdict according to the direction of the court, against their own opinion, judgment, and conscience?" The jury is still described as "the conscience of the community."[4]

Of course, the jury is not the only source of community conscience. Government in a representative democracy does in some degree represent the conscience of the community. Chief Judge Bazelon, describing the jury as "community conscience," added: "I do not contend that the jury is the exclusive spokesman of the community conscience. When the legislature enacts a criminal prohibition it too speaks on behalf of that conscience." The judiciary also can decide on the basis of community conscience. This was explicit in a unanimous 1952 decision of the Supreme Court reversing a state conviction for unlawful drug possession because of police misconduct. The police had had the defendant stomach-pumped by force and the resulting vomited matter analyzed to obtain the evidence. The Court called this "conduct that shocks the conscience," making it clear that it was referring to the conscience of the community rather than only the consciences of the individual members of the Court.[5]

Yet the fact that government can be a source of community conscience does not in any way diminish the role of the jury as community conscience. Serving as community conscience is an aspect of the political roles of the jury, which constitute its worth to society. In any event, the citizenry has little trust in any branch of government (see chapter 3), so would not be likely to accept any branch of government as the exclusive and ultimate source of community conscience.

Certainly, to have the jury able to decide on the basis of conscience entails the risk that sometimes a jury will reach a morally abhorrent verdict (see chapter 8). But in the centuries-long course of development of the jury system, society has chosen to accept that risk in return for the benefits of the political roles of the jury. There is no way to eliminate the risk of abhorrent jury decisions without eliminating the political roles of the jury, which would render the jury system essentially worthless. Recall again Madison's pertinent observation: "Some degree of abuse is inseparable from the proper use of every thing."[6] In any event, this same risk of morally abhorrent decisions attaches to a range of recourse roles in society, including particularly those of police and prosecutor.

THE JUROR'S OATH AND PROMISE

Before a jury trial can begin, every juror is required to take an oath. The form of oath varies from one jurisdiction to another, but mostly within a quite narrow range. The California form, which conveys the general sense, requires each juror to respond affirmatively to: "Do you, and each of you, understand and agree that you will well and truly try the cause now pending before this court, and a true verdict render according only to the evidence presented to you and to the instructions of the court?"[7]

A number of eminent jurists have claimed that any exercise of the nullification power of the jury violates the juror's oath. It was on this basis that Blackstone described the exercise of the nullification power as "pious perjury"—perjury being defined as the violation of an oath within the judicial process. Two members of the Supreme Court acknowledged that "[a] jury may, at times, afford a higher justice by refusing to enforce harsh laws," but questioned "whether the jury system is to be defended on the ground that jurors sometimes disobey their oaths." In England, the *Criminal Courts Review* insists that for jurors to exercise the nullification power "is contrary to their oath or affirmation."[8]

Some judges have insisted to the jurors during the course of trial that the exercise of the nullification power would violate their oath. This occurred in the case of *US v Krzyske*, as noted in chapter 9. In the California case of *People v Williams*, during jury deliberations the jury foreperson informed the judge that one juror believed the law to be wrong and refused to uphold it. The judge then questioned this juror alone. After reminding him that he had taken an oath, the judge said: "You understand that if you would not follow the instructions that have been given to you by the court that you would be violating that oath? Do you understand that?"[9]

Remarkably, none of these jurists offer any argument or analysis to support their view that the exercise of the nullification power of the jury violates the juror's oath. It would seem that they consider it obvious. But it is not at all obvious. On the contrary, the exercise of the nullification power of the jury can reasonably be viewed as consistent with the juror's oath. The point is that this oath, as a legal expression, has acquired its meaning from its context and the history of its interpretation. Juries have exercised the nullification power for centuries, yet in all of this time no juror has ever been prosecuted for perjury for doing so. Throughout these centuries, government has consistently, even if sometimes grudgingly, condoned the exercise of the nullification power of the jury. This long historical record undermines any accusation of perjury against a juror who exercises the nullification power.

Also, a number of other eminent jurists clearly believe that the exercise of the nullification power of the jury is consistent with the juror's oath. As noted at various points in part III, federal appellate judge Bazelon and federal district judges Dwyer and Weinstein have approved the nullification power of the jury and recognized that it is crucial to the role of the jury in society, and federal district judge Fisher strongly encouraged a jury to exercise its nullification power. Indeed, the Supreme Court decision in *Duncan v Louisiana* relied on the jury to exercise its nullification power to safeguard against government overreaching (see chapter 7). Eminent English judges have taken a similar view.[10] Not one of these experienced judges refers at all to the juror's oath in relation to the nullification power of the jury. But it is also true that none of these jurists would condone perjury. The only possible conclusion is that none of them has viewed the exercise of the nullification power of the jury as in any way a violation of the juror's oath.

Certainly, the courts could, if they wished, devise a new form of oath that would avoid the history of interpretation of the usual form of oath, and as a result far better support the accusation that the exercise of the nullification power violates the juror's oath. For example, they could append to the usual form of oath something like the following: "Do you understand and agree that you will render your verdict without regard to your assessment of the legitimacy or justice of the law, and even if your conscience or moral judgment should imperatively demand otherwise?" But courts do not do so.[11]

Yet even a fully explicit oath not to exercise the nullification power would not be an insurmountable barrier against the exercise of the nullification power. The crux is that even if a juror swears an explicit oath not to exercise the nullification power, he still possesses the nullification power, whether he wants it or not. We can consider the implications of this along with the implications of a further promise that jurors are generally asked to give. In addition to the oath, the judge will normally ask each prospective juror in *voir dire* for assurance that he will accept the law as the judge gives it in her instructions. A prospective juror who gives the judge this assurance is arguably promising her that if he is empanelled on the jury he will not exercise the nullification power. But despite having given this promise, he still possesses the nullification power, whether he wants it or not.

What this amounts to is that the juror has now become subject to two potentially conflicting sets of responsibilities. On the one hand, he bears the responsibilities imposed by his promise that he will not exercise the nullification power, as well as by any explicit oath not to exercise the nullification power. On the other hand, he still bears the responsibilities imposed by his possession of the nullification power. A person who bears responsibilities cannot simply cast them off by promising another person (even a person in authority) that he will not fulfill them, or even by swearing an explicit oath that he will not fulfill them.

Plainly, the responsibilities imposed by possession of the nullification power of the jury must ultimately take precedence if the exercise of that power is necessary to prevent serious injustice. In blunt terms, if the juror's oath or promise turns out to require him to do wrong, that promise must yield. A declaration of commitment to act in a way that turns out to be wrongful is not binding.[12] We would not applaud the jurors in the trial of Penn and Mead (the precursor of *Bushell's Case*) or in *US v Morris* (the case under the Fugitive Slave Act) if they had convicted because of an oath or promise not to exercise the nullification power.

As Conrad explains, the juror must weigh against any oath or promise "an equally important—if not overridingly important—fundamental human obligation not to commit or contribute to an injustice. This nation expects jurors to remember this obligation when they step into court."[13] This view is in harmony with the instructions that federal judge Fisher gave to the jurors in the Camden 28 case, strongly encouraging them to exercise the nullification power if they found government behavior to be offensive and unjust. Clearly, this federal trial judge considered that anything that the juror's oath and promise might signify must yield to the obligation not to permit an injustice.

Nevertheless, any explicit oath or promise not to exercise the nullification power is not to be taken lightly. Conrad explains that such commitments by the jurors "should serve to remind them of the seriousness of the decision which lies before them, and the importance of making that decision with cool, clear minds, committed to justice."[14] Specifically, these commitments should remind jurors that their obligation is to apply the law as the judge has instructed unless they have a weighty reason to exercise the nullification power.

A remaining issue is whether the prospective juror ought in the first place to avoid becoming subject to these two potentially conflicting sets of responsibilities. After all, it is open to any prospective juror to avoid this predicament by respectfully informing the judge in *voir dire* that he would not be able to reach a verdict against his conscience. Recall, though, that many trial judges will respond by simply dismissing him from the jury (see chapter 9). So the unfortunate truth is that individuals who are aware of the crucial political dimensions of the role of jury duty, and are forthright and honest about their commitment to that role, are generally excluded from juries.

This leads to the question whether it would be right for individuals who are aware of the political dimensions of the role of jury duty to deceive the judge in *voir dire* as to their intentions if they are empanelled on the jury. A few jurists have considered this regarding jury duty in capital-murder cases, where it is established that prospective jurors "who firmly believe that the death penalty is unjust" are not permitted to serve unless "they state clearly that they are willing to temporarily set aside their own beliefs in deference to the rule of law." Butler in particular supports direct deception: "I believe with all my heart that capital punishment is morally wrong, and I would have no compunction about lying about this belief during *voir dire* if my lie could prevent the government from killing a human being."[15]

Note, though, that a juror who wishes to exercise the nullification power may also have to deceive his fellow jurors. If he does not, they may report his intentions to the judge, who will then likely dismiss him from the jury. So a juror who wishes to be sure of exercising the nullification power will have to insist during jury deliberations that he is voting to acquit only because he finds the evidence against the defendant insufficiently persuasive to support a conviction—even if the evidence is obviously overwhelmingly persuasive.

In sum, there is no ideal course of behavior for the prospective juror who is aware of the political dimensions of the role of jury duty. If she is forthright and honest, the judge will likely prevent her from fulfilling her civic obligation to undertake jury duty. This means she will be unable to take her share of social responsibility as a juror for preventing injustice. But her alternative is to use deception as a policy intended to achieve the good of society. This is also an imperfect course of action,[16] although in particular cases it may arguably be the lesser evil.

Overall, though, it would be best for the citizenry in general to become aware of the political roles of the jury, committed to fulfilling those roles, and willing to declare this commitment to the judge in *voir dire*. It is only while relatively few prospective jurors take this position that judges are, as a practical matter, able to dismiss them so readily. Also, if many prospective jurors took this position, the judiciary might focus on its responsibility for fostering rather than obstructing the political roles of the jury.

PRINCIPLES OF JUROR RESPONSIBILITY

If jurors are properly committed to the coherent fulfillment of their role, they will apply the law as the judge has instructed them, unless there is a weighty reason to exercise their nullification power. But if there *is* a weighty reason—political, moral, or in terms of conscience—the juror bears the affirmative responsibility of determining whether it is appropriate to exercise the nullification power. As Adams insisted in 1771 regarding the juror: "It is not only his right, but his duty ... to find the verdict according to his own best understanding, judgment, and conscience, though in direct opposition to the direction of the court."[17]

Exactly the same view of the responsibility of the juror is the basis of the Supreme Court decision in *Duncan v Louisiana*. To understand this, consider what would have happened if Duncan had been tried before a jury. The judge would surely have instructed the jury—correctly—that touching a person on the elbow without his consent could be enough to constitute simple battery according to the law. Since Duncan admitted touching the white boy on the elbow, a jury that followed the instructions of the judge on the law would be bound to find Duncan guilty. Yet the whole point of the Supreme Court's decision is that it is the proper function of the jury to acquit the defendant in a case such as this. The Court makes it clear that a jury that convicted Duncan would not be fulfilling its responsibilities. The Court expected that any juror in a case such as that against Duncan would recognize not only his right but also his duty to find the verdict according to his own best understanding, judgment, and conscience, though in direct opposition to the direction of the court.

This responsibility is not a matter for the juror either to celebrate or to treat lightly. Rather, it is a burdensome responsibility to approach with solemnity and awe. As Bazelon, one of the more learned and insightful judges to serve in the federal courts, stated in a lecture: "when jurors have to use a law to send a man to prison, they are forced to think long and hard about the justice of the law."[18] What *forces* jurors to think long and hard about the justice of the law is the responsibility—political, moral, or in terms of conscience—that is integral to the recourse role of jury duty.

The jury cannot evade this responsibility. In particular, if it follows the instructions of the judge, it is responsible for its decision to do so. Certainly, the jury cannot pass its responsibility back to the judge. Yet some jurists have claimed that if the jury applies the law as the judge instructs, it incurs no responsibility. This is plainly and simply wrong. A typical example of this view is the 1830 case of *US v Wilson*, which has been cited as justification by more modern proponents of the same view. In that case, the trial judge instructed the jury on the law but also told them, as was not unusual at the time, that it was entitled to reach its own decision on the law. But the judge then also told the jury: "by taking the law as given by the court you incur no moral responsibility."[19]

This view is completely unacceptable. The core of the jury's responsibility is the fulfillment of its political roles. The jury fulfills these political roles in crucial part by determining whether to exercise its nullification power—that is, by determining whether to accept the judge's instructions on the law. So it is fundamentally a contradiction in terms to suggest that the jury has no responsibility—whether political, moral, or in terms of conscience—if it follows the judge's instructions.

Moral responsibility is the specific focus of the court in *US v Wilson* and of later proponents of the same view. But in regard to moral responsibility, the issue of following the instructions of authority extends far beyond the role of the jury in relation to the judge. It is an indisputable principle that one adult human being of sound mind cannot escape moral responsibility by following the instructions of another human being. Of course, persons such as great leaders or spokespersons for institutions—or great judges—may provide guidance to others regarding moral reasoning, decisions, and conduct. But an individual who adopts the guidance of a person or institution as moral authority has made a moral decision to be guided by that person or institution, and remains morally responsible for that decision and all that she does in reliance on it.

It is particularly egregious to suggest that moral responsibility can be avoided by following the instructions of a person who exercises government authority. On the contrary, it is every citizen's ultimate moral responsibility to determine for himself when it is right and when it is wrong to follow the instructions of government authority. Certainly, government has no power to absolve a person who perpetrates a wrongful act from moral responsibility for the act.

The juror might fear reprisals for going against the instructions of the judge. Apart from relatively unusual circumstances, the juror generally has nothing to fear (see chapter 9). But of course a juror might not know that she has nothing to fear. Yet even a genuine fear of reprisals does not diminish the burden of moral responsibility that rests on the juror. On the contrary, a fear of reprisals will only pile further moral burdens onto the juror. In addition to considering issues of justice for the defendant, she now has her own interests to take into account.

So suppose that the juror determines that the defendant is guilty as charged but also determines that it would be grossly unjust to convict him. That is, on balance it would be right to exercise the nullification power of the jury. The juror may, despite this, decide not to exercise the nullification power because of fear of the consequences to herself or to others who depend on her for their welfare. Or she may decide to exercise the nullification power despite the possible consequences. Either way, the decision is hers, as is the moral responsibility for making that decision.

The juror is not an automaton, and he knows that he is not an automaton. He knows that he has the capability of uttering the words "not guilty," and that if he does so, the defendant will go free (or at least there will be a mistrial). In other words, every juror knows that he possesses the nullification power, even if he does not know the terms in which to describe it.

The juror cannot avoid knowing in this way that he possesses the nullification power. This is true even if the judge instructs him categorically that if he finds certain facts, he *must* reach a verdict of guilty (see chapter 9). The point is that the juror cannot avoid knowing that he is still *capable* of saying "not guilty," whatever facts he may find and regardless of what the judge has told him that he must do. The juror might, taking everything into account, decide that he ought to obey the judge. But if this is his decision, he, and not the judge, bears the responsibility for it.

Note particularly that whether or not the judge informs the jury that it possesses the nullification power can make no difference at all to the level of responsibility that rests on the jury. Some jurists have wrongly claimed that it does make a difference. For example, an academic writer asserts that "instructing the jury that it may acquit for good reason ... increases its moral responsibility if it convicts. For, if jurors have legal authority to engage in rule departures, they can no longer completely disavow responsibility for convictions by relying on a lack of authority to do otherwise."[20]

This is false reasoning. The level of moral responsibility that any individual bears is not affected by whether government chooses to tell her that she bears responsibility. Equally, no one could "completely disavow" moral responsibility on the basis that government has not explicitly authorized her to take responsibility. This is especially true for citizens of the United States, a country proud of its deeply entrenched sense of individual autonomy and of limited government. Americans are neither accustomed nor entitled to rely on the instructions of government to determine the extent of our moral responsibilities.

The responsibilities of good citizenship are burdensome. There is a particular burden on jurors who properly think long and hard about the justice of a law that may send a defendant to prison, possibly for many years. The judge cannot lift this burden from the jurors, regardless of how she instructs them.

In every case where there is a weighty issue of government overreaching, the jurors are certainly under the obligation to *consider* whether to exercise their nullification power. But there are no general rules or formulas to prescribe for them in every case whether or not they should actually do so. Rather, the burden of this determination rests squarely on them, within the discretion of the recourse role of jury duty.

THE REACH OF JUROR RESPONSIBILITY THROUGH THE JUSTICE SYSTEM

As explained in chapter 7, a jury verdict of guilty has a twofold effect. First, it legitimates the entire process of the justice system up to that point. That is, it legitimates every phase of the justice system's dealings with the defendant: the investigation of the defendant by the police and associated authorities, the law under which the defendant has been prosecuted, and the prosecution of this particular defendant for his particular violation of that law. Second, a jury verdict of guilty authorizes the judge to impose punishment on the defendant.

The nullification power of the jury enables it to refuse to legitimate what has gone before and to refuse to authorize what is to follow. A jury that delivers a verdict of guilty has declined to exercise its nullification power and must take responsibility for doing so. It follows that the responsibility of the jury in a criminal trial, whether cast as political or moral or in terms of conscience, extends through every phase of the justice system's dealings with the defendant.

The cases discussed in chapter 6 include examples of the jury taking responsibility for each of these phases. An example of the jury exercising its nullification power to reject government overreaching in the police investigation stage is the Camden 28 case. An example of the jury exercising its nullification power to reject an unjust law is the case of *US v Morris*. An example of the jury exercising its nullification power to reject the prosecution of particular defendants as unjust is the cases of theft of coal by miners during the Depression.

Blackstone's "pious perjury" theft cases, and many others discussed in chapter 6, illustrate the jury exercising its nullification power to reject an unjust punishment. The issue of the responsibility of the juror regarding unjust punishment has been a continuing subject of debate for many years. In nineteenth-century England it influenced substantial political changes. A great number of offenses then carried the death penalty, and jurors were keenly aware of this and of their own role in relation to the penalty. In 1810, William Grant, then both a member of Parliament and a senior appellate judge, speaking on a parliamentary bill to reduce the range of capital offenses, declared:

> [I]t now has become almost a matter of course for jurymen to avail themselves of every possible circumstance to acquit the prisoner of the capital part of the charge. They know, indeed, that the executions are few; they cannot be unmindful of the lenity of the judges: but notwithstanding this, they are unwilling to risk any thing; they will not trust to another the use of a discretion which they have the power and disposition to exercise themselves.[21]

An 1831 petition for eliminating the death penalty as the punishment for a range of crimes went directly to the main point: "That in the present state of the law, juries feel extremely reluctant to convict where the penal consequences of the offence excite a conscientious horror on their minds, lest the rigorous performance of their duty as jurors should make them accessory to judicial murder."[22]

In terms of moral responsibility, this "conscientious horror" that weighed on the jurors was well founded. Every juror knows that delivering a verdict of guilty has consequences, in the form of the accused defendant being sentenced. Every person has moral responsibility for the reasonably foreseeable consequences of her actions, which includes responsibility for making possible the reasonably foreseeable actions of another party. The fact that the other party is government can make no difference to the moral responsibility of the person who makes it possible for government to act. So from a moral viewpoint, if the death penalty for the offenses in question was so inappropriate as to constitute judicial murder, then it is fair to say that any jurors whose verdict enabled the judge to impose that penalty were indeed accessory to judicial murder.

Writing in the mid-nineteenth century, the American political philosopher Lysander Spooner summed up the situation: "It is absurd . . . to say that jurors have no moral responsibility for any cruel or unreasonable *sentence* that may be inflicted even upon a *guilty* man, when they consent to render a verdict which they have reason to believe will be used by the government as a justification for the infliction of such sentence."[23]

So it is impossible to accept a wholly contrary view that the Supreme Court expressed in a 1994 case. The Court asserted that "juries are not to consider the consequences" of a guilty verdict, in terms of the sentence that the judge imposes on the defendant.[24] This view is frankly morally repugnant. There is no context whatsoever in which any adult of sound mind is "not to consider the consequences" of her actions of any kind whatsoever.

In addition, this statement of the Court is false to the political history and the development of the political roles of the jury, as discussed in part III. It wrongly denies the political role of the jury as safeguard against government, including the courts, which the Court itself recognized in *Duncan v Louisiana*. The role of jury duty as developed over several centuries is a recourse role, so the responsibility of jurors for the reasonably foreseeable consequences of their verdict, in terms of the punishment that the judge imposes, is incorporated as a crucial part of the role.

Juror responsibility can also encompass systemic social issues that reach through all phases of the justice system process. In this vein, Butler, focusing on systemic racial discrimination, has argued that African American jurors should use the nullification power to "prevent the application of one particularly destructive instrument of white supremacy—American criminal justice— to some African-American people":

> Let us assume that there is a black defendant who, the evidence suggests, is guilty of the crime with which he has been charged, and a black juror who thinks that there are too many black men in prison. The black juror has two choices: She can vote for conviction, thus sending another black man to prison and implicitly allowing her presence to support public confidence in the system that puts him there, or she can vote "not guilty," thereby acquitting the defendant, or at least causing a mistrial. In choosing the latter, the juror makes a decision not to be a passive symbol of support for a system for which she has no respect. . . . [She] invokes the political nature of her role in the criminal justice system and votes "no."[25]

Butler argues further that African American jurors are able to assess the interests of the African American community, and that this community is better served by not imprisoning a range of offenders who could instead be reabsorbed into the community. "Black people have a community that needs building, and children who need rescuing, and as long as a person will not hurt anyone, the community needs him there to help. Assuming that he actually will help is a gamble, but not a reckless one."[26] Butler here evokes the medieval English jury that was relatively unconcerned with legal issues but rather to a great extent based its verdict on whether the defendant's character and reputation indicated that he might be reabsorbed into the community (see chapter 1).

The discussion of *Duncan v Louisiana* in chapter 7 and this chapter certainly supports the argument that the responsibility of the juror extends to considering systemic racial bias in the justice system, in regard to the possible exercise of the nullification power. A good deal of the extensive debate on Butler's proposals has focused on the likely effect of these proposals in practice, taking a range of issues into account.[27]

JUROR RESPONSIBILITY IN PRACTICE

In the case of *US v Antwuan Ball*, a juror wrote an open letter to the judge after the trial (see chapter 10). This juror had delivered his verdicts on the defendants in the belief that they would result in probation or relatively brief imprisonment. The actual sentences were fifteen years and more, which the juror plainly considered inappropriate and even unjust.

A guilty verdict authorizes government to proceed with punishment of the defendant. But in the case of *US v Antwuan Ball*, the jurors could not reasonably be considered responsible for authorizing government to impose these lengthy prison sentences. A person is responsible only for the *foreseeable* consequences of his actions. Acquitted-conduct sentencing, which allowed for these sentences, is not something that the average juror in that case could have imagined possible. In fact, even many lawyers do not realize that acquitted-conduct sentencing is possible.

Yet any reader of this book *is* now aware of acquitted-conduct sentencing. So suppose the following situation. Someone who is aware of acquitted-conduct sentencing is serving on a jury in a case where the defendant is charged with offenses of varying levels of seriousness. Her assessment of the evidence is that it establishes the defendant's guilt on a minor offense beyond a reasonable doubt. She is willing to convict the defendant for this offense and to accept the responsibility for a proportionate punishment being imposed on him.

Suppose also, though, that this juror is not willing to convict the defendant on any of the more serious offenses that he is charged with. This might be because, like the jurors in the case of *US v Antwuan Ball*, she finds that there is really no evidence at all to support the more serious charges. Or she might consider it quite likely that the defendant is guilty of the more serious charges but recognize that the evidence presented at trial is not clear enough to establish his guilt beyond a reasonable doubt. Or she might find that the evidence does establish the defendant's guilt on the more serious charges beyond a reasonable doubt but determine that there are sufficiently weighty reasons to exercise the nullification power of the jury to acquit him of those charges. All of these reasons are valid in the fulfillment of the recourse role of the juror.

However, this juror is aware that if she delivers a verdict of guilty on the minor offense, the defendant may be sentenced as if she had convicted him of the more serious offenses as well. She might or might not find this acceptable. But in any event, the possibility of acquitted-conduct sentencing is now foreseeable to her. If she delivers a verdict of guilty on a lesser charge, she is aware that she is authorizing the judge to impose a sentence based on the more serious offenses. As a result, if the judge does so, then she, the juror, bears responsibility.

She may, though, wish to accept this responsibility. After all, she can avoid the responsibility for foreseeable acquitted-conduct sentencing only by acquitting the defendant on all charges. If she does this, she bears the responsibility for any foreseeable consequences of allowing the defendant to go free, returning him into society.

It is characteristic of cases where the likely punishment is unjust that jurors are faced with a choice between two unpalatable alternatives. Failure to exercise the nullification power will result in legitimating an unjust punishment, but exercising the nullification power will result in unjustly freeing the defendant into society. There are no general rules or formulas to guide jurors to a decision as to whether or not to actually exercise their nullification power in a case of likely unjust punishment. Rather, they bear the burden of deciding which of the undesirable alternatives is less bad, within their discretion in the recourse role of jury duty.

The recourse role of jury duty is a heavy responsibility. If the view is that it is too heavy a responsibility for the average person, or that the average person does not possess the qualities needed to fulfill this role, then there is no point in the jury system. Judges decide most cases alone and do so far more cheaply than do juries. Unless juries fulfill their political roles, it would benefit society to simply have judges deciding all cases alone.

It might seem that the juror who knows less bears less responsibility. But the juror is not entitled to be willfully ignorant of the consequences of a guilty verdict. Jurors are drawn from a populace that largely distrusts office holders through the entire system of government (see chapter 3). What this generally amounts to is that the juror is faced with deciding whether to commit the defendant to be punished by a judge that she does not particularly trust, under laws made by legislators that she does not particularly trust. So it is incumbent on her to be aware, as far as reasonably possible, of the likely real consequences of a verdict of guilty. Again, if we do not believe that jurors possess the qualities needed for this, there is no point in having a jury system.

The more the juror is aware of the likely consequences of her verdict, the greater is her capacity to fulfill her political roles. Of course, this does not mean that the juror should know precisely how many years imprisonment would follow from a verdict of guilty. The juror cannot be expected to be familiar with the federal sentencing guidelines that currently take up a 583-page manual or with their equivalent in any of the state justice systems.

Also, in accordance with present-day judicial policy, the judge will not give the jury any information as to the likely punishment. The Supreme Court has declared: "Information regarding the consequences of a verdict is . . . irrelevant to the jury's task. Moreover, providing jurors sentencing information invites them to ponder matters that are not within their province, distracts them from their factfinding responsibilities, and creates a strong possibility of confusion."[28] The politically responsible juror simply cannot accept this view. It is topsy-turvy, both politically and morally. Jurors undertake their fact-finding within the framework of the political and moral responsibilities of their recourse role of jury duty. In this framework, it is the *lack* of information regarding the consequences of their verdict that can create a strong possibility of confusion.

Yet despite the complexities of sentencing guidelines and the obstructive practices of the judiciary, there are many circumstances in which the juror is able to form a sufficient sense of what kind of punishment is likely to be imposed on the defendant if he is found guilty.

A helpful illustration is an issue of federal punishments that the federal government itself eventually recognized as unjust. This is the issue of punishments for possession of crack cocaine, which were widely recognized as excessive compared to the punishments for possession of powder cocaine. The issue has strong race and class overtones: users of crack cocaine "tend to be poorer than those who use powder—and disproportionately African-American," and prosecutors have tended to focus exclusively on African American users.[29]

The issue of disparity between punishments for possession of crack and powder cocaine was widely discussed over many years in television programs and newspaper articles. In fact, eliminating this disparity was an "oft-repeated campaign promise" of Barack Obama in 2008, in his bid for the presidency.[30]

It was widely recognized that this disparity was unjust, and that a substantial reduction in sentences for possession of crack cocaine was needed to correct the injustice. In fact, this was so widely recognized that in 2010 Congress was moved to enact a statute, with bipartisan support, that somewhat reduced the disparity. The statute even explicitly acknowledged the prior injustice in sentencing, in that it described itself formally as "an act to restore fairness to federal cocaine sentencing."[31]

Because of this wide recognition of the issue, in any prosecution for possession of crack cocaine jurors could be expected to be aware of the high and disparate punishments, and also aware that the punishments for possession of crack cocaine were recognized as unjust.

Jurors are obliged to apply the law as the judge has instructed them unless there is a weighty reason to exercise their nullification power. But the prospect of a recognized unjust punishment, in any case where possession of crack cocaine was proved against the defendant, certainly constituted a weighty reason for the jurors. This, of course, did not mean that jurors were obliged to exercise the nullification power to acquit in any such case. However, it did mean that in every such case jurors were obliged to consider whether it was appropriate to exercise the nullification power. A jury that did not at least consider exercising the nullification power in a case where possession of crack cocaine was proved against the defendant failed to fulfill the responsibilities of its political roles.

As is characteristic of cases where the likely punishment is unjust, the jurors in these cases were faced with the choice between legitimating an unjustly disproportionate punishment (if they did not exercise the nullification power) and unjustly freeing the defendant into society (if they did exercise the nullification power). Jurors have the responsibility to ensure that the criminal defendant is treated justly, but they also have the responsibility to ensure that the rule of law is maintained in society. When the likely punishment is unjust, these responsibilities are in harsh conflict. It is politically and morally unsatisfactory for a jury to be faced with such a dire choice. But as long as there are foreseeable unjust punishments, jurors will be faced with choices of this kind.

Chapter 13

Juror Responsibility for Unjust Prison Conditions

Chapter 6 described how jurors have exercised their nullification power in many cases over the centuries to avoid imposing an unjust punishment on the defendant. Chapter 12 went further and explained that jurors must bear responsibility for authorizing and legitimating a foreseeable unjust punishment. That chapter particularly focused on responsibility for injustice arising from excessively long prison sentences.

Excessively long sentences are not the only form of unjust punishment. In fact, unjust punishment can take place as part of any sentence of imprisonment, however short. This is the case when the conditions of imprisonment for which government is responsible are systemically unjust. Note that although, for convenience, this chapter generally refers to prisons (state or federally administered incarceration facilities), the systemically unjust conditions that it discusses are equally of concern regarding jails (locally administered incarceration facilities).

Of course, government cannot reasonably be considered responsible for every incident that occurs in prison. But government must certainly be held responsible for forms of injustice that are systemic in American prisons. From a political and moral perspective—and also as a matter of plain fact—systemically unjust conditions of imprisonment must be regarded as part of the punishment that government imposes on inmates.[1]

Indeed, government has acknowledged that it bears responsibility for some of the worst systemic forms of injustice in American prison conditions. This chapter considers those forms of injustice. Specifically, it first considers two forms of injustice that the federal courts have recognized as the responsibility of government: injustice resulting from systemic conditions of overcrowding and injustice resulting from systemically inadequate medical care. This chapter then considers a form of injustice that Congress has recognized as the responsibility of government: the rape of inmates that is systemic in American prisons.

Yet despite the fact that government is responsible and has recognized that it is responsible for these three forms of systemic injustice in American prison conditions, government has failed to take sufficient measures to eradicate the injustice, as this chapter will explain. This failure to eradicate known systemic injustices is a matter of concern to jurors. In fulfilling their political roles as safeguard against government and as legitimation of government, conscientious jurors must be concerned with any systemic injustice in prison conditions for which government is responsible.

A great deal of information regarding each of these systemic forms of injustice in prison conditions is readily available to the public, so that in many cases jurors could foresee the possibility of unjust punishment. Because of this, jurors must bear responsibility in regard to the possible exercise of the nullification power. If the jury delivers a verdict of guilty, it fulfills its political role as legitimation of government. Specifically, it legitimates the punishment that its verdict of guilty authorizes government to impose—including any foreseeable injustice in the punishment that is likely to result from systemic conditions of imprisonment.

The prospect of injustice resulting from systemic conditions of imprisonment certainly constitutes a weighty reason for jurors to consider exercising the nullification power. This, of course, does not mean that jurors are obliged to exercise the nullification power to acquit in every case, so that no one is ever sent to prison. But it does mean that in every criminal case jurors are obliged to consider whether the prospect of the defendant suffering injustice resulting from systemic prison conditions makes it appropriate to exercise the nullification power. A jury that does not do so fails to fulfill the responsibilities of its political roles.

Chapter 12 discussed the conflicting responsibilities that face jurors whenever there is a prospect of the defendant suffering an unjust punishment. These same conflicting responsibilities face jurors when injustice may result from systemic conditions of imprisonment. That is, jurors have the responsibility to ensure that the criminal defendant is treated justly, but they also have the responsibility to ensure that the rule of law is maintained in society. They are faced with the choice between legitimating an unjust punishment resulting from systemic conditions of imprisonment (if they do not exercise the nullification power) and unjustly freeing the defendant into society (if they do exercise the nullification power). This is the grim choice that must face jurors as long as there are foreseeable unjust punishments, including those that result from systemic conditions of imprisonment.

Some jurors might decide that existing prison conditions, regardless of how unjust they may be, are good enough for someone found guilty of a criminal offense. The discretionary power of jurors within their recourse role of jury duty permits them to reach such a decision. Every jury possesses this discretionary power, and bears its responsibilities, regardless of the political and moral attitudes of its members. But jurors are not free to ignore the issue. The political roles of the juror do not permit him to imagine that he need not be concerned with the systemic conditions of imprisonment that government will likely impose on the defendant if he is convicted.

Chapter 12 has already considered and rejected the contrary view expressed by the Supreme Court. The Court's view, that "juries are not to consider the consequences" of a guilty verdict, denies the political roles of the jury that constitute the value of the jury system to society. In addition, this view is morally repugnant.

There are no general rules or formulas to guide the juror in determining whether to exercise the nullification power to avoid subjecting the defendant to the risk of unjust prison conditions. But there are factors that the jury could well take into account. Overall, jurors might reflect long and hard on whether it is absolutely necessary to the benefit of society that the individual defendant in the case should be committed to the kind of prison system that this chapter will describe. They might also consider whether the particular defendant in the case will be disproportionately likely to suffer injustice in this prison system, to an extent that justifies the exercise of the nullification power to release him back into society.

INJUSTICE RESULTING FROM SYSTEMIC PRISON OVERCROWDING

In 2011, the Supreme Court decided an important case that gives insight into the injustice resulting from overcrowding in American prisons. The case, *Brown v Plata*, brought together in a single decision two federal class actions, one of which had first been filed twenty years earlier and the other more than ten years earlier. Both of these actions derived from cases brought by inmates of the California prison system, so the opinion in *Brown v Plata* focuses on conditions in that system. But although overcrowding is particularly marked in California prisons, severe systemic overcrowding results in injustice to inmates throughout American prison systems.

Overcrowding is a long-standing problem of the entire American prison system. Forty years ago, Warren Burger, as chief justice of the Supreme Court, spoke of prisons "built 100 years ago for 600 inmates . . . crowded with

1500 men with almost no recreational facilities, obsolete vocational training, little or no counselling, and two men living—or existing—in a cell 6 by 8 feet." Thirty years ago two members of the Court observed: "There can be little question that our prisons are badly overcrowded and understaffed and that this in large part is the cause of many of the shortcomings of our penal systems."[2] Today, virtually every state has yet more severely overcrowded prison systems.[3]

The case of *Brown v Plata* became a matter of continuing public concern. There was particular concern that the federal courts might demand very costly improvements to the California prison system, raising the possibility of state tax increases. Television news reports and current-affairs programs, as well as newspaper articles and opinion pieces, brought the issues continuingly before the public. In any California criminal prosecution, jurors could be expected to be aware of the issues regarding prison conditions that this case dealt with. But it would also be hard for anyone anywhere in America to be unaware that an enormous and growing prison population has led to severe overcrowding throughout the American prison system, and that this systemic overcrowding has resulted in unjust conditions.

The Supreme Court in *Brown v Plata* affirmed the decision of a special three-judge federal trial court, which had described conditions in California prisons as follows:

> Since reaching an all-time population record of more than 160,000 in October 2006, the state's adult prison institutions have operated at almost double their intended capacity. As Governor Schwarzenegger observed in declaring a prison state of emergency that continues to this day, this creates "conditions of extreme peril" that threaten "the health and safety of the men and women who work inside severely overcrowded prisons and the inmates housed in them." Thousands of prisoners are assigned to "bad beds," such as triple-bunked beds placed in gymnasiums or day rooms, and some institutions have populations approaching 300% of their intended capacity.[4]

As an attorney for plaintiffs submitted to the Court: "Areas that once provided recreation space are now lined with bunk beds, some three high. The dormitory is jammed with hundreds of prisoners, many suffering from mental illness, contagious disease a constant threat. Broom closets have been turned into medical units, and makeshift metal cages lined up along the walls and in hallways serve as holding cells for prisoners on suicide watch." In addition, a 2010 article in the *Federal Sentencing Reporter* notes "reports of prisoners in at least one prison being confined to large cages called holding cells for days at time without beds and toilets."[5]

The Court notes in its opinion in *Brown v Plata* many examples of injustice resulting from overcrowding. One example is: "suicidal inmates may be held for prolonged periods in telephone-booth sized cages without toilets … an inmate who had been held in such a cage for nearly 24 hours [was observed] standing in a pool of his own urine, unresponsive and nearly catatonic. Prison officials explained they had 'no place to put him.'" Another example is: "Two prisoners committed suicide by hanging after being placed in cells that had been identified as requiring a simple fix to remove attachment points that could support a noose. The repair was not made because doing so would involve removing prisoners from the cells, and there was no place to put them."[6]

The Supreme Court upheld the decision of the lower court requiring the state to reduce its prison population to no more than 37.5 percent above the capacity of its prisons. This reduction, which is to take place by 2013, will require reducing the number of prison inmates by more than thirty thousand. Even if this is accomplished, California prisons will still be systemically overcrowded, although perhaps this will result in less injustice than at present.

The state has responded by instituting a policy known as "realignment."[7] This provides for a number of individuals convicted of relatively minor offenses to be assigned to county jails rather than the state prisons that were the subject of the Court's order. The offenses must be nonviolent, nonsexual, and nonserious; both the offenses and the offenders are now generally known as "non-non-nons" or "triple-nons." A positive assessment of this new policy states: "The legislation offers counties an unprecedented amount of flexibility in most areas of community supervision, including sentencing and early release for low-level offenders, alternative sanctions (ankle bracelets, substance abuse rehabilitation, etc.), supervised probation and parole, and delivery of social services."[8]

However, Los Angeles District Attorney Steve Cooley points out that "despite being labeled 'non-non-nons,' the group of criminals reassigned to county jails includes those convicted of serious offenses: possession of assault weapons, drug trafficking and large-scale identity theft and insurance fraud."[9] To maintain and guard these and other new inmates, the counties will need substantial, continuing state funding. They will also need substantial funding for the proposed programs of community supervision, alternative sanctions, and so forth. It is not clear that the state legislature will reliably provide the necessary funds.

Also, to some extent the "realignment" policy may merely shift systemic overcrowding from state prisons to county jails. Los Angeles, because of its size, will likely receive about a third of the offenders to be "realigned" from the state prison system. But even now, before the main influx of "realigned" offenders, "violence and overcrowding in Los Angeles' county jail is arguably even worse than it is in state prisons."[10]

As a recent legal article explains, any long-term solution to the problem of prison overcrowding and the injustice that results from it requires a shift in attitudes toward criminal punishment. But there is deep-seated resistance to this within the political system, in California and elsewhere in America (see chapter 10). There is concern that the California government will drift toward minimal compliance with the order in *Brown v Plata*, seek to terminate this order as soon as possible, and revert as far as possible to the old ways.[11]

The history of prevarication by the California government during the course of the *Brown v Plata* litigation can only reinforce this concern. In 2005, the original federal district trial court in one of the two class actions brought together in *Brown v Plata* explained why it was compelled to take the extraordinary step of ordering the appointment of a receiver to manage the state's prison system: "The Court has attempted to move defendants toward meeting constitutional standards by issuing a series of court orders with detailed objectives and measures. Unfortunately, defendants have repeatedly delayed their progress and ultimately failed to achieve even a semblance of compliance. . . . It is resoundingly clear to the Court that continued insistence on defendants' compliance with Court orders would lead to nothing but further delay."[12]

Similarly, in 2007 the original federal district trial court in the other class action complained: "It has been almost twelve years since this court found widespread violations of the Eighth Amendment. . . . [F]or more than eleven years this court has issued numerous orders . . . and the system still falls woefully short of meeting the requirements of the Eighth Amendment. Defendants have had more than sufficient time to comply with the mandate required by the court's 1995 order and the numerous orders issued since then."[13]

In addition, the resolution of these cases in *Brown v Plata* does nothing about systemic prison overcrowding elsewhere in America. In fact, federal courts rarely order states to reduce their prison populations. One reason for this—and also a reason why the litigation in *Brown v Plata* took so many years—is that a 1996 federal statute, the Prison Litigation Reform Act (PLRA), makes it particularly difficult for the federal courts to order a state to reduce its prison population.

The required procedure under the PLRA is that first a regular federal district trial court must find that there is a constitutional violation (the particular violation in *Brown v Plata* was a failure to provide adequate medical and mental health care, as discussed shortly). The court must then enter an order requiring the state to take measures less drastic than reducing its prison population and must allow the state a reasonable time to comply. If this does not remedy the constitutional violation, the district court may then authorize a three-judge federal trial court to be convened. If the three-judge court finds by clear and convincing evidence that overcrowding is the primary cause of the constitutional violation, and that nothing other than reducing overcrowding will remedy the violation, then—and only then—it may order the state to reduce its prison population.[14]

These PLRA provisions constitute a high barrier, so that only the most extreme circumstances allow the federal courts to order a state to reduce its prison population. So overcrowding persists, and results in injustice, in prison systems throughout America without any realistic prospect of a judicial remedy.

A jury verdict of guilty authorizes the judge to sentence the defendant to a prison system that risks injustice resulting from systemic overcrowding. This prospect of injustice is surely a sufficiently weighty reason to oblige jurors to consider whether it is appropriate to exercise their nullification power. Jurors might then think long and hard as to whether it is absolutely necessary to the overall benefit of society that the individual defendant in the case should be subject to any risk of confinement at all under such unjust conditions.

In particular, jurors might think long and hard as to the appropriate verdict in a case where the defendant is charged only with a minor offense. An example is the case noted in chapter 11 where the defendant was charged only with stealing a dollar in change from the coin box of a parked car—especially since in some American jurisdictions a guilty verdict could, for someone with a prior criminal record, result in imprisonment for life. Jurors might in fact take this approach more broadly to offenders classified as "triple-non" whose actual offenses are truly nonserious. But this and other matters must be for the jurors themselves to weigh, within their discretion in the recourse role of jury duty.

INJUSTICE RESULTING FROM SYSTEMICALLY INADEQUATE MEDICAL CARE

The two federal class actions consolidated in *Brown v Plata* were a complaint of inadequate treatment of inmates with serious mental disorders (*Coleman v Brown*) and a complaint of inadequate treatment of inmates with serious medical conditions (*Plata v Brown*), throughout the California prison system. These cases eventually led to the order to reduce the prison population, because over the years of litigation it became clear that severe systemic overcrowding was preventing any progress being made.[15]

The Court in *Brown v Plata* held that prisoners have a constitutional right to adequate care: "As a consequence of their own actions, prisoners may be deprived of rights that are fundamental to liberty. Yet...[p]risoners retain the essence of human dignity inherent in all persons.... A prison that deprives prisoners of basic sustenance, including adequate medical care, is incompatible with the concept of human dignity and has no place in civilized society."[16]

Precisely what level of care is appropriate for prisoners on a system-wide basis is a potential source of controversy. After all, many Americans outside prison do not have adequate medical or mental health care. It would be hard to argue that convicted criminals are entitled to better care than members of society who are guilty of no criminal offense. But no such controversy arises from the litigation in *Brown v Plata*, as the three-judge federal trial court set a minimal standard that even the defendant state of California did not contest: "The United States Constitution does not require that the state provide its inmates with state-of-the-art medical and mental health care, nor does it require that prison conditions be comfortable. California must simply provide care consistent with the minimal civilized measure of life's necessities ... sufficient to prevent the unnecessary and wanton infliction of pain or death."[17]

As the court described, the actual standard of care falls grotesquely short of this minimal level throughout the California prison system:

> Tragically, California's inmates have long been denied even that mini-
> mal level of medical and mental health care, with consequences that have
> been serious, and often fatal. Inmates are forced to wait months or years
> for medically necessary appointments and examinations, and many
> receive inadequate medical care in substandard facilities that lack the
> medical equipment required to conduct routine examinations or afford
> essential medical treatment. Seriously mentally ill inmates languish in
> horrific conditions without access to necessary mental health care, rais-
> ing the acuity of mental illness throughout the system and increasing
> the risk of inmate suicide. A significant number of inmates have died
> as a result of the state's failure to provide constitutionally adequate medi-
> cal care. As of mid-2005, a California inmate was dying needlessly *every
> six or seven days*.[18]

The opinion of the original district court in one of the class actions that led to *Brown v Plata* describes conditions of prison medical care in some detail. The court obtained expert testimony, and the judge himself made prison visits, resulting in the court's 2005 order to appoint a receiver to manage the California prison system. Conditions had not improved in 2008, when that court authorized the formation of a three-judge court. Conditions had still not improved in 2011, when the Supreme Court upheld the order of the three-judge court to reduce the California prison population. The following accounts therefore describe the present-day reality of conditions throughout the California prison system.

In terms of facilities for medical care, the district court found: "The physical conditions in many CDCR [California Department of Corrections and Rehabilitation] clinics are completely inadequate for the provision of medical care. Many clinics did not meet basic sanitation standards. Exam tables and counter tops, where prisoners with infections such as Methicillin-Resistant Staph Aureus (MRSA) and other communicable diseases are treated, were not routinely disinfected or sanitized. Many medical facilities required fundamental repairs, installation of adequate lighting and such basic sanitary facilities as sinks for hand-washing."[19]

The court opinion describes the judge's own prison visit: "The Court observed first-hand at San Quentin that even the most simple and basic elements of a minimally adequate medical system were obviously lacking. For example, the main medical examining room lacked any means of sanitation—there was no sink and no alcohol gel—where roughly one hundred men per day undergo medical screening, and the Court observed that the dentist neither washed his hands nor changed his gloves after treating patients into whose mouths he had placed his hands."[20]

In terms of staffing, this court found: "Many of the CDCR physicians have prior criminal charges, have had privileges revoked from hospitals, or have mental health related problems.... The Court Experts testified that the care provided by such doctors repeatedly harms prisoner patients. The Court finds that the incompetence and indifference of these CDCR physicians has directly resulted in an unacceptably high rate of patient death and morbidity."[21]

The court described a number of incidents of inmate death resulting from lack of proper treatment, or indeed lack of any treatment whatsoever. A typical example is:

[A]t 6:00 a.m., the nurse and physician determined that further care was unnecessary at that time and released the inmate from the infirmary. On his return to the transport van, the inmate began staggering, went down on his hands and knees and went prone. As the inmate was helped into the van, a medical provider told a correctional officer that the inmate "was fine and just needed sleep." When the inmate arrived at his housing unit fifteen minutes later, he stumbled out of the van, went down on his hands and knees, then went prone and became unresponsive. By 6:30 a.m., the inmate had no vital signs, and at 7:02 a.m. he was pronounced dead.[22]

The court also noted instances of cruelty on the part of prison medical staff: "[A] prisoner arrived at the clinic after a fight and was unable to move his legs. As the patient had sustained a neck injury, the medical staff should have immobilized his neck to prevent further injury. When the patient failed to respond as the doctor stuck needles in his legs, the doctor said that the patient was faking, and moved his neck from side to side, paralyzing the patient, assuming he was not already paralyzed."[23]

Beyond the particular situation in California that was the subject of the litigation leading to *Brown v Plata*, the level of medical and mental health care is generally desperately low throughout prison systems in America. One important way in which states ensure that the level of care remains low is by charging inmates for medical care, setting the fees at a level that inmates cannot pay. A federal government report informs: "In the majority of States, legislatures have passed laws authorizing correctional agencies to charge prisoners for medical care—fees . . . that are beyond the means of many prisoners."[24]

A jury verdict of guilty authorizes the judge to sentence the defendant to a prison system that a systemically low standard of medical and mental health care renders unjust. This injustice is certainly a sufficiently weighty reason to oblige jurors at least to consider whether it is appropriate to exercise their nullification power. Again, it is surely appropriate for them to think particularly long and hard as to whether it is absolutely necessary to the overall benefit of society that anyone guilty of a relatively minor offense should be subject to any risk of confinement at all under such systemic conditions, whether in California or elsewhere in America. This and other matters must, as always, be for the jurors themselves to weigh, within their discretion in the recourse role of jury duty.

THE INJUSTICE OF SYSTEMIC PRISON RAPE

Rapes are perpetrated throughout the American prison system, with great frequency and in extremely large numbers. My book on prison rape gives a full account of the subject.[25] The summary here focuses on the issues facing the juror in fulfilling her political roles.

Most of the rapists of female inmates are male prison officers. But the rapists of male inmates include both prison officers and other male inmates. Two members of the Supreme Court assessed the state of affairs:

> The atrocities and inhuman conditions of prison life in America are almost unbelievable; surely they are nothing less than shocking. . . . Weaker inmates become the property of stronger prisoners or gangs, who sell the sexual services of the victim. Prison officials either are disinterested in stopping abuse of prisoners by other prisoners or are incapable of doing so, given the limited resources society allocates to the prison system. . . . Even more appalling is the fact that guards frequently participate in the brutalization of inmates.[26]

This was written in 1980. The situation did not improve. In fact, with increased prison overcrowding the incidence of rape likely increased. In 2003, Congress found that in the previous twenty years more than a million inmates had likely been the victim of rape or other sexual assault, and that many of them had suffered repeated assaults. Recognizing government responsibility for systemic prison rape in America, and declaring a commitment to eliminate it, Congress enacted, by unanimous vote in both houses, the Prison Rape Elimination Act (PREA).

Yet rape remains prevalent throughout the American prison system. In fact, there is no evidence that the incidence of systemic prison rape has substantially declined since the enactment of the PREA. Although some prison authorities have instituted programs that have very greatly lowered the incidence of all forms of sexual abuse in their particular facilities, there has simply not been enough positive action of this kind to have any great effect on the overall level of systemic prison rape in America.

Evidence that rape remains prevalent overall in the American prison system comes particularly from a range of federal government reports. These include a series of annual reports assessing the prevalence and nature of sexual abuse in incarceration that the PREA requires the Bureau of Justice Statistics of the Department of Justice to carry out.

A further important report comes from the National Prison Rape Elimination Commission (NPREC), a body set up by the PREA to study the impact of prison rape on society, holding public hearings as needed, and to recommend national standards for eliminating prison rape. The NPREC delivered its report in 2009. While this report acknowledges some limited positive developments, it does not recognize any substantial overall decrease in the level of sexual abuse, including rape, in the American prison system since the PREA was enacted. A 2011 Department of Justice report on proposed national standards has also not suggested that any kind of sexual abuse in incarceration has substantially decreased.

Enactment of the PREA was an important development. By enacting it, government publicly acknowledged its own responsibility for the systemic sexual abuse of prison inmates. Certainly, government does have responsibility—including responsibility for the systemic rape of inmates by other inmates. After all, government exercises close control over inmates, and so can implement appropriate policies and practices to deal with systemic prison rape. Indeed, some prison facilities have succeeded in doing so, showing that it can be done.

The fact that government is responsible for the systemic sexual abuse of prison inmates is crucial for invoking the political roles of the jury. These political roles entail the jury acting as safeguard against government and as legitimation of government. From the political and moral perspective that the juror must take, systemic sexual abuse must be considered as part of the punishment imposed on inmates.

The PREA is also important in that it continues to stimulate a range of reforms. But it has not fulfilled its declared promise to eliminate prison rape in America, and it is far from clear that it will do so. One reason is that, although the PREA directs the attorney general to finalize and promulgate national standards for implementation of the requirements of the PREA, he delayed doing this until May 2012. There are also major unresolved issues regarding funding for needed prison improvements.

Another factor that, despite the PREA, impedes any great reduction in the level of systemic prison rape is the indifference, and even the hostility, of many prison officers. Many inmate reports of rape are not properly investigated, and many victims and potential victims are denied protective custody. Prison officers have used the ever-present threat of rape to maintain control or obtain information. Officers have even made "gifts" of vulnerable inmates to stronger, dominant inmates, to punish the former for an infraction or to reward the latter for cooperation. And, of course, officers themselves perpetrate a considerable proportion of the rapes of inmates.

The accounts of physical and psychological damage to inmate victims of years of repeated multiple rapes are harrowing. As well as devastating internal ripping and tearing, victims suffer beatings and knifings, and contract a range of diseases, including HIV/AIDS. The psychological damage has led some victims to commit suicide. Others have mutilated themselves. Victims who survive to be released back into society have difficulty in integrating and maintaining employment, and so are more likely to become homeless or require government assistance.

Some inmates are particularly likely to be raped in prison. Young and small inmates are very vulnerable, as are nonviolent offenders and anyone not affiliated with a gang. Developmentally disabled inmates are also more likely to be raped. But even someone who is in no particularly vulnerable category may become a rape victim if he or she fails to maintain and demonstrate the continuing strength that prison culture demands.

Victims and potential victims of prison rape have very little support from the justice system. The federal government has powers under a 1980 statute (the Civil Rights of Institutionalized Persons Act) that could be used to compel alleviation of prison conditions conducive to rape, but in practice it does not often use these powers. A few states have enacted their own statutes but have made only limited progress in implementation.

Prison officers who rape prisoners are rarely prosecuted. Prisoners who rape other prisoners are virtually never prosecuted. Very few cases are even referred to prosecutors, and many prosecutors are uninterested in those few cases that are referred to them. Courts virtually never issue an injunction requiring prison authorities to take steps to prevent an inmate being raped, or raped again.

It is also extremely difficult for inmate rape victims to obtain any form of compensation. The barriers in the federal judicial system illustrate the typical difficulties that an inmate faces. Before a prison inmate—state or federal— can gain access to the federal courts, a provision of the PLRA requires him or her to exhaust all available administrative remedies. This includes prison internal grievance procedures. Prison authorities throughout America have responded by implementing highly complex and cumbersome grievance procedures marked by very short deadlines. Inmate rape victims often fall foul of these and so are denied all access to the courts. In addition, the courts themselves have set up a barrier in the form of a restricted interpretation of the Eighth Amendment that prevents many inmates from obtaining justice from the courts.[27]

In sum, the justice system routinely fails to intervene on behalf of victims. In large part as a result of this, many inmates are repeatedly raped throughout their entire term of imprisonment, while the perpetrators have effective impunity.

A jury verdict of guilty authorizes the judge to sentence the defendant to a prison system that systemic prison rape renders unjust. This injustice is certainly a sufficiently weighty reason to oblige jurors to consider whether it is appropriate to exercise their nullification power. Once again, it is surely appropriate for them to think particularly long and hard as to whether it is absolutely necessary to the overall benefit of society that anyone guilty of a relatively minor offense should be subject to any risk of confinement at all under such unjust conditions. This and other matters must, as always, be for the jurors themselves to weigh, within their discretion in the recourse role of jury duty.

Notes

INTRODUCTION

1. Duncan v Louisiana, 391 US at 155–56 (footnote omitted).

CHAPTER 1

1. See Lacey, "Responsibility and Modernity in Criminal Law," 257, 259–61, 263.

2. See Fonteyne, "A New Hi-Tech Method."

3. Carpenter and Whitington, *Liber Albus*, 333; Masschaele, *Jury, State, and Society*, 207.

4. See Vidmar, *World Jury Systems*; Kaplan and Martín, *Understanding World Jury Systems*.

5. Most references in this book to England or the English legal system also apply to Wales, which has not had a separate legal system since the sixteenth century. The Scottish system developed differently; see Gane, "The Scottish Jury."

6. Adams, *The Works of John Adams*, vol. 2, 253.

7. The scope of the Seventh Amendment requirement is controversial. See Oldham, *Trial by Jury*, 5–9.

8. See chapter 7. In this book, references to the states apply also to the District of Columbia, and references to the Supreme Court, or simply to the Court (capitalized in each case), always mean the US Supreme Court.

The federal Fifth Amendment provision on the grand jury and the Seventh Amendment provision on the jury in civil trials have not been held applicable to the states.

9. See Hans and Vidmar, *Judging the Jury*, 31.

10. The Administration of Justice (Miscellaneous Provisions) Act 1933 abolished the grand jury in England. Juries decide only around 1 percent of criminal cases and less than 1 percent of civil cases in England. See Elliott and Quinn, *English Legal System*, 199–200.

The *Criminal Courts Review* particularly denies the popular idea that a constitutional right to jury trial can be derived from the Magna Carta, the thirteenth-century English charter that requires any action against a freeman to be "by the lawful judgment of his peers" (the usual translation of "per legale judicium parium" in the thirty-ninth clause of the Magna Carta). See Auld, *Criminal Courts Review*, ch. 5, 137–38 (paras. 7–8); Holdsworth, *A History of English Law*, vol. 1, 59–63.

For the contrary view, see Blackstone, *Commentaries*, bk. 3, 350 (ch. 23) (civil trials); bk. 4, 342–43 (ch. 27) (criminal trials).

For the jury system as "a hallowed institution," see Auld, *Criminal Courts Review*, ch. 5, 135 (para. 1).

11. Dwyer, *In the Hands of the People*, 132.

12. In Singer v US, the Supreme Court held that a defendant has no constitutional right to a bench trial. For the various approaches of American jurisdictions, see ibid., 380 US at 35.

13. The database of driver's license holders will include holders of the "non-driver's card" issued by the Department of Motor Vehicles in any state. For categories of exclusion, see chapter 9.

14. The terminology *tales* juror, or *talesman*, is also found. For the history of pressing bystanders into jury duty, see Masschaele, *Jury, State, and Society*, 101, 125; Oldham, *Trial by Jury*, 129; R v Dolby.

15. See Kamisar et al., *Modern Criminal Procedure*, 1368–69.

16. For a summary of the constitutional requirements, see Jonakait, *The American Jury System*, 95–96.

17. See Carrington, "The Seventh Amendment," 43–47; Sherrill White Construction v South Carolina National Bank; Vidmar, "The Performance of the American Civil Jury," 893–95.

18. For the sentencing hearing, see chapter 10. The principle that the judge alone determines the sentence has one exception. Most of the states that implement the death penalty limit its application to murder committed with certain "aggravating circumstances." The Supreme Court held in Ring v Arizona that it is for the jury to decide whether such circumstances are present and hence whether the death penalty is to be imposed.

The federal Constitution does not forbid prosecution appeal against the sentence; see Stith-Cabranes, "The Criminal Jury in Our Time," 141.

19. US v Cox, 627 F3d at 1084–85.

CHAPTER 2

1. See Postal Service.

2. See National Center for State Courts, *State-of-the-States Survey*, 7, table 3; ibid., 8.

3. See ibid., 19.

4. Jury-information web pages generally refer to the "average" length of trial without specifying what kind of average. It is presumably the arithmetic mean. "Average" in this chapter is always the arithmetic mean.

A Department of Justice survey of civil jury trials in the seventy-five largest American counties finds the average length to be 4.3 days. Cohen and Smith, *Civil Trial Cases*, 8. Of course, these trials may not be representative of civil trials generally, or of criminal trials.

For examples of substantial time commitments required of jurors, see Schwartz, Behrens, and Silverman, *The Jury Patriotism Act*, 2–3.

5. For the statistics, see National Center for State Courts, *State-of-the-States Survey*, 20–21. Over half of American courts compute this jury yield, which the *State-of-the-States Survey* calls the "summoning yield." For these courts, the overall jury yield is 45.8 percent. This percentage of the almost thirty-two million persons who are summoned comes (after rounding down) to fourteen million persons. Of these, one and a half million are actually empanelled on juries. This leaves over twelve million who are not empanelled.

6. United States Department of Labor, Bureau of Labor Statistics, *Employment Situation Summary*. The civilian labor force includes noncitizens, who are not liable for jury duty. But noncitizens are only a small proportion of the total and so have little effect on the calculated results.

7. See, e.g., Commission on the Future of the West Virginia Judicial System, *Final Report*, Appendix C, C–10 (estimating 67% of those summoned for jury duty employed full or part time, as against 53% of the state populace; "a negligible part" unemployed, as against 9% of the state populace). The situation appears similar in England, see Slapper and Kelly, *The English Legal System*, 309.

8. For the average cost of wages, etc., see United States Department of Labor, Bureau of Labor Statistics, *Employer Costs for Employee Compensation*. For the average working week, see United States Department of Labor, Bureau of Labor Statistics, *Employment Situation Summary*.

9. The paid employment of some people must itself be attributed to the jury system. This is the case for administrative officials of the jury system and for a range of other categories considered later in this chapter. If any such individual performs jury duty, then strictly speaking the $190 a day average estimated for his work ought not to be ascribed to the jury system; to do so constitutes double counting. But the time that these individuals spend on jury duty is a negligible proportion of the nine million person-days devoted each year to

the jury system, so this double counting does not have any substantial effect on the eventual overall cost assessment for the jury system.

10. For the number of counties, and for the breakdown of counties by population in the following paragraph in the text, see National Center for State Courts, *State-of-the-States Survey*, 3, table 1. For jury management employees, see National Center for State Courts web page, where the category is broken down into jury supervisors, jury analysts, and jury clerks; accessed December 23, 2011, http://www.ncsconline.org/D_KIS/jobdeda/Jobs _JuryMgmt(15).htm.

11. See United States Department of Labor, Bureau of Labor Statistics, *Employer Costs for Employee Compensation.*

12. Fay v People of State of New York, 332 US at 271; Mazzarella, "Avoiding Contact with Jurors," 12.

13. For the recent lengthy *voir dire* questioning, see Graczyk, "Testimony Set to Start." For estimates of the median length of *voir dire* in criminal and civil trials in the various states of the United States, see National Center for State Courts, *State-of-the-States Survey*, 77–78. These estimates support the estimate in the text. So also do the estimates for the duration of "a typical noncapital felony *voir dire*" in *Jury Summit* 2001, Survey Results, 4.

14. Ball, *Theater Tips and Strategies for Jury Trials*, is one of the more forthrightly entitled books for trial attorneys addressing this need.

15. See Gershman, "The Eyewitness Conundrum," 25–26; Kamisar et al., *Modern Criminal Procedure*, 744–46.

16. See National Center for State Courts, *Best Practices in Jury System Management*, 1.

17. See, e.g., DecisionQuest.

18. See, e.g., Bennett, under *Consulting Services.*

19. Strier, "Whither Trial Consulting?," 94.

20. Center for Jury Studies web page, accessed December 23, 2011, http:// www.ncsconline.org/D_Research/cjs/. National Center for State Courts web page inviting contributions, accessed December 23, 2011, https://www .ncsconline.org/D%5FDev/fotc/.

21. For examples of state studies, see Clark, *Report and Recommendations;* Vermont Committee on Jury Policy, *Reports and Information.* Some participants in the committees that create these various reports may serve without fee, but, as explained in the text, the value of their time is still a cost of the jury system. A nongovernment study is Klerman, *A Look at California Juries.*

22. Dwyer, *In the Hands of the People*, 161.

23. The conference hotel room rate was $198 plus taxes, amounting to over $226, and the conference entailed a three-night stay (January 31–February 3, 2001). See *Jury Summit 2001*, under *Attendee Registration.* If only two hundred

of the nearly four hundred participants stayed at the hotel, the lodging cost alone was over $135,000.

24. A book example is Kressel and Kressel, *Stack and Sway*. For citations to a selection of law-journal articles, see Jonakait, *The American Jury System*, 314–15.

25. Carrington, "The Seventh Amendment," 39. This writer's subject is the jury in civil trials, but his explanation applies equally to criminal trials.

26. See Doran, Jackson, and Seigel, "Rethinking Adversariness," 3–4.

27. The following description in the text is drawn from United States Courts, *The Rulemaking Process*.

28. An example of a case that went through all three levels of federal courts on a habeas corpus challenge to the jury instruction is Weeks v Angelone. Note that the costs of a retrial ordered as part of further legal proceedings have already been included in the earlier estimates in this chapter, which cover all jury trials including those that are retrials.

29. See Wellons v Hall, 130 S. Ct. at 729.

30. See Serio, "A Process Right Due?," 1178–80, for a survey of judicial decisions regarding the right of an indigent to a jury consultant.

31. National Center for State Courts, *Best Practices in Jury System Management*, 4.

CHAPTER 3

1. Mitchell v Harmony, 54 US at 142.

2. Lincoln, *Gettysburg Address*, 2–3.

3. Apprendi v New Jersey, 530 US at 498 (Scalia J, concurring).

4. See *Economist, Anglo-Saxon Attitudes*.

5. For the data in this and the next paragraphs, see American Bar Association, *Perceptions of the US Justice System*, 50. A later survey, American Bar Association, *Jury Service*, in fact makes little reference to the jury system in the context of the justice system, and so is largely irrelevant here.

6. American Bar Association, *Perceptions of the US Justice System*, 65. The remainder in each case neither agreed nor disagreed.

7. Ibid., 63. Despite this clear expression of the populace's low opinion of the justice system, the Executive Summary of the ABA report on this survey strains to find a positive slant. It declares as a "key finding" of the survey that "People strongly believe in the justice system, though they also identify areas that warrant improvement." Ibid., 6. This is directly misleading. Unfortunately, many citations of the survey refer to the misleading Executive Summary rather than to the tabulated response data in the ABA report.

8. Ibid., 59.

9. See Moyers, "Justice for Sale." For discussion of judicial elections, see chapter 4.

10. Armshaw, "Why Every State Should Have a Jury Patriotism Act"; Ehisen, "Will Jury Patriotism Act Deepen Jury Pool?," 2; Schwartz, Behrens, and Silverman, *The Jury Patriotism Act*, 1; *Crime Control Digest*, "Juror No-Shows Soar to 'Crisis' High"; Munsterman, *Improving Juror Response Rates in the District of Columbia*, 1.

11. Auld, *Criminal Courts Review*, ch. 5, 218–25 (paras. 214–27).

12. Dwyer, *In the Hands of the People*, 162.

13. *Associated Press*, "Getting Out of Jury Duty Is a National Pastime"; Parker, "Jury Duty Is Getting Harder to Shirk."

14. *Associated Press*, "Getting Out of Jury Duty Is a National Pastime."

15. Schwartz, Behrens, and Silverman, *The Jury Patriotism Act*, 7.

16. Jonakait, *The American Jury System*, 126.

17. Auld, *Criminal Courts Review*, ch. 5, 218 (para. 214).

18. Munsterman, *Improving Juror Response Rates in the District of Columbia*, i.

19. Klerman, *A Look at California Juries*, 2; Dwyer, *In the Hands of the People*, 162; see Schwartz, Behrens, and Silverman, *The Jury Patriotism Act*, 5 (emphasis added).

20. See Tyler, *Why People Obey the Law*, 3–4.

21. See ibid. The influence of a person's social group (friends, colleagues, family, and so forth) may also affect her compliance with the law. However, this is not an entirely separate perspective on compliance, but may be viewed as a combination of instrumental and normative influences. See ibid., 23–24.

22. Ibid., 64 (paragraph break suppressed). For details of Tyler's studies, see ibid., 8–13, 179–229.

23. Ibid., 22–23 (internal citations and quotation marks suppressed).

24. Kadish and Kadish, *Discretion to Disobey*, 3. For a similar view in English legal philosophy, see Hart, *The Concept of Law*, 39.

25. This is also true, although to a lesser extent, in England, where the *Criminal Courts Review* acknowledges in regard to jury duty "that public perception of it as a civic duty is far from universal." Auld, *Criminal Courts Review*, ch. 5, 140 (para. 13).

26. The basis for Amish rejection of jury duty appears to be the biblical injunction "Judge not, that ye be not judged" in Matt. 7:1 (AV). For the excusal of Amish from jury duty, as well as for the tendency of Amish not to register to vote to avoid being summoned for jury duty in the first place, see Esau, *The Amish and Litigation*, n. 105 and accompanying text. Out of concern at Amish being discouraged from voting, the state of Ohio has enacted their exemption from jury duty into statutory law. Ohio, *Revised Code: Commissioners of Jurors*, c. 2313, §16(A)(7).

27. For England, Practice Direction, Jury Service: Excusal; this Practice Direction has now been superseded in consequence of statutory changes. For

discussion regarding Australia and New Zealand, see Parliament of Victoria, *Jury Service in Victoria*, 87–89. For Hong Kong, see, e.g., Re Lau Ko Yuen Tom. For Scotland, see Gane, "The Scottish Jury," 264. For application to religious groups, see Parliament of Victoria, *Jury Service in Victoria*, 88.

28. The Supreme Court upheld this practice of exclusion in Lockhart v McCree. See also chapter 12.

29. Butler, "Racially Based Jury Nullification," 680; Gates, *Thirteen Ways of Looking at a Black Man*, 109. For similar expressions, see, e.g., sources cited in Butler, "Racially Based Jury Nullification," 691 n. 76, 692 n. 78, and in Washington v Lambert, 98 F3d at 1187–88.

30. Butler, *Let's Get Free*, 20.

31. Martin, "Let Judges Do Their Jobs."

CHAPTER 4

1. For the first survey, see Kalven and Zeisel, *The American Jury*. For the methodology problems with that survey, see Greene et al., *Wrightsman's Psychology*, 291. For the more recent studies, see Vidmar and Hans, *American Juries*, 148–51; Eisenberg et al., "Judge-Jury Agreement in Criminal Cases," 179–85; Jonakait, *The American Jury System*, 226, with references to original sources; Greene et al., *Wrightsman's Psychology*, 292–93, with references to original sources.

2. See Thorpe, *The Federal and State Constitutions*, 3060; Macdonald, *Select Charters*, 359.

3. Strauder v West Virginia, 100 US at 308; United States Department of State, *Rights of the People*, ch. 7, "Trial by Jury."

4. For support of this from neuroscience research, see Molnar-Szakacs et al., "Do You See What I Mean?," and sources cited there.

5. See Stuntz, *The Collapse of American Criminal Justice*, 141, 325 n. 46.

6. For discussion, see Kirby, "The Jury of the Future," 5–6, 7–13.

7. Chandler, *American Criminal Trials*, 274; see Munsterman, *Multi-Lingual Juries*.

8. Hernandez v New York, 500 US at 352.

9. Gallagher v Delaney, 139 F3d at 350; ibid. at 342.

10. The Court established this in Gitlow v New York, refining its holding in later decisions. See also chapter 7.

11. Miller v California, 413 US at 32 (footnote omitted).

12. Ibid. at 31.

13. See, e.g., Jonakait, *The American Jury System*, 64, 67–74.

14. Ibid., 79.

15. Condorcet, *Essai*; see Singer, *The Legacy of Positivism*, chs. 1, 2.

16. Condorcet, *Essai*, xxiv.

17. Three among many articles are Edelman, "On Legal Interpretations of the Condorcet Jury Theorem"; Levmore, "Ruling Majorities and Reasoning Pluralities"; Stearns, "The Condorcet Jury Theorem and Judicial Decisionmaking."

18. Note also that the mathematical reasoning of Condorcet's theorem works equally well if each of the people in the group deciding the question is more likely than not to choose the *incorrect* answer. The theorem then shows that the larger the group, the greater is the probability of an incorrect majority decision.

19. For the belief that groups reach better decisions, see, e.g., Jonakait, *The American Jury System*, 42–46. For studies on juries, etc., see, e.g., Surowiecki, *The Wisdom of Crowds*, 183–84. For development of the theory of groupthink, see Janis, *Groupthink*. For a juror's claim that other jurors pressured him into agreeing to a verdict—in this instance, a verdict of guilty in a capital-murder case—see Jackman, "Mistrial in Fairfax Murder, Rape Case." For a survey of physical threats and attacks during jury deliberations, see Peltz, "For Jurors, the Real Drama Is Often Found outside the Courtroom"; see also chapter 5.

20. Railroad Company v Stout, 84 US at 664.

21. Barry, *Dave Barry Slept Here*, 68; Twain, *Sketches New and Old*, 211; Auld, *Criminal Courts Review*, ch. 5, 140 (para. 13).

22. Tanner v US, 483 US at 115–16; see King, "Juror Delinquency," 2723–24.

23. See Wellons v Hall, 130 S. Ct. at 729. As noted in chapter 1, in some capital cases the jury determines whether to impose the death penalty.

24. Knox, "The Game's Up."

25. R v Young. The retrial also resulted in a unanimous guilty verdict.

26. See cases cited in Tanner v US, 483 US at 119; ibid. at 121.

27. See, e.g., Dwyer, *In the Hands of the People*, 143–44, 173–75; Jonakait, *The American Jury System*, 50–51, 233–44.

28. Jonakait, *The American Jury System*, 238.

29. See Rohde, "Do Diplomas Make Jurors Any Better?"; Jonakait, *The American Jury System*, 45.

30. Minow, "Stripped Down Like a Runner," 1210–11; Jonakait, *The American Jury System*, 239.

31. R v Fricker (case report has no page or paragraph numbers); Haralambous, "Juries and Extraneous Material," 532.

32. Jefferson, "Notes on the State of Virginia, Query XIV," 37–38. Arguably, this view goes back to medieval England, see Masschaele, *Jury, State, and Society*, 118.

33. For a comprehensive list of statutes, see Thompson, *The Albany Law Journal*, 56–57. For these statutes as judicial control of juries, see Thayer, *A Preliminary Treatise on Evidence*, 147–55.

34. See Lubasch, "Juror Is Convicted of Selling Vote to Gotti"; United States Department of Justice, "Federal Jury Convicts Former El Paso Criminal District Court Judge Manuel Barraza."

35. US v Greenspan, 26 F3d at 1006.

36. For discussion, with reference to original sources, see King, *Nameless Justice*, 126–29, 130–34, 158. See also Langhofer, "Unaccountable at the Founding," 1823 n. 7.

37. Criminal Justice Act 2003, § 44; R v T, B, C & H, paras. 5, 6, 7–9, 33, sentences confirmed in R v Twomey.

38. Regarding the likelihood of bias, Conrad, *Jury Nullification*, 191–92, cites to Johnson, "Black Innocence and the White Jury," 1620–21, for a study finding that "jury verdicts came much closer to treating black and white defendants equally than did the decisions of judges." But in fact Johnson's article does not reach, and does not support, this conclusion. For the argument that a judge is a greater danger, see, e.g., Jonakait, *The American Jury System*, 34–35. The quotation regarding racist societies is ibid., 80.

39. See Moyers, "Justice for Sale"; Bright, "Can Judicial Independence Be Attained in the South?," 844–55. In Caperton v Massey, the Supreme Court did impose some limit. A party to a case pending in a state's highest court had contributed generously to the campaign of a person seeking election as a judge of that same court. That person was duly elected and was one of a bare majority deciding the case in favor of the campaign contributor. The Supreme Court held that he should have removed himself from the case.

40. Moyers, "Justice for Sale" (statement of Gammage).

41. For bias and the need for reform, see Jonakait, *The American Jury System*, 34–35; Moyers, "Justice for Sale"; Sandra Day O'Connor Project on the State of the Judiciary. For a limited reform, see, e.g., California, *Code of Civil Procedure*, § 170.1(a)(9)(A), a 2010 statute disqualifying a judge from any case involving a party or lawyer who has contributed substantially to the judge's past or upcoming election.

42. See Vidmar and Hans, *American Juries*, 148; Eisenberg et al., "Judge-Jury Agreement in Criminal Cases," 181.

43. See Vidmar and Hans, *American Juries*, 149; Eisenberg et al., "Judge-Jury Agreement in Criminal Cases," 185–89.

44. See Vidmar and Hans, *American Juries*, 149; Chesterton, *Tremendous Trifles*, 85–86 (paragraph break suppressed).

45. See Vidmar and Hans, *American Juries*, 149.

46. Jonakait, *The American Jury System*, 79. The following discussion in the text refers to Vidmar and Rice, "Assessments of Noneconomic Damage Awards," 897 n. 59, and to Diamond and Casper, "Blindfolding the Jury to Verdict Consequences," 544–46.

47. The following variable pairs provide a counter-example: [10, 9]; [11, 15]; [12, 19.5]; [13, 3]; [14, 27.5]; [15, 31]; [16, 34]; [17, 38]; [18, 150]; [20, 47]. The standard calculation for the correlation coefficient yields 0.62. The overall increasing trend is clear. But although for the first variable the highest value (20) is only twice the lowest (10), yet for the second variable the highest value (150) is fifty times the lowest (3).

CHAPTER 5

1. Auld, *Criminal Courts Review*, ch. 5, 219 (para. 216). In some circumstances, merely being examined in *voir dire* as a prospective juror may involve issues of promoting democratic citizenship. However, these entail the political roles of the jury, discussed in chapter 12.

2. Dividing two billion (the number of dollars) by one and a half million (the number of jurors), and then dividing this by two (the number of days per juror) yields $667 per juror per day. But despite official claims, the actual average length of a jury trial might be more than two days. This would reduce the daily cost per juror. However, at least partially balancing this out, a longer average trial length would increase the total cost estimate of the jury system. Rounding down from $667 to merely "more than $600" per juror per day allows a margin that sufficiently takes care of this issue.

3. Tocqueville, *De la démocratie en Amérique*, vol. 2, ch. 8, 213–15; Dwyer, *In the Hands of the People*, 152; Auld, *Criminal Courts Review*, ch. 5, 135 (para. 1).

4. Tocqueville, *De la démocratie en Amérique*, vol. 2, ch. 8, 213–15.

5. Amar, "The Bill of Rights as a Constitution," 1186 (footnote omitted); Jefferson, "Notes on the State of Virginia, Query XIV," 37–38.

6. Pendleton, *Criminal Justice in England*, ix; ibid., 380 (punctuation altered).

7. Dwyer, *In the Hands of the People*, 157; Conrad, *Jury Nullification*, 258; Jonakait, *The American Jury System*, 196.

8. See American Association of School Administrators, "Citizenship, Democracy and Public Schools."

9. For the average expenditure, see National Education *Association, Rankings and Estimates*, 57, table H–16. The amount quoted is a proper economic-cost evaluation of current expenditures; see the definition of "Current Expenditures," ibid., xiii–xiv.

Typically for state statutes, Alaska, *Public Schools Generally*, § 30 requires 180 days per year "in session," but up to 10 of these days may be diverted to teacher training. Under § 40, a day "in session" is defined as "devoted to the instruction of pupils or to study periods for the pupils."

10. Burns, *The Death of the American Trial*, 73 (emphasis in original). Tocqueville introduced these ideas, in reference to civil trials only, in *De la démocratie en Amérique*, vol. 2, ch. 8, 213.

11. United States Department of State, *Rights of the People*, ch. 7, "Trial by Jury."

12. Illinois, *Citizen Participation Act*, § 110/5.

13. Lincoln, *Gettysburg Address*, 2–3; Mathews, "How Concepts of Politics Control Concepts of Civic Responsibility," 150 (emphasis omitted).

14. Schultz, "Local Government Needs More Citizen Participation"; Energize, *Citizen Involvement* (paragraph breaks suppressed).

15. See, e.g., South Carolina, *Government Volunteers*.

16. Schultz, "Local Government Needs More Citizen Participation."

17. See, e.g., Energize, *Citizen Involvement*.

18. Williams, *The Proof of Guilt*, 284. Williams gives no source of support for this claim.

19. Dwyer, *In the Hands of the People*, 136, with other such reminiscences ibid., 138–39, 151; Ragins, "Justice at the Grass Roots."

20. Finkelstein, "Tempers Seem to Be Growing Shorter in Many Jury Rooms" (paragraph break suppressed).

21. See Peltz, "For Jurors, the Real Drama Is Often Found outside the Courtroom"; People v Keenan, 758 P2d at 1120–22, and cases referenced there. A government-sponsored survey of English jurors claimed: "Some jurors indicated that meeting . . . people from other walks of life with different occupations and outlooks was regarded as being one of the most positive aspects of the experience." Matthews, Hancock, and Briggs, *Jurors' Perceptions*, 42. But the report supports this with the statements of just 2 jurors out of the 361 interviewed, and gives no indication of what any of the other jurors thought about this. Also, this survey is unreliable, as the report acknowledges that it does "not know for certain how representative those who initially consented to be interviewed were of all the eligible jurors at the study courts." Ibid., 17.

22. American Bar Association, *Perceptions of the US Justice System*, 29, 36. Of the respondents, 646 had an "active" role court experience. Of these, 423 found the experience positive, and 82 percent of these reported that their opinions about the justice system "remained the same"; 223 found the experience negative, and 48 percent of these reported that their opinions about the justice system "remained the same." So the total number whose opinions about the justice system "remained the same" is $0.82 \times 423 + 0.48 \times 223$, amounting to 454 respondents. This is 70 percent of the 646 respondents.

Of the 423 respondents who found their experience positive, 15 percent reported a "positive change" in their opinions about the justice system, while 3 percent reported a "negative change." Of the 223 respondents who found their experience negative, none reported a "positive change" in their opinions about the justice system, while 52 percent reported a "negative change." So the total number who reported a "positive change" was 0.15×423, which is about 63, or 10 percent of the 646 respondents—or about one-third of those who reported a change in their opinions. The total number who reported a "negative change" was $0.03 \times 423 + 0.52 \times 223$, which is about 129, or 20 percent of the 646 respondents—or about two-thirds of those who reported a change in their opinions.

23. American Bar Association, *Jury Service*, 18. Even this modest conclusion is not fully supported by the survey data, because the survey posed its question about jury experience to every respondent who had ever been *called* for jury duty, regardless of whether they actually served. Less than half of the people who have at some time been called for jury duty have ever actually served on a jury. Ibid., 17–18.

24. *Fair and Independent Courts.*

25. Typical questionnaires may be found at American Judicature Society, *Jury Exit Questionnaires*. Dwyer incautiously takes at face value an Ohio survey claiming astonishingly positive juror responses. Dwyer, *In the Hands of the People*, 137–38; court officials provided the survey reports, see ibid., 213. In England, the *Criminal Courts Review* recognizes the need for cautious assessment of a survey by the Court Service (a government agency) showing extraordinarily high levels of juror satisfaction. Auld, *Criminal Courts Review*, ch. 5, 218–19 (paras. 215–16).

26. Jonakait, *The American Jury System*, 83, claims that "surveys of those who have served overwhelmingly indicate that former jurors have confidence in the jury system." He gives no reference to any survey, and in any event confidence in the jury system would not equate to confidence in the trial or justice system.

Some English surveys focus on the effect of jury duty on a person's view of the justice system, in particular Matthews, Hancock, and Briggs, *Jurors' Perceptions*, and the annual *Crown Court Survey of Jurors*. However, the English experience of jury duty is not necessarily comparable to the American. Also, these English surveys are unreliable because of sampling problems: they requested individuals who had completed jury duty to participate, but it is not known how representative were those who agreed to participate. In any event, these surveys show little or no overall change in confidence in the justice system as a result of jury duty.

CHAPTER 6

1. See Penn, *The Peoples Ancient and Just Liberties Asserted*, 9; 11–27 (spelling slightly altered; pages not numbered, counted here from the title page as 1).

2. Bushell's Case, 124 Eng. Rep. at 1010.

3. In earlier years, "nullification" appears to have referred to any practice whereby the *judge* was able to circumvent a verdict of the jury that was contrary to his wishes. See, e.g., Bentham, *The Elements of the Art of Packing*, 7 n.

4. See, e.g., US v Jackson, 436 F2d at 42 (referring to "the jury's dispensing power—the power to decide against the law and the facts").

5. See, e.g., Conrad, *Jury Nullification*, 6–7.

6. Green, *Verdict according to Conscience*, xiii, xv, and xvii; Dwyer, *In the Hands of the People*, 71–77; Sixth Form Law, *Juries—Stephen Owen*; Auld, *Criminal Courts Review*, ch. 5, 173–76 (paras. 99–108).

7. See, e.g., Conrad, *Jury Nullification*, 48–63, 65–75, 88–98.

8. See Green, *Verdict according to Conscience*, 177–99; Pease, *The Leveller Movement*, 296–97.

9. Dwyer, *In the Hands of the People*, 73. Christie, "Lawful Departures from Legal Rules," 1298, is simply incorrect in claiming: "Almost all the older cases [of jury nullification] are based on the notion that the jury had the ultimate responsibility for determining the law applicable in a criminal prosecution."

10. Dwyer, *In the Hands of the People*, 73. For an attempt to classify the forms of injustice to which juries have responded by exercising the nullification power, see Brown, "Jury Nullification within the Rule of Law." This book does not adopt Brown's classificatory scheme.

11. See Jonakait, *The American Jury System*, 255; Leipold, "The Dangers of Race-Based Jury Nullification," 126.

12. See Pease, *The Leveller Movement*, 330–48. Despite the verdict, Oliver Cromwell, who was installed as Lord Protector shortly afterward, kept Lilburne in prison.

13. For discussion of an important colonial case, see Conrad, *Jury Nullification*, 32–37.

14. See Abramson, *We the Jury*, 80–82; US v Morris, 26 F Cas. at 1331.

15. This occurred in US ex rel. Wheeler v Williamson.

16. For an account of the legal developments, with reference to original sources, see Conrad, *Jury Nullification*, 106–8.

17. The Supreme Court upheld exactly this procedure in In re Debs, 158 US at 594–96.

18. Hopkins v Oxley Stave Co., 83 F at 939.

19. Dwyer, *In the Hands of the People*, 77, drawing on Kalven and Zeisel, *The American Jury*, 291–93.

20. Dwyer, *In the Hands of the People*, 81.

21. See Adamic, *My America*, 316–24; Leuchtenburg, *Franklin D. Roosevelt and the New Deal*, 25.

22. Jonakait, *The American Jury System*, 109.

23. See Dwyer, *In the Hands of the People*, 75–76.

24. US v Anderson, transcript at 8729, reprinted in Scheflin and Van Dyke, "Jury Nullification," 53.

25. See Morton, "Sir Anthony McCowan"; Corley, *Case Report—R v Ponting*; Lloyd-Bostock and Thomas, "Decline of the 'Little Parliament,' " 10.

26. See Sixth Form Law, *Juries—Stephen Owen*.

27. For the relatively recent extension of jury duty to the citizenry as a whole in America and England, see Hostettler, *The Criminal Jury Old and New*, 13. For discussion of property qualifications, see Oldham, *Trial by Jury*, 299 n. 9. For the New York data and statutory juror qualifications, see Fay v People of State of New York, 332 US at 266–67 (punctuation amended). For discriminatory application of criteria, see, e.g., Carter v Jury Commission of Greene County.

28. Fay v People of State of New York, 332 US at 298–99 (Murphy J, dissenting). For discussion in that era, see Ketler, "The Constitutionality of Blue Ribbon Juries."

29. For the federal courts, see Rabinowitz v US. In the 1970 case of Carter v Jury Commission of Greene County, the Supreme Court rejected a constitutional challenge to an Alabama system of jury selection that effectively excluded persons of color. A decade later, the same court signaled the end of the era of such systems in Duren v Missouri.

30. A few American states have at various times given the jury sentencing power, but most have now abandoned this except in death-penalty cases. See Iontcheva, "Jury Sentencing as Democratic Practice," 314–39.

31. See Green, *Verdict according to Conscience*, 29.

32. Blackstone, *Commentaries*, bk. IV, 239 (ch. 17) (spelling slightly altered).

33. Romilly, Speech, col. xvi. For several cases in the 1730s in which the jury found the value of property stolen to be obviously and blatantly far less than its actual value (including when cash was stolen), see ibid., cols. xv–xvi.

34. Blackstone, *Commentaries*, bk. IV, 239 (ch. 17). The "nullification" terminology is more recent; see Stuntz, *The Collapse of American Criminal Justice*, 30.

35. See Langbein, "Shaping the Eighteenth-Century Criminal Trial," 22.

36. Kirby, "The Jury of the Future."

37. See Radzinowicz, *A History of English Criminal Law*, Appendix 3, 730, citing to *The Petition of Bankers from 214 Cities and Towns*.

38. Steckler v US, 7 F2d at 60. The other case was Marshallo v US. In each of these cases, the defendant, hoping to avoid a penalty entirely, appealed on the ground that the conviction could not stand because it was inconsistent with the acquittal. The appeals were rejected. One of the courts blandly declared: "It is permissible for a jury to convict on one count and acquit on the other, where it was also within their province to convict on both counts on the same evidence." Marshallo v US, 298 F at 76. The other acknowledged: "That the conviction may have been the result of some compromise [by the jury] is, of course, possible; but to consider so is to consider too curiously, unless all verdicts are to be upset on speculation." Steckler v US, 7 F2d at 60.

39. For example, Mississippi, Title 63, c. 3, § 1201, defines reckless driving and declares: "Reckless driving shall be considered a greater offense than careless driving." Careless driving is defined in § 1213, which declares: "Careless driving shall be considered a lesser offense than reckless driving."

40. Dwyer, *In the Hands of the People*, 151.

41. Crook, "Jury System" (paragraph break suppressed). Crook could not "talk about the details" because revealing what occurred in the jury room is prohibited in England by the Contempt of Court Act, 1981, § 8.

42. For discussion and references, see Scheflin and Van Dyke, "Jury Nullification," 69–71.

43. See, e.g., Vidmar and Hans, *American Juries*, 228, 234–36; TXO Production Corp. v Alliance Resources, 509 US at 464 (Stevens J, plurality opinion), at 490–92 (O'Connor J, dissenting).

CHAPTER 7

1. In favor, Butler, "Racially Based Jury Nullification," 701 (footnote omitted); against, Stern, "Between Local Knowledge and National Politics," 1816.

2. US v Polizzi, Appendix A, 549 F Supp. 2d at 450–54, gives a "selected bibliography" of books, periodicals, and other materials on the specific topic of "historic powers of jurors when the Sixth Amendment was adopted." It contains one hundred items. As noted in chapter 6, the controversy over the right to exercise the nullification power is interwoven with a controversy over whether the jury has the right to decide the law as well as the facts in a case. This too has generated an immense literature. For references, see Conrad, *Jury Nullification*, 48–63, 65–75, 88–98.

There is also a good deal of dispute as to how far the views of the Framers should determine what the law is in present-day America. For an account, although a sardonic and partisan one, of the difference in views on this issue between two current members of the Supreme Court, see Apprendi v New Jersey, 530 US at 498–99 (Scalia J, concurring).

3. Sparf v US, 156 US at 74. For the majority opinion, see ibid. at 74, 101–3; for the dissenting opinion, see ibid. at 114, 148–49. Butler ascribes the hostility to the nullification power of the jury in Sparf v US to economic and political shifts in America: "At this time big business became a political force, and the rich guys wanted the law to be very settled, predictable, and probusiness, which meant taking power out of the hands of the people." Butler, *Let's Get Free*, 67.

4. "The vast majority of case law condemns nullification as 'lawless.'" Brown, "Jury Nullification within the Rule of Law," 1149 n. 7, citing to several illustrative cases.

5. US v Thomas, 116 F3d at 614. For a similar view in the California Supreme Court, see People v Williams, 21 P3d at 1213–14.

6. See Duncan v Louisiana, 391 US at 146–47.

7. Usually the Bill of Rights refers to the first ten amendments to the federal Constitution. But the Ninth and Tenth are irrelevant to the incorporation doctrine discussed here, so that in the context of incorporation it is common simply to refer to the first eight amendments as the Bill of Rights. The incorporation doctrine is based on the Court's interpretation of the Fourteenth Amendment to the Constitution, which denies the states the power to "deprive any person of life, liberty, or property, without due process of law."

8. Duncan v Louisiana, 391 US at 146.

9. Ibid. at 155–56 (footnote omitted). The two dissenters on the Court in fact agreed that the function of the jury was to protect against government, but argued that there was no longer a need for such protection (see chapter 8). So all nine members of the Court agreed that the jury system could only be justified as a protection against government.

10. Ibid. at 157 (footnote omitted).

11. Duncan v Perez, where the court also recounts harassment in the first prosecution: Duncan was subjected to multiple arrests and otherwise harassed; his chief counsel was arrested "on a baseless charge of the unlawful practice of law . . . made in bad faith and for purposes of harassment" and had to obtain a federal court injunction against being prosecuted himself.

12. Apprendi v New Jersey, 530 US at 477 (Court's internal quotation marks and insertions omitted).

13. Taylor v Louisiana, 419 US at 529; ibid., n. 7; US v Polizzi, 549 F Supp. 2d at 406.

14. Dwyer, *In the Hands of the People*, 73, 79, 81 (paragraph breaks suppressed).

15. US v Dougherty, 473 F2d at 1130–32 (paragraph breaks suppressed).

16. Adams, *The Works of John Adams*, vol. 2, 253.

17. Pollock and Maitland, *The History of English Law*, vol. 2, 624; see Campbell, *Lives of the Lord Chancellors*, vol. 5, 348 (ch. 148).

18. United States Department of State, *Rights of the People*, ch. 7, "Trial by Jury" (emphasis added).

19. See Pennock, "Political Representation," 10–15, and sources cited there.

20. Smith v Texas, 311 US at 130 (footnote omitted). For references to earlier cases, see Kamisar et al., *Modern Criminal Procedure*, 1365–66.

21. For the fair cross section requirement, see Taylor v Louisiana, 419 US at 530. For women as a group, see ibid. at 531; African Americans and Hispanics, US v Biaggi, 909 F2d at 676–79; Jews, US v Gelb, 881 F2d at 1161. For discussion of standards of proportion, see Kamisar et al., *Modern Criminal Procedure*, 1365.

The fair cross section requirement does not extend to other kinds of groups, such as certain occupational groups that some studies have shown to be under-represented. For a survey of the studies and an assessment of government measures to deal with the issues, see Darbyshire, Maughan, and Stewart, *What Can the English Legal System Learn from Jury Research*, 3–9.

22. Taylor v Louisiana, 419 US at 538; Apodaca v Oregon, 406 US at 413.

23. Berghuis v Smith. As this case acknowledges, the federal courts grant this latitude to the state courts according to the terms of the Antiterrorism and Effective Death Penalty Act of 1996, which restricts the power of the federal courts to grant habeas corpus relief, and which the federal courts have upheld as constitutional.

24. For techniques of avoidance of Batson v Kentucky restrictions, see, e.g., Jonakait, *The American Jury System*, 143–49, and sources cited there; Kamisar et al., *Modern Criminal Procedure*, 1384–86, and sources cited there. The case excluding Latino jurors was Hernandez v New York.

25. See chapter 3. The scholar Richard H. Fallon has distinguished three concepts of legitimacy. An entity or action of government possesses *sociological legitimacy* if the populace regards it as being "deserving of support for reasons beyond fear of sanctions or mere hope for personal reward"; it has *legal legitimacy* if it accords with the legal norms of the society; it possesses *moral legitimacy* if it is deserving of support for moral reasons. Fallon, "Legitimacy and the Constitution," 1794–99. Overall, a government is best able to function if it can lay claim to all forms of legitimacy.

26. Masschaele, *Jury, State, and Society*, 207. Masschaele does not analyze the concept of legitimacy, nor does he treat the legitimating function of the jury in any structural way.

27. American Bar Association, *Perceptions of the US Justice System*, 59.

28. Dwyer, *In the Hands of the People*, 153; Douglas, *We the Judges*, 389.

29. Williams v Florida, 399 US at 100 (emphasis added).

30. Local 36 of International Fishermen and Allied Workers of America v US, 177 F2d at 339.

CHAPTER 8

1. All references in this chapter to this dissent are Duncan v Louisiana, 391 US at 188 (Harlan and Stewart JJ, dissenting).

2. The only constitutional provision that might arguably be used to actually prevent prosecutions for purposes of racial harassment is the equal protection clause of the Fourteenth Amendment. But the Court has not applied the equal protection clause in this way. As Stuntz points out, it would be hard to do so without data in the form of extensive trial records showing racial discrimination in decisions to prosecute; but no jurisdictions kept sufficiently extensive

records at the time, and few do so now. Stuntz, *The Collapse of American Criminal Justice*, 212–15. In addition, defendants face legal barriers against discovering government records regarding discrimination in decisions to prosecute, see US v Armstrong. Stuntz also notes (*The Collapse of American Criminal Justice*, 368–69 n. 72) that the decision of a federal appellate court in Duncan v Perez, issuing an injunction against further prosecution of Duncan on the ground that this new prosecution was "instituted in bad faith and for purposes of harassment," seems to be unique and indicates a jurisprudential path that courts might have more generally taken but did not take. See also chapter 11.

3. US v Dougherty, 473 F2d at 1132.

4. Auld, *Criminal Courts Review*, ch. 5, 175 (para. 105).

5. Wolfram, "The Constitutional History of the Seventh Amendment," 671 (footnote omitted). The writer's subject here is the jury in civil cases. The point is yet stronger for criminal trials.

6. Chapter 6 discussed the ruling of the trial judge in the English trial of Clive Ponting that the "interests of the state" had to be interpreted as meaning the "interests of the government of the day." The jury, in acquitting Ponting, rejected this identification of interests.

7. Sobolewski, "Electors and Representatives," 106.

8. Leipold, "The Dangers of Race-Based Jury Nullification," 127. Concern about the potential for inconsistency in the exercise of jury powers goes back at least as far as comments by Story J in the 1835 case of US v Battiste, 24 F Cas. at 1042–43. For differing interpretations of this case, see US v Polizzi, 549 F Supp. 2d at 423; Conrad, *Jury Nullification*, 66.

9. US v Dougherty, 473 F2d at 1143–44 (Bazelon CJ, concurring and dissenting) (footnotes omitted).

10. People v Williams, 21 P3d at 1223 (citations and references omitted).

11. The quotations are from US v Dougherty, 473 F2d at 1134; ibid. at 1130.

12. Auld, *Criminal Courts Review*, ch. 5, 175 (para. 105).

13. Gertner, "Circumventing Juries, Undermining Justice," 439.

14. Brown, "Jury Nullification within the Rule of Law," 1194–95 (footnotes omitted). For a similar argument, see Conrad, *Jury Nullification*, 167–90, 202.

15. Madison, "Report on the Virginia Resolutions," 571.

16. US v Dougherty, 473 F2d at 1143 (Bazelon CJ, concurring and dissenting) (footnotes omitted).

CHAPTER 9

1. See Stern, "Between Local Knowledge and National Politics," 1841, for this account and references to original sources.

2. Bentham, *Elements of the Art of Packing*, 43 (emphasis in original). Bentham withheld publication of this work for thirteen years after completing it in 1808, because of the clear threat that both author and printer would be prosecuted. For discussion of special juries and of Bentham's work, with references to original sources, see Oldham, *Trial by Jury*, 137, 140–42, 164–73.

3. Juries Act 1949, § 28.

4. For jury vetting, see Hostettler, *The Criminal Jury Old and New*, 129, and original sources cited there. For current guidelines, see Crown Prosecution Service, "Jury Vetting."

5. For discussion and history, see King, "Silencing Nullification Advocacy," 459–67. In a typical case, the judge asked, "I'll have to ask you . . . whether you're willing to accept the law from me as I give it in instructions?" The juror responded, "I don't know." He explained, "Something may come up that I'd feel very strongly about." The judge did not allow him to serve. US v James, 2.

6. See King, "Silencing Nullification Advocacy," 438–40, and sources cited there. For one prospective juror's experience of this, see Collins-Chobanian, "Analysis of Paul Butler's Race-Based Jury Nullification," 523.

7. See, e.g., Turney v State, US v Heicklen. See also King, "Silencing Nullification Advocacy," 492–94.

8. See Fay v People of State of New York, 332 US at 267.

9. For discussion, see Robins, "Judge and Jury."

10. For a charming account, see Cooke, "No Exempt Categories."

11. For a discussion of these concerns and the arguments in favor of dismissing them, see Auld, *Criminal Courts Review*, ch. 5, 146–48 (paras. 29–32).

12. R v Abdroikof, [2007] UKHL 37, opinion of Lord Bingham of Cornhill at paras. 23–24. "Serving police officers remain ineligible for jury service in Scotland, Northern Ireland, Australia, New Zealand, Canada, Hong Kong, Gibraltar and a number of states in the United States." Ibid., at para. 24.

13. Criminal Justice Act 2003, sched. 33, § 321 abolished these exemption categories. R v Khan, [2008] 3 All ER 502 at para. 132, stipulates that the trial judge must ascertain whether any prospective juror "is or has been, a police officer or a member of the prosecuting authority, or is a serving prison officer."

14. For Giuliani, see Cooke, "No Exempt Categories." For Bloomberg, see Grynbaum, "Bloomberg Reports for Jury Duty."

15. Robins, "Judge and Jury," quoting Andrew Prynne QC; ibid., quoting John McDonnell QC.

16. See In re Fahy, 2009 WL 567997 at 3.

17. Ibid. at 5.

18. People v Williams, 21 P3d at 1213 (emphasis removed).

19. US v Dougherty, 473 F.2d at 1130–37; US v Rosenthal, 454 F3d at 946.

20. US v Krzyske, 836 F2d at 1021.

21. See US v Krzyske (reconsideration hearing), 857 F2d at 1095 (Merritt J, dissenting) (paragraph numbers omitted and paragraph breaks suppressed).

22. US v Dougherty, 473 F.2d at 1136–37 (footnote omitted) (Leventhal J); Dwyer, *In the Hands of the People*, 81–82. For discussion, see Diamond, "Dispensing with Deception," and sources cited there.

23. US v Dougherty, 473 F.2d at 1140–41 (Bazelon CJ, concurring and dissenting).

24. US v Polizzi, 549 F Supp. 2d at 340–41.

25. See Dann, " 'Must Find the Defendant Guilty' Jury Instructions," 12 (emphasis added); ibid. See also King, "Silencing Nullification Advocacy," 475 n. 158.

26. Eleventh Circuit, US Court of Appeals, *Pattern Jury Instructions*, 5 (para. 2.1) (emphasis added).

27. Middlebrooks, "Reviving Thomas Jefferson's Jury," 421.

28. US v Thomas, 116 F3d at 614.

29. Ibid. at 623–24.

30. People v Williams, 21 P3d at 1214.

31. Dwyer, *In the Hands of the People*, 50.

32. US v Rosenthal, 454 F3d at 950 (footnote omitted).

33. R v McKenna, [1960] 1 All ER at 329.

34. See, e.g., Clark v US.

35. People v Kriho, 996 P2d at 165–70.

36. US v Krzyske, 836 F2d at 1021. Note for completeness a bizarre 1997 English case, in which a trial judge imprisoned two jurors for "contempt of court in refusing to deliver a verdict," because they could not come to any decision in the case. R v Schot, [1997] 2 Cr. App. R. at 383–87. The Court of Appeal quickly overturned the convictions for contempt, in terms that rebuked the trial judge for numerous serious failings in dealing with the matter, and insisted that it can be only on "very rare occasions [that] . . . the possibility of contempt by a juror arises." Ibid. at 398–400.

CHAPTER 10

1. There has been a strong shift toward defining criminal offenses by statute to replace offenses that were created by the common law in earlier years. Many jurisdictions have wholly abolished common-law criminal offenses. See, e.g., Ohio, *Crimes—Procedure*, c. 2901, § 03(A) ("No conduct constitutes a criminal offense against the state unless it is defined as an offense in the Revised Code.").

The federal Constitution limits the sentence that a federal or state court can impose to the maximum specified by the statute that defines the offense. Some statutes specify a maximum sentence but allow increases above that maximum if there are "aggravating factors." If the case is tried before a jury, the Constitution requires any aggravating factors to be proved to the jury. Among the main cases dealing with these issues are Apprendi v New Jersey, Blakely v Washington, Cunningham v California, and US v Booker.

Federal loan-sharking offenses are formally designated as "Making or Financing an Extortionate Extension of Credit; Collecting an Extension of Credit by Extortionate Means." They are defined, and the penalty specified, in 18 USC §§ 892–894.

2. Gertner, "Circumventing Juries, Undermining Justice," 424–25.

3. See, e.g., the description in Rita v US, 551 US at 342–44. For discussion of the role of the probation officer in the sentencing hearing, see Stith, "The Arc of the Pendulum," 1437.

4. Gall v US, 128 S. Ct. at 593.

5. Among the many federal and state courts that have insisted on this are US v Grier, 475 F3d at 570 n. 9; People v Huey, 505 A2d at 1245–46.

6. US v O'Brien, 130 S. Ct. at 2174.

7. So the federal statute establishing the United States Sentencing Commission, discussed shortly in the text, stipulates that "rehabilitating the defendant" should not be taken into account in sentencing. 28 USC § 994(k). For suggestions that state and federal budget crises may now to some extent be causing a swing back toward rehabilitation, see Kamisar et al., *Modern Criminal Procedure*, 1488–89, and sources cited there.

For an account, with references to sources, of the developments in sentencing policy as discussed in the following text paragraphs, see Gertner, "Circumventing Juries, Undermining Justice," 425–28. See also Stith and Koh, "The Politics of Sentencing Reform."

8. United States Sentencing Commission, *Federal Sentencing Guidelines Manual and Sentencing Table*. For the following discussion, the Guidelines Manual deals with loan-sharking offenses at 197–98 (§ 2E2.1), and with criminal history category at 380–94 (§ 4A1).

9. US v Booker, 543 US at 245.

10. Gall v US, 128 S. Ct. at 594, 596–97.

11. Ibid. at 597.

12. People v Beatty, 80 P3d at 855 (court's citations to precedent omitted).

13. Martinez, "Wesley Snipes Heads to Prison" (paragraph breaks suppressed).

14. This is a simplified version, sufficient for the discussion here, of the standard definition, as found in e.g., American Law Institute, *Model Penal Code*, § 1.13(9).

15. "Elements of a crime must be charged in an indictment and proved to a jury beyond a reasonable doubt." US v O'Brien, 130 S. Ct. at 2174.

16. Gertner, "Circumventing Juries, Undermining Justice," 431–32 (emphasis in original, footnote omitted, paragraph break suppressed). It is

often not clear, from the statute or otherwise, whether something should be treated as an element of the offense or as a sentencing factor. The trial judge decides this, and either the prosecution or the convicted defendant can appeal against the decision.

17. United States Sentencing Commission, *Federal Sentencing Guidelines Manual*, 358–61 (§ 3C1.1).

18. US v Dunnigan, 507 US at 91.

19. Ibid. at 96–97.

20. US v Snipes, 611 F3d at 863, 871.

21. For the account of the initial proceedings as given here, see Witte v US, 515 US at 392–95. For the scope of "relevant conduct" and its impact on sentencing, see United States Sentencing Commission, *Federal Sentencing Guidelines Manual*, 22–32 (§ 1B1.3).

22. Witte v US, 515 US at 395.

23. Ibid. at 399–400. The Court states that Witte would not ultimately suffer unfairness, because a provision in the sentencing guidelines "operates to mitigate the possibility that the fortuity of two separate prosecutions will grossly increase a defendant's sentence," and that "he would be able to vindicate his interests through appropriate appeals should the Guidelines be misapplied in any future sentencing proceeding." Ibid. at 405. But the provision to which the Court refers, *Federal Sentencing Guidelines Manual*, 452 (§ 5G1.3), is a mere "policy statement" that the sentencing judge has broad discretion to apply or not. It is disingenuous to suggest that a defendant could appeal against misapplication of this provision, given that appellate courts are so extremely deferential to the trial judge on sentencing. Indeed, the Supreme Court insists that this deference must apply equally when the sentencing judge departs from the guidelines on the basis of a policy disagreement with the guidelines. Spears v US, 129 S. Ct. at 843–44.

24. Williams v New York, 337 US at 244.

25. People v Gitlow, 136 NE at 324 (Pound and Cardozo JJ, dissenting).

26. US v Watts, 519 US at 149–50.

27. Ibid. at 150–51.

28. Ibid. at 151 (citing to 18 USC § 3661); ibid. at 155.

29. The cases raising doubt regarding US v Watts were those noted earlier in this chapter, declaring the sentencing guidelines to be advisory rather than mandatory and establishing that the trial judge may not impose a sentence beyond the statutory maximum. The Court rejected the Fifth Amendment challenge in US v Booker, 543 US at 240–41. For discussion, see US v White, 551 F3d at 383–84.

30. Some of the cases are US v Settles (DC Circuit), US v Grier (3d Circuit), US v White (6th Circuit), US v Horne (7th Circuit), US v Canania (8th Circuit), US v Duncan (11th Circuit).

31. US v White, 551 F3d at 383 n. 1. Federal appellate courts usually sit as a panel of three judges. For particularly important or controversial cases, an *en banc* panel may be convened, consisting of all the judges on that court of appeal, or at least a much larger number than three.

32. US v Hurn, 496 F3d at 785–88.

33. US v White, 551 F3d at 387–88 (Merritt J, dissenting).

34. People v Woodlief, 90 SE at 139–40.

35. Wisconsin v Leitner, 646 NW2d at 353 (footnotes omitted); for Connecticut, People v Huey, 505 A2d at 1245; for Colorado, People v Beatty, 80 P3d at 856 (the acquittal had occurred in a different trial, but the point is similar, and in any event the court's approval of US v Watts is explicit and unreserved); for New York, see Sterback, "Getting Time for an Acquitted Crime," 1241–44.

36. US v White, 551 F3d at 394 (Merritt J, dissenting).

37. US v Horne, 474 F3d at 1007.

38. For the following account and the quotation from the sentencing record, see US v Juarez-Ortega, 866 F3d at 747–49.

39. US v Canania, 532 F3d at 776 (Bright J, concurring).

40. Courts that have considered applying a higher evidentiary standard include US v Hopper, 177 F3d at 833; US v Hurn, 496 F3d at 788–89. For recognition that it would probably make no great difference, see Gertner, "Circumventing Juries, Undermining Justice," 439.

41. US v Ibanga, 454 F Supp. at 536.

42. US v Ibanga, 271 Fed. Appx. at 3. The Supreme Court precedent on which the appellate court relied was Gall v US, which was decided after the trial court's decision on sentencing.

43. Federal Bureau of Investigation, Washington Field Division. "First of Five Remaining Congress Park Defendants."

44. Caron to Roberts.

45. Some jurists have suggested that requiring juries to give reasons to justify their verdicts would improve the quality of jury verdicts. See, e.g., Auld, *Criminal Courts Review*, ch. 5, 176 (para. 106). For discussion of how this would compromise the ability of the jury to serve as safeguard against government, see, e.g., US v Spock, 416 F2d at 182; Jackson, *Making Juries Accountable*, 530; Kadish and Kadish, *Discretion to Disobey*, 52–53.

CHAPTER 11

1. For the development of social role concepts, see Parsons, *The Social System*.

2. For the following account, see Kelsey, *Twentieth-Century Doctor*.

3. See Kadish and Kadish, *Discretion to Disobey*, 27.

4. Oakley and Cocking, *Virtue Ethics and Professional Roles*, 153–55.

5. Kadish and Kadish, *Discretion to Disobey*, 27–28, 62.

6. Ibid., 27–35, 143–44.

7. Ibid., 29.

8. Ibid., 29–30.

9. Ibid., 29.

10. "In effect, the procedure used when conscientious individuals depart from roles that do not provide for justifiable rule departures [that is, nonrecourse roles] must be incorporated as a feature of roles that do provide for justifiable departures [that is, recourse roles]." Ibid., 30.

11. Ibid., 73–74 (footnotes omitted, paragraph break suppressed).

12. Butler, *Let's Get Free*, 63 (paragraph break suppressed).

13. Kadish and Kadish, *Discretion to Disobey*, 76. See also Miller and Remington, "Procedures before Trial," 115; Kamisar et al., *Modern Criminal Procedure*, 969–70.

14. Kadish and Kadish, *Discretion to Disobey*, 81 (footnote omitted). See also Kamisar et al., *Modern Criminal Procedure*, 955–1006.

15. In some states, the attorney general or governor has the power to override a decision of the local prosecutor not to prosecute. See, e.g., Johnson v Pataki, where a local prosecutor in the state of New York publicly declared his policy not to seek the death penalty, and the state governor instructed the attorney general to assume control of a prosecution in order to seek the death penalty. But powers of this kind are rarely exercised.

In cases where the state offense is also a federal offense, the federal authorities can prosecute. This occurred regarding violence against African Americans and against civil rights workers in the South, where state prosecutors failed to prosecute. It also occurs in a number of areas, such as drug offenses, where federal and state laws criminalize the same conduct.

16. Bordenkircher v. Hayes, 434 US at 364.

17. For setting government enforcement priorities, see Wayte v US, 470 US at 607. For the new discretion-limiting policy, see Stith, "The Arc of the Pendulum," 1440–41; for why it has failed, see ibid., 1450–52.

18. Bordenkircher v. Hayes, 434 US at 364. For discussion, see Kamisar et al., *Modern Criminal Procedure*, 973–94.

19. For explanation, see Stuntz, *The Collapse of American Criminal Justice*, 119–21, referring to US v Armstrong. See also chapter 8.

20. See Driscoll, "Understanding the Power of Prosecution," 31.

21. In England, the Crown Prosecution Service, a government department created in 1985 that is responsible for determining criminal charges and bringing prosecutions, bases any decision to prosecute on "whether a prosecution is needed in the public interest." Crown Prosecution Service, "The Principles We Follow."

22. See Atiyah and Summers, *Form and Substance in Anglo-American Law*, 185. For a discussion of American state and federal drafting procedures that suggest reasons for this, see ibid., 315–23.

23. The offense was abolished by the Suicide Act, 1961. For nonprosecution in the preceding years, see R v Commissioner *ex parte* Blackburn, [1968] 1 All ER at 769 (observation by Denning MR).

24. US v Hiveley, 61 F3d at 1363–65 (Bright J, concurring) (paragraph breaks suppressed); see Newman, *Conviction*, 174–78.

25. The following summary of the California three-strikes law is taken from Ewing v California, 538 US at 15–17, and contains direct quotes from this case that are not specifically noted as such.

26. See Bazelon, "Arguing Three Strikes," 1–2.

27. Lockyer v Andrade, where the Supreme Court held that this sentence did not violate the Eighth Amendment ban on cruel and unusual punishment. The Court reached a similar conclusion in Ewing v California.

28. Bazelon, "Arguing Three Strikes," 5.

CHAPTER 12

1. Scheflin and Van Dyke, "Jury Nullification," 87.

2. See Kadish and Kadish, *Discretion to Disobey*, 59–66.

3. Ibid., 66.

4. Adams, *The Works of John Adams*, vol. 2, 254; US v Spock, 416 F2d at 182.

5. US v Dougherty, 473 F2d at 1140 n. 5 (Bazelon CJ, concurring and dissenting); Rochin v California, 342 US at 172.

6. Madison, "Report on the Virginia Resolutions," 571.

7. California Judicial Branch, *Jury Info.* For a sampling of oaths from other states, see Conrad, *Jury Nullification*, 240.

8. Duncan v Louisiana, 391 US at 187 (Harlan and Stewart JJ, dissenting) (footnote omitted); Auld, *Criminal Courts Review*, ch. 5, 174 (para. 101).

9. See People v Williams, 21 P3d at 1212–13.

10. Plainly on the basis of the nullification power, Denning MR described the jury as "the bulwark of our liberties," Ward v James, [1966] 1 QB at 295, and Patrick Devlin described it as "the lamp that shows that freedom lives," Devlin, *Trial by Jury*, 164. Both Denning and Devlin served as trial-court judges before distinguished careers as appellate judges.

11. "[I]n general jurors are not required to swear that they will follow the instructions given to them by the judge regardless of how deeply it violates their personal moral or conscientious convictions." Conrad, *Jury Nullification*, 239.

12. Some scholars assert this directly; others argue that the obligation created by the promise is outweighed by other considerations. See, e.g., Gilbert, *A Theory of Political Obligation*, 82–83, and sources cited there.

13. Conrad, *Jury Nullification*, 261.

14. Ibid., 265.

15. Lockhart v McCree, 476 US at 176; Butler, "Racially Based Jury Nullification," 725 n. 236.

16. More than two centuries ago, the German philosopher Immanuel Kant insisted that deception as a policy intended to achieve the good of society is likely, on the contrary, to undermine societal foundations. Kant, "Über ein vermeintes Recht, aus Menschenliebe zu lügen," 305.

17. Adams, *The Works of John Adams*, vol. 2, 255.

18. Bazelon, *The Adversary Process*, 12679, col. 2.

19. US v Wilson, 28 F Cas. at 708. A typical modern expression of this view, relying on US v Wilson, is Christie, "Lawful Departures from Legal Rules," 1304. For the issue of the jury deciding the law, see chapter 6.

20. Christie, "Lawful Departures from Legal Rules," 1304. For a similar view, see US v Dougherty, 473 F.2d at 1136. For discussion of these views, see Scheflin and Van Dyke, "Jury Nullification," 108–11.

21. Grant, Speech, col. lxvii.

22. See Radzinowicz, *A History of English Criminal Law*, Appendix 4, 731, citing to *The London Jurors' Petition*, 1831.

23. Spooner, *An Essay on the Trial by Jury*, 190 (emphasis in original). Spooner, ibid. 189–91, links this responsibility to the issue of whether the jury should decide the law and to rights claimed to derive from the Magna Carta, which are irrelevant here. Also irrelevant here are the proto-libertarian and anarchist sentiments that Spooner purports to derive from the moral responsibility of the juror.

24. Shannon v US, 512 US at 579.

25. Butler, "Racially Based Jury Nullification," 680, 714.

26. Ibid., 716–17.

27. See, e.g., Leipold, "The Dangers of Race-Based Jury Nullification"; Collins-Chobanian, "Analysis of Paul Butler's Race-Based Jury Nullification."

28. Shannon v US, 512 US at 579.

29. For the observation about users of crack cocaine, see Wilson, "Obama Signs Fair Sentencing Act." For the tendency of prosecutors to focus exclusively on African American users, and an explanation of how they are able to do so despite supposed constitutional safeguards against discriminatory prosecution, see Stuntz, *The Collapse of American Criminal Justice*, 119–21.

30. See Perazzo, "Obama: Tilting at Racial Windmills."

31. Fair Sentencing Act of 2010, preamble (capitalization amended). For history and analysis of this legislation, see Gotsch, *"After" the War on Drugs*. Even before enactment of this statute, some federal trial judges were exercising their discretion to impose somewhat less excessive sentences for

possession of crack cocaine; see Kimbrough v US and Spears v US. See also chapter 10.

CHAPTER 13

1. The concept of "punishment," as viewed from a political and moral perspective, is necessarily broader than a special definition of "punishment" that the Supreme Court has developed as a term of art to restrict the application of the Eighth Amendment guarantee against cruel and unusual punishments in individual cases. According to the Court's definition, if a prison inmate suffers harm as a result of conditions of imprisonment, the courts will not intervene—however unjust the conditions might be—unless the inmate can prove at trial that some prison official was subjectively aware that he was at substantial risk of harm. It is not even enough for the inmate to show that an official was aware of facts from which the risk of harm to him could readily be inferred; the inmate must show that the official did actually draw the inference. The Court stresses this point: "an official's failure to alleviate a significant risk that he should have perceived but did not, while no cause for commendation, cannot under our cases be condemned as the infliction of punishment." Farmer v Brennan, 511 US at 837–38.

The Court's Eighth Amendment jurisprudence, and in particular its special definition of "punishment," cannot control the juror, whose political role as a safeguard against government requires her to do justice precisely when the courts will not. In fact, because the Court's restricted interpretation of the Eighth Amendment can often prevent inmates from obtaining justice from the courts, jurors must be all the more vigilant to take the prospect of punishment in the form of unjust systemic prison conditions into account in reaching their verdict.

2. Burger, Address by the Chief Justice, 21–22; US v Bailey, 444 US at 424 (Blackmun and Brennan JJ, dissenting).

3. For example, see Bartlett, "Post-Conviction Bonds" (New Jersey "has about 26,000 inmates crammed into a system designed for around 17,000"); Hogan, "Overcrowding of State Prisons Demands Action" ("Michigan prisons . . . are at a bursting point as prisoner overcrowding has reached a critical point"); King, *The State of Sentencing 2008*, 10 (Kentucky, Pennsylvania, and South Carolina measures to combat overcrowding); Whyte, "The 3 Most Crowded State Prison Systems in America" ("Alabama . . . is currently incarcerating 25,593 inmates, while the intended capacity of all of its facilities combined only amounts to 13,403 inmates"; "Massachusetts, with 11,327 total inmates and an intended capacity of just 7,979").

4. Coleman v Schwarzenegger, 2009 WL 2430820 at sec. I (internal citation and internal brackets omitted). The name of the case changed several times over the years: the named plaintiff switched between the original plaintiffs in

the two cases that the courts joined together; the named defendant was whoever was governor of California at the time; the order of the parties changed
as the case went through the appeals process. The proclamation by Governor
Schwarzenegger that the Court refers to was Prison Overcrowding State of
Emergency Proclamation (Proclamation 4278), October 4, 2006.

5. For broom closets, etc., see Driscoll, "Studying Prison Realignment," 8,
quoting from seminar presentation by Michael W. Bien. For holding cells,
see Specter, "Everything Revolves around Overcrowding," 197.

6. Brown v Plata, 131 S. Ct. at 1924; ibid. at 1934.

7. The enactment is Assembly Bill 109 (2011).

8. Driscoll, "Studying Prison Realignment," 8.

9. See Gould, "As California Fights Prison Overcrowding."

10. Ibid.

11. See Lopez, "*Coleman/Plata*," 113–20.

12. Plata v Schwarzenegger, at 27, 43 (paragraph breaks suppressed).

13. Coleman v Schwarzenegger [district court], opinion at 8.

14. For discussion, see Brown v Plata, 131 S. Ct. at 1929. The two original
federal class actions were assigned to the same three-judge trial court and then
brought together into a single litigation.

15. In the course of the litigation, the state stipulated to an injunction
providing for remedial measures in the district court in 2001 but failed to comply with that injunction. In 2005 the district court appointed a receiver to manage the entire California prison health care system. In 2008 the receiver
reported that overcrowding made it impossible to remedy the situation. This
satisfied the provisions of the PLRA, and accordingly a three-judge court was
convened. This court ordered the reduction in prison population. See Brown
v Plata, 131 S. Ct. at 1926–28.

16. Ibid. at 1928.

17. Coleman v Schwarzenegger, 2009 WL 2430820 at sec. I, *1 (internal
quotation marks omitted).

18. Ibid. (emphasis in original).

19. Plata v Schwarzenegger, at 21 (internal citations omitted).

20. Ibid. at 22.

21. Ibid. at 8 (internal citations omitted).

22. Ibid. at 12 (internal citations omitted). An example of other such
accounts that the court gives is: "the prisoner went to the prison emergency
room with ... indications of seriously deficient blood flow and probable
shock. .... Rather than being sent to a community hospital emergency room
for immediate treatment, as would have been appropriate, the patient was sent
to the prison's Outpatient Housing Unit for observation. He died shortly
thereafter from cardiac arrest." Ibid. at 9. Another example is: "a prisoner
repeatedly requested to see a doctor regarding acute abdominal and chest

pains; the triage nurse canceled the medical appointment, thinking the prisoner was faking illness. . . . A doctor did see the prisoner a few weeks later but refused to examine him because the prisoner had arrived with a self-diagnosis and the doctor found this unacceptable. The prisoner died two weeks later." Ibid. at 9–10.

23. Ibid. at 13 (internal citations omitted).

24. National Prison Rape Elimination Commission, Report, 16.

25. Singer, *Prison Rape: An American Institution?* This book gives full citations to all sources referred to in the text.

26. US v Bailey, 444 US at 421–22 (Blackmun and Brennan JJ, dissenting) (paragraph breaks suppressed).

27. Note 1 explains this interpretation as the Supreme Court developed it in Farmer v Brennan regarding individual cases. The Court's jurisprudence in prison rape cases has not as yet taken into account the systemic nature of prison rape in America.

Bibliography

BOOKS, ARTICLES, REPORTS, ETC.

Abramson, Jeffrey B. *We, the Jury: The Jury System and the Ideal of Democracy.* Cambridge, MA: Harvard University Press, 2000.

Adamic, Louis. *My America, 1928–1938.* New York: Harper, 1938.

Adams, Charles Francis. *The Works of John Adams, Second President of the United States, with a Life of the Author.* Vol. 2. Boston, 1850.

Amar, Akhil Reed. "The Bill of Rights as a Constitution." *Yale Law Journal* 100 (1991): 1131–209.

American Association of School Administrators. "Citizenship, Democracy and Public Schools." Accessed December 20, 2011. http://www.aasa.org/content.aspx?id=196.

American Bar Association. *Jury Service: Is Fulfilling Your Civic Duty a Trial?* Harris Interactive, July 2004. Accessed December 21, 2011. http://www.abanow.org/wordpress/wp-content/files_flutter/1272052715_20_1_1_7_Upload_File.pdf.

American Bar Association. *Perceptions of the US Justice System.* Report, 1999. Accessed December 21, 2011. http://www.abanow.org/wordpress/wp-content/files_flutter/1269460858_20_1_1_7_Upload_File.pdf.

American Judicature Society. *Jury Exit Questionnaires.* Accessed December 21, 2011. http://www.ajs.org/jc/exit_questionnaires.asp.

American Law Institute. *Model Penal Code.* Philadelphia: American Law Institute, 1962.

Armshaw, Kristin. "Why Every State Should Have a Jury Patriotism Act." *FindLaw*, July 14, 2004. Accessed December 21, 2011. http://writ.news .findlaw.com/commentary/20040714_armshaw.html.

Associated Press. "Getting Out of Jury Duty Is a National Pastime." July 27, 2007. Accessed July 30, 2007. http://www.cnn.com/2007/US/law/07/27/ reluctant.jurors.ap/index.html [page no longer available].

Atiyah, P. S., and Robert S. Summers. *Form and Substance in Anglo-American Law: A Comparative Study in Legal Reasoning, Legal Theory and Legal Institutions*. Oxford: Oxford University Press, 1987.

Auld, Robin. *Review of the Criminal Courts of England and Wales* [cited as Auld, *Criminal Courts Review*]. London: The Stationery Office, 2001.

Ball, David. *Theater Tips and Strategies for Jury Trials*. 3rd ed. Notre Dame, IN: National Institute for Trial Advocacy, 2003.

Barry, Dave. *Dave Barry Slept Here: A Sort of History of the United States*. New York: Random House, 1997.

Bartlett, Dennis. "Post-Conviction Bonds Could Solve N.J. Prison Overcrowding and Save Taxpayer Money." *Newsroom Jersey*, March 5, 2010. Accessed January 8, 2012. http://www.newjerseynewsroom.com/ commentary/post-conviction-bonds-could-solve-nj-prison-overcrowding -and-save-taxpayer-money.

Bazelon, David. *The Adversary Process: Who Needs It?* 12th Annual James Madison Lecture, New York University School of Law, April 1971. Reprinted in US Congressional Record, vol. 117, part 10, 12675–79 (Senate, April 29, 1971).

Bazelon, Emily. "Arguing Three Strikes." *New York Times*, May 17, 2010. Accessed December 21, 2011. http://www.nytimes.com/2010/05/23/ magazine/23strikes-t.html.

Bennett, Cathy E. & Associates. Accessed December 23, 2011. http://www .cebjury.com/.

Bentham, Jeremy. *The Elements of the Art of Packing, as Applied to Special Juries, particularly in Cases of Libel Law*. London, 1821.

Blackstone, William. *Commentaries on the Laws of England*. Oxford, 1768.

Bright, Stephen B. "Can Judicial Independence Be Attained in the South? Overcoming History, Elections, and Misperceptions about the Role of the Judiciary." *Georgia State University Law Review* 14 (1998): 817–60.

Brown, Darryl K. "Jury Nullification within the Rule of Law." *Minnesota Law Review* 81 (1997): 1149–200.

Burger, Warren E. Address to the Bar of the City of New York. *Record of the Association of the Bar of the City of New York* 25 (March 1970 Supp.): 14–24.

Burns, Robert P. *The Death of the American Trial*. Chicago: University of Chicago Press, 2009.

Butler, Paul. *Let's Get Free: A Hip-Hop Theory of Justice*. New York: New Press, 2009.

Butler, Paul. "Racially Based Jury Nullification: Black Power in the Criminal Justice System." *Yale Law Journal* 105 (1995): 677–725.

California Judicial Branch. *Jury Info: Step 1: Selection of a Jury.* Accessed January 3, 2012. http://www.courts.ca.gov/2240.htm.

Campbell, John. *Lives of the Lord Chancellors and Keepers of the Great Seal of England, from the Earliest Times till the Reign of King George IV.* London, 1846.

Caron, Jim to The Honorable Richard W. Roberts, May 16, 2008. *Washington Times*, May 16, 2008. Accessed August 31, 2008. http://video1.washingtontimes.com/video/docs/letter.pdf [page no longer available].

Carpenter, John, and Richard Whitington. *Liber Albus.* London, 1419. Translated from the original Latin and Anglo-Norman by Henry Thomas Riley as *Liber Albus: The White Book of the City of London.* London, 1861.

Carrington, Paul D. "The Seventh Amendment: Some Bicentennial Reflections." *University of Chicago Legal Forum* (1990): 33–86.

Chandler, Peleg W. *American Criminal Trials.* Vol. 1. Boston, 1841.

Chesterton, G. K. *Tremendous Trifles.* New York: Dodd, Mead, 1920.

Christie, George C. "Lawful Departures from Legal Rules: 'Jury Nullification' and Legitimated Disobedience." *California Law Review* 62 (1974): 1289–310.

Clark, Joseph T. et al. *Report and Recommendations of the Supreme Court of Ohio Task Force on Jury Service.* February 2004. Accessed December 23, 2011. http://www.sconet.state.oh.us/publications/juryTF/jurytf_proposal.pdf.

Cohen, Thomas H., and Steven K. Smith. *Civil Trial Cases and Verdicts in Large Counties, 2001.* United States Department of Justice, Bureau of Justice Statistics Bulletin, April 2004. Accessed December 23, 2011. http://bjs.ojp.usdoj.gov/content/pub/pdf/ctcvlc01.pdf.

Collins-Chobanian, Shari. "Analysis of Paul Butler's Race-Based Jury Nullification and His Call to Black Jurors and the African American Community." *Journal of Black Studies* 39 (2009): 508–27.

Commission on the Future of the West Virginia Judicial System. *Final Report.* 1998. Accessed December 23, 2011. http://www.state.wv.us/wvsca/future/report/appendc.pdf.

Condorcet, Marquis de. *Essai sur l'application de l'analyse à la probabilité des décisions rendues à la pluralité des voix.* Paris, 1785.

Conrad, Clay. *Jury Nullification: The Evolution of a Doctrine.* Durham, NC: Carolina Academic Press, 1998.

Cooke, Alistair. "No Exempt Categories." Letter from America, BBC News, September 13, 1999. Accessed December 30, 2011. http://news.bbc.co.uk/1/hi/programmes/letter_from_america/445738.stm.

Corley, Vyvienne Y. A. *Case Report—R v Ponting. Criminal Law Review* (1985): 318–20.

Crime Control Digest. "Juror No-Shows Soar to 'Crisis' High." July 2, 2004. Accessed December 26, 2011. http://www.washingtoncrime.org/.

Crook, Frances. "Jury System: A Bulwark of Freedom." *Frances Crook's blog,* May 2008. Accessed December 21, 2011. http://www.howardleague.org/francescrookblog/jury-system-a-bulwark-of-freedom.

Crown Court Survey of Jurors. London: Ministry of Justice. Annual Survey. Survey report 2010 accessed December 21, 2011. http://www.justice.gov.uk/publications/docs/crown-court-jurors-survey-2010.pdf.

Crown Prosecution Service. "Jury Vetting." Accessed December 21, 2011. http://www.cps.gov.uk/legal/h_to_k/jury_vetting/.

Crown Prosecution Service. "The Principles We Follow." Accessed December 21, 2011. http://www.cps.gov.uk/about/principles.html.

Dann, B. Michael. " 'Must Find the Defendant Guilty' Jury Instructions Violate the Sixth Amendment." *Judicature* 91, no. 1 (July–August 2007): 12–19.

Darbyshire, Penny, Andy Maughan, and Angus Stewart. *What Can the English Legal System Learn from Jury Research Published up to 2001?* Kingston University, Occasional Paper Series 49. Kingston upon Thames, UK: Kingston Business School/Kingston Law School, 2002.

DecisionQuest. Accessed December 23, 2011. http://www.decisionquest.com.

Devlin, Patrick. *Trial by Jury.* London: Stevens, 1956.

Diamond, Shari Seidman. "Dispensing with Deception, Curing with Care: A Response to Judge Dann on Nullification." *Judicature* 91, no. 1 (July–August 2007): 20–25.

Diamond, Shari Seidman, and Jonathan D. Casper. "Blindfolding the Jury to Verdict Consequences: Damages, Experts, and the Civil Jury." *Law and Society Review* 26 (1992): 513–63.

Doran, Sean, John D. Jackson, and Michael L. Seigel. "Rethinking Adversariness in Nonjury Criminal Trials." *American Journal of Criminal Law* 23 (1995): 1–58.

Douglas, William O. *We the Judges: Studies in American and Indian Constitutional Law from Marshall to Mukherjea.* Garden City, NY: Doubleday, 1956.

Driscoll, Sharon. "Studying Prison Realignment in Real Time." *Stanford Lawyer* 85 (Fall 2011): 8–9, 79.

Driscoll, Sharon. "Understanding the Power of Prosecution." *Stanford Lawyer* 83 (Fall 2010): 31–32, 80.

Dwyer, William L. *In the Hands of the People: The Trial Jury's Origins, Triumphs, Troubles, and Future in American Democracy.* New York: Thomas Dunne Books, St. Martin's Press, 2002.

Economist. Anglo-Saxon Attitudes: A Survey of British and American Views of the World. March 2008. Polimetrix (America) and YouGov (England). Accessed December 26, 2011. http://www.economist.com/media/pdf/FullPollData.pdf.

Edelman, Paul H. "On Legal Interpretations of the Condorcet Jury Theorem." *Journal of Legal Studies* 31 (2002): 327–49.

Ehisen, Rich. "Will Jury Patriotism Act Deepen Jury Pool?" *State Net Capitol Journal* 12, no. 10 (March 8, 2004). Accessed December 26, 2011. http://www.statenet.com/capitol_journal/.

Eisenberg, Theodore, Paula L. Hannaford-Agor, Valerie P. Hans, Nicole L. Waters, G. Thomas Munsterman, Stewart J. Schwab, and Martin T. Wells. "Judge-Jury Agreement in Criminal Cases: A Partial Replication of Kalven and Zeisel's *The American Jury*." *Journal of Empirical Legal Studies* 2 (2005): 171–207.

Eleventh Circuit, US Court of Appeals. *Pattern Jury Instructions (Criminal Cases) 2003*. Accessed December 30, 2011. http://www.ca11.uscourts.gov/documents/jury/crimjury.pdf.

Elliott, Catherine, and Frances Quinn. *English Legal System*. 9th ed. Harlow, UK: Longman, 2008.

Energize, Inc. *Citizen Involvement in Boulder County Government, Colorado.* Accessed December 21, 2011. http://www.energizeinc.com/art/vvgovt.html.

Esau, Alvin. "The Amish and Litigation." July 1998. Accessed February 2, 2008. http://www.umanitoba.ca/Law/Courses/esau/lr/lr_amish.html [page no longer available].

Fair and Independent Courts: A Conference on the State of the Judiciary. Report of conference at Georgetown University Law Center, Washington DC, September 28–29, 2006. Accessed December 21, 2011. http://www.law.georgetown.edu/judiciary/documents/Summary_smgroups.pdf.

Fallon, Richard H., Jr. "Legitimacy and the Constitution." *Harvard Law Review* 118 (2005): 1787–853.

Federal Bureau of Investigation, Washington Field Division. "First of Five Remaining Congress Park Defendants Is Sentenced to 180 Months in Prison." Press Release, May 1, 2008. Accessed December 26, 2011. http://washingtondc.fbi.gov/dojpressrel/pressrel08/wfo050108b.htm [page no longer available].

Finkelstein, Katherine E. "Tempers Seem to Be Growing Shorter in Many Jury Rooms." *New York Times*, August 3, 2001. Accessed December 21, 2011. http://www.nytimes.com/2001/08/03/nyregion/03JURY.html.

Fonteyne, Ronald. "A New Hi-Tech Method for Checking the Mesh Size of Fishing Nets." International Council for the Exploration of the Sea (ICES). Accessed December 23, 2011. http://www.ices.dk/marineworld/omega.asp.

Gane, Christopher. "The Scottish Jury." *Revue internationale de droit pénal* 72 (2001): 259–72.

Gates, Henry L. Jr. *Thirteen Ways of Looking at a Black Man*. New York: Random House, 1997.

Gershman, Bennett L. "The Eyewitness Conundrum: How Courts, Police and Attorneys Can Reduce Mistakes by Eyewitnesses." *New York State Bar Association Journal* 81, no. 1 (January 2009): 24–32.

Gertner, Nancy. "Circumventing Juries, Undermining Justice: Lessons from Criminal Trials and Sentencing." *Suffolk University Law Review* 32 (1999): 419–39.

Gilbert, Margaret. *A Theory of Political Obligation: Membership, Commitment, and the Bonds of Society*. Oxford: Clarendon Press, 2006.

Gotsch, Kara. *"After" the War on Drugs: The Fair Sentencing Act and the Unfinished Drug Policy Reform Agenda*. Washington, DC: American Constitution Society for Law and Policy, 2011.

Gould, Jens Erik. "As California Fights Prison Overcrowding, Some See a Golden Opportunity." *Time US*, September 29, 2011. Accessed January 8, 2012. http://www.time.com/time/nation/article/0,8599,2094840,00 .html#ixzz1eFnmQYVk.

Graczyk, Michael. "Testimony Set to Start in Infamous Texas KFC Mass Slayings Case." *Associated Press*, October 13, 2007, reported in various newspapers, including *Weatherford Democrat*, October 15, 2007. Accessed December 23, 2011. http://weatherforddemocrat.com/statenews/x1 155979264/Testimony-set-to-start-in-infamous-Texas-KFC-mass-slayings -case.

Grant, Sir William. Speech on Sir Samuel Romilly's Bills, May 1, 1810. Parliamentary Debates, House of Commons (1st series) 19 (1812): Appendix, cols. lxv–lxix.

Green, Thomas Andrew. *Verdict according to Conscience: Perspectives on the English Criminal Trial Jury 1200–1800*. Chicago: University of Chicago Press, 1985.

Greene, Edie, Kirk Heilbrun, William H. Fortune, and Michael T. Nietzel. *Wrightsman's Psychology and the Legal System*. 6th ed. Belmont, CA: Thomson Wadsworth, 2007.

Grynbaum, Michael M. "Bloomberg Reports for Jury Duty." *New York Times*, August 6, 2007. Accessed December 21, 2011. http://cityroom.blogs .nytimes.com/2007/08/06/mayor-bloomberg-reports-for-jury-duty/.

Hans, Valerie P., and Neil Vidmar. *Judging the Jury*. New York: Plenum, 1986.

Haralambous, Nicola. "Juries and Extraneous Material: A Question of Integrity." *Journal of Criminal Law* 71 (2007): 520–33.

Hart, H. L. A. *The Concept of Law*. Oxford: Oxford University Press, 1961.

Hogan, Jeff. "Overcrowding of State Prisons Demands Action." *County Press*, September 23, 2009. Accessed January 8, 2012. http://thecountypress

.mihomepaper.com/news/2009-09-23/Opinion/Overcrowding_of_state _prisons_demands_action.html.

Holdsworth, William Searle. *A History of English Law*. Vol. 1. 3rd ed. Boston: Little, Brown, 1922.

Hostettler, John. *The Criminal Jury Old and New: Jury Power from Early Times to the Present Day*. Winchester, UK: Waterside Press, 2004.

Iontcheva, Jenia. "Jury Sentencing as Democratic Practice." *Virginia Law Review* 89 (2003): 311–83.

Jackman, Tom. "Mistrial in Fairfax Murder, Rape Case." *Washington Post*, July 4, 2007. Accessed December 26, 2011. http://www.washingtonpost .com/wp-dyn/content/article/2007/07/03/AR2007070301173_pf.html.

Jackson, John D. "Making Juries Accountable." *American Journal of Comparative Law* 50 (2002): 477–530.

Janis, Irving Lester. *Groupthink: Psychological Studies of Policy Decisions and Fiascoes*. 2nd ed. Boston: Houghton Mifflin, 1982.

Jefferson, Thomas. "Notes on the State of Virginia, Query XIV (1782)." In *The Works of Thomas Jefferson*, vol. 4, Federal Edition, edited by Paul Leicester Ford, 37–65. New York: Putnam, 1904.

Johnson, Sheri Lynn. "Black Innocence and the White Jury." *Michigan Law Review* 83 (1985): 1611–708.

Jonakait, Randolph N. *The American Jury System*. New Haven, CT: Yale University Press, 2003.

Jury Summit 2001. Conference Information and Survey Results. Accessed December 23, 2011. http://www.jurysummit.com.

Kadish, Mortimer R., and Sanford H. Kadish. *Discretion to Disobey: A Study of Lawful Departures from Legal Rules*. Stanford, CA: Stanford University Press, 1973.

Kalven, Harry, Jr., and Hans Zeisel. *The American Jury*. Boston: Little, Brown, 1966.

Kamisar, Yale, Wayne R. LaFave, Jerold H. Israel, Nancy J. King, and Orrin S. Kerr. *Modern Criminal Procedure*. 12th ed. St Paul, MN: Thomson/West, 2008.

Kant, Immanuel. "Über ein vermeintes Recht, aus Menschenliebe zu lügen." *Berlinische Blätter*, September 10, 1797: 301–14.

Kaplan, Martin F., and Ana M. Martín, eds. *Understanding World Jury Systems through Social Psychological Research*. New York: Psychology Press, 2006.

Kelsey, Mavis P., Sr. *Twentieth-Century Doctor: House Calls to Space Medicine*, College Station: Texas A & M University Press, 1999.

Ketler, David W. "The Constitutionality of Blue Ribbon Juries." *Journal of Criminal Law and Criminology* 38 (1947): 369–75.

King, Nancy J. "Juror Delinquency in Criminal Trials in America, 1796–1996." *Michigan Law Review* 94 (1996): 2673–751.

King, Nancy J. "Nameless Justice: The Case for the Routine Use of Anonymous Juries in Criminal Trials." *Vanderbilt Law Review* 49 (1996): 123–59.

King, Nancy J. "Silencing Nullification Advocacy inside the Jury Room and outside the Courtroom." *University of Chicago Law Review* 65 (1998): 433–500.

King, Ryan S. *The State of Sentencing 2008: Developments in Policy and Practice.* Washington, DC: The Sentencing Project, 2009. Accessed January 8, 2012. http://sentencingproject.org/doc/sl_statesentencingreport2008.pdf.

Kirby, Michael Donald. "The Jury of the Future." Australian Bar Association Conference, Dublin, Ireland, July 9, 1998: Delivering Justice in a Democracy III. Accessed December 22, 2011. http://www.hcourt.gov.au/assets/publications/speeches/former-justices/kirbyj/kirbyj_dublin1.htm.

Klerman, Daniel. *A Look at California Juries: Participation, Shortcomings and Recommendations.* Washington, DC: American Tort Reform Association, September 2002. Accessed December 23, 2011. http://www.atra.org/reports/CA_juries/report.pdf.

Knox, Malcolm. "The Game's Up: Jurors Playing Sudoku Abort Trial." *Sydney Morning Herald* (Australia), June 11, 2008. Accessed December 26, 2011. http://www.smh.com.au/news/national/the-games-up-jurors-playing-sudoku-abort-trial/2008/06/10/1212863636766.html.

Kressel, Neil J., and Dorit F. Kressel. *Stack and Sway: The New Science of Jury Consulting.* Boulder, CO: Westview Press, 2002.

Lacey, Nicola. "Responsibility and Modernity in Criminal Law." *Journal of Political Philosophy* 9 (2001): 249–76.

Langbein, John H. "Shaping the Eighteenth-Century Criminal Trial: A View from the Ryder Sources." *University of Chicago Law Review* 50 (1983): 1–136.

Langhofer, Kory A. "Unaccountable at the Founding: The Originalist Case for Anonymous Juries." *Yale Law Journal* 115 (2006): 1823–31.

Leipold, Andrew D. "The Dangers of Race-Based Jury Nullification: A Response to Professor Butler." *UCLA Law Review* 44 (1996): 109–41.

Leuchtenburg, William E. *Franklin D. Roosevelt and the New Deal, 1932–40.* New York: Harper Torchbooks, 1963.

Levmore, Saul. "Ruling Majorities and Reasoning Pluralities." *Theoretical Inquiries in Law* 3 (2002). Accessed December 26, 2011. http://www.bepress.com/til/default/vol3/iss1/art4.

Lincoln, Abraham. *Gettysburg Address.* Bliss Copy, November 19, 1863.

Lloyd-Bostock, Sally, and Cheryl Thomas. "Decline of the 'Little Parliament': Juries and Jury Reform in England and Wales." *Law and Contemporary Problems* 62 (1999): 7–40.

Lopez, Amanda. "*Coleman/Plata*: Highlighting the Need to Establish an Independent Corrections Commission in California." *Berkeley Journal of Criminal Law* 15 (2010): 97–126.

Lubasch, Arnold H. "Juror Is Convicted of Selling Vote to Gotti." *New York Times*, November 7, 1992. Accessed December 21, 2011. http://www.nytimes.com/1992/11/07/nyregion/juror-is-convicted-of-selling-vote-to-gotti.html.

Macdonald, William. *Select Charters and Other Documents Illustrative of American History, 1606–1775*. New York, 1899.

Madison, James. "Report on the Virginia Resolutions" (House of Delegates, Session of 1799–1800). In *The Debates in the Several State Conventions on the Adoption of the Federal Constitution*, vol. 4, 2nd ed., edited by Jonathan Elliot, 546–80. N.p., 1836.

Martin, John S., Jr. "Let Judges Do Their Jobs." *New York Times*, June 24, 2003. Accessed December 21, 2011. http://www.nytimes.com/2003/06/24/opinion/let-judges-do-their-jobs.html.

Martinez, Michael. "Wesley Snipes Heads to Prison on Tax Conviction." *CNN*, December 9, 2010. Accessed December 30, 2011. http://edition.cnn.com/2010/SHOWBIZ/celebrity.news.gossip/12/09/snipes.jail/index.html?hpt=T2 December 9, 2010.

Masschaele, James. *Jury, State, and Society in Medieval England*. Basingstoke, UK: Palgrave Macmillan, 2008.

Mathews, David. "How Concepts of Politics Control Concepts of Civic Responsibility." In *Civic Responsibility and Higher Education*, edited by Thomas Ehrlich, 149–63. Phoenix: Oryx Press, 2000.

Matthews, Roger, Lynn Hancock, and Daniel Briggs. *Jurors' Perceptions, Understanding, Confidence and Satisfaction in the Jury System: A Study in Six Courts*. London: Home Office, May 2004. Accessed December 21, 2011. http://webarchive.nationalarchives.gov.uk/20110218135832/http://rds.homeoffice.gov.uk/rds/pdfs2/rdsolr0504.pdf.

Mazzarella, Wendy Patrick. "Avoiding Contact with Jurors." *California Bar Journal* (July 2009): 12, 14.

Middlebrooks, Donald M. "Reviving Thomas Jefferson's Jury: *Sparf and Hansen v United States* Reconsidered." *American Journal of Legal History* 46 (2004): 353–421.

Miller, Frank W., and Frank J. Remington. "Procedures before Trial." *Annals of the American Academy of Political and Social Science* 339 (1962): 111–24.

Minow, Martha. "Stripped Down Like a Runner or Enriched by Experience: Bias and Impartiality of Judges and Jurors." *William and Mary Law Review* 33 (1992): 1201–18.

Molnar-Szakacs, Istvan, Allan D. Wu, Francisco J. Robles, and Marco Iacoboni. "Do You See What I Mean? Corticospinal Excitability during Observation of Culture-Specific Gestures." *PloS ONE* (2007), e626. Accessed December 26, 2011. doi: 10.1371/journal.pone.0000626.

Morton, James. "Sir Anthony McCowan: Judge in the Trial of Clive Ponting." Obituary. *Independent on Sunday* (UK), September 1, 2003. Accessed

July 18, 2010. http://www.independent.co.uk/news/obituaries/sir-anthony
-mccowan-548678.html [page no longer available].

Moyers, Bill. "Justice for Sale." *Bill Moyers Journal.* PBS, February 19, 2010.
Accessed December 26, 2011. Transcript, http://www.pbs.org/moyers/
journal/02192010/transcript4.html.

Munsterman, G. Thomas. *Improving Juror Response Rates in the District
of Columbia.* Council for Court Excellence, March 2006. Accessed
January 19, 2012. http://www.courtexcellence.org/PublicationsNew/
policy_reform_reports/FINAL%20JURY%20WHEEL%20REPORT
.EVERYTHING.2006.pdf.

Munsterman, G. Thomas. *Multi-Lingual Juries.* Future Trends in State Courts,
National Center for State Courts 1999–2000. Accessed December 26, 2011.
http://contentdm.ncsconline.org/cgi-bin/showfile.exe?CISOROOT=/
juries&CISOPTR=221.

National Center for State Courts. *Best Practices in Jury System Management.*
Accessed December 23, 2011. http://www.ncsconline.org/d_research/cjs/
BPinJurySystemMgmt-v3.pdf.

National Center for State Courts/State Justice Institute. *The State-of-the-States
Survey of Jury Improvement Efforts: A Compendium Report,* by Gregory E.
Mize, Paula Hannaford-Agor, and Nicole L. Waters [cited as National
Center for State Courts, *State-of-the-States Survey*]. April 2007. Accessed
December 23, 2011. http://www.ncsconline.org/D_Research/cjs/pdf/
SOSCompendiumFinal.pdf.

National Education Association. *Rankings and Estimates: Rankings of the
States 2010 and Estimates of School Statistics 2011.* NEA Research,
December 2010. Accessed December 20, 2011. http://www.nea.org/assets/
docs/HE/NEA_Rankings_and_Estimates010711.pdf.

National Prison Rape Elimination Commission. *Report.* June 23, 2009.
Accessed January 8, 2012. https://www.ncjrs.gov/pdffiles1/226680.pdf.

Newman, D. *Conviction: The Determination of Guilt or Innocence without Trial.*
Boston: Little, Brown, 1966.

Oakley, Justin, and Dean Cocking. *Virtue Ethics and Professional Roles.*
Cambridge: Cambridge University Press, 2001.

Oldham, James. *Trial by Jury: The Seventh Amendment and Anglo-American
Special Juries.* New York: New York University Press, 2006.

Parker, Laura. "Jury Duty Is Getting Harder to Shirk." *USA Today,*
November 7, 2006. Accessed December 26, 2011. http://www.usatoday
.com/news/nation/2006-11-06-no-show-jury_x.htm.

Parliament of Victoria, Law Reform Committee. *Jury Service in Victoria: Final
Report.* Vol. 1. Melbourne: Government Printer, 1997.

Parsons, Talcott. *The Social System.* London: Routledge and Kegan Paul, 1951.

Pease, Theodore Calvin. *The Leveller Movement: A Study in the History and Political Theory of the English Great Civil War.* Washington, DC: American Historical Association, 1916.

Peltz, Jennifer. "For Jurors, the Real Drama Is Often Found outside the Courtroom." *Washington Post*, October 11, 2009, A10.

Pendleton, Howard. *Criminal Justice in England: A Study in Law Administration.* New York: Macmillan, 1931.

[Penn, William]. *The Peoples Ancient and Just Liberties Asserted, in the Tryal of William Penn, and William Mead.* London, 1670.

Pennock, J. Roland. "Political Representation: An Overview." In *Representation*, edited by J. Roland Pennock and John W. Chapman, 3–27. New Brunswick, NJ: AldineTransaction, 2007.

Perazzo, John. "Obama: Tilting at Racial Windmills." *FrontPageMagazine.com*, December 16, 2008. Accessed January 21, 2012. http://archive.frontpagemag .com/readArticle.aspx?ARTID=33432.

Pollock, Frederick, and Frederic William Maitland. *The History of English Law.* 2nd ed., 1898. Reprint, Cambridge: Cambridge University Press, 1923. Page references are to the 1923 reprint.

Postal Service. Accessed December 23, 2011. http://www.usps.com.

Practice Direction, Jury Service: Excusal. [1988] 1 WLR 1162.

Radzinowicz, Leon. *A History of English Criminal Law and Its Administration from 1750: The Movement for Reform, 1750–1833.* New York: Macmillan, 1948.

Ragins, Sanford. "Justice at the Grass Roots." *Judicature* 83 (2000): 312–14.

Robins, Jon. "Judge and Jury." *TheLawyer.com*, August 23, 2004. Accessed December 21, 2011. http://www.thelawyer.com/cgi-bin/item.cgi?id=111 658&d=11&h=24&f=23.

Rohde, David. "Do Diplomas Make Jurors Any Better? Maybe Not." *New York Times*, April 10, 2000. Accessed December 21, 2011. http://www.nytimes .com/2000/04/10/nyregion/do-diplomas-make-jurors-any-better-maybe -not.html.

Romilly, Sir Samuel. Speech on Sir Samuel Romilly's Bills, February 9, 1810. Parliamentary Debates, House of Commons (1st series) 19 (1812): Appendix, cols. i–xliii.

Sandra Day O'Connor Project on the State of the Judiciary at Georgetown Law Center. Accessed December 21, 2011. http://www.law.georgetown.edu/ judiciary/index.html.

Scheflin, Alan, and Jon Van Dyke. "Jury Nullification: The Contours of a Controversy." *Law and Contemporary Problems* 43 (1980): 51–115.

Schultz, Mark. "Local Government Needs More Citizen Participation." *MetroWest Daily News* (Framingham, MA), March 24, 2008. Accessed

December 21, 2011. http://www.metrowestdailynews.com/opinions/opinion_columnists/x1556060711.

Schwartz, Victor E., Mark A. Behrens, and Cary Silverman. *The Jury Patriotism Act: Making Jury Service More Appealing and Rewarding to Citizens.* Washington, DC: American Legislative Exchange Council, 2003.

Serio, Steven C. "A Process Right Due? Examining Whether a Capital Defendant Has a Due Process Right to a Jury Selection Expert." *American University Law Review* 53 (2004): 1143–86.

Singer, Michael. *Prison Rape: An American Institution?* Westport, CT: Praeger, forthcoming.

Singer, Michael. *The Legacy of Positivism.* Basingstoke, UK: Palgrave Macmillan, 2005.

Sixth Form Law. *Juries—Stephen Owen.* Accessed December 27, 2011. http://sixthformlaw.info/01_modules/mod1/1_5_lay_people/1_5_2_juries/16_stephen_owen.htm.

Slapper, Gary, and David Kelly. *The English Legal System 2009–10.* Abingdon, UK: Routledge-Cavendish, 2009.

Sobolewski, Marek. "Electors and Representatives: A Contribution to the Theory of Representation." In *Representation,* edited by J. Roland Pennock and John W. Chapman, 95–107. New Brunswick, NJ: AldineTransaction, 2007.

Specter, Donald. "Everything Revolves around Overcrowding: The State of California's Prisons." *Federal Sentencing Reporter* 22, no. 3 (February 2010): 194–99.

Spooner, Lysander. *An Essay on the Trial by Jury.* Boston, 1852.

Stearns, Maxwell L. "The Condorcet Jury Theorem and Judicial Decisionmaking: A Reply to Saul Levmore." *Theoretical Inquiries in Law* 3 (2002). Accessed December 26, 2011. http://works.bepress.com/maxwell_stearns/4.

Sterback, Megan. "Getting Time for an Acquitted Crime: The Unconstitutional Use of Acquitted Conduct at Sentencing and New York's Call for Change." *Touro Law Review* 26 (2011): 1223–49.

Stern, Simon. "Between Local Knowledge and National Politics: Debating Rationales for Jury Nullification after *Bushell's Case.*" *Yale Law Journal* 111 (2002): 1815–59.

Stith, Kate, and Steve Y. Koh. "The Politics of Sentencing Reform: The Legislative History of the Federal Sentencing Guidelines." *Wake Forest Law Review* 28 (1993): 223–90.

Stith, Kate. "The Arc of the Pendulum: Judges, Prosecutors, and the Exercise of Discretion." *Yale Law Journal* 117 (2008): 1420–97.

Strier, Franklin. "Whither Trial Consulting? Issues and Projections." *Law and Human Behavior* 23 (1999): 93–115.

Stuntz, William J. *The Collapse of American Criminal Justice.* Cambridge, MA: The Belknap Press of Harvard University Press, 2011.

Surowiecki, James. *The Wisdom of Crowds: Why the Many Are Smarter Than the Few and How Collective Wisdom Shapes Business, Economies, Societies, and Nations.* New York: Doubleday, 2004.

Thayer, James Bradley. *A Preliminary Treatise on Evidence at the Common Law.* Boston, 1898.

Thompson, Isaac Grant. *The Albany Law Journal: A Weekly Record of the Law and the Lawyers.* Vol. 6, July 1872–January 1873. Albany, NY, 1873.

Thorpe, Francis Newton. *The Federal and State Constitutions, Colonial Charters, and Other Organic Laws of the States, Territories, and Colonies Now or Heretofore Forming the United States of America.* Vol. 5. Washington, DC: Government Printing Office, 1909.

Tocqueville, Alexis de. *De la démocratie en Amérique.* Vol. 2. Brussels, 1835.

Twain, Mark. *Sketches New and Old.* New York: Harper, 1922.

Tyler, Tom R. *Why People Obey the Law.* Princeton: Princeton University Press, 2006.

United States Courts. *The Rulemaking Process: A Summary for the Bench and Bar.* Accessed December 23, 2011. http://www.uscourts.gov/RulesAnd Policies/FederalRulemaking/RulemakingProcess/SummaryBench Bar.aspx.

United States Department of Justice. "Federal Jury Convicts Former El Paso Criminal District Court Judge Manuel Barraza." US Attorney's Office, Western District of Texas, February 4, 2010. Accessed January 19, 2012. http://www.justice.gov/usao/txw/press_releases/2010/Barraza_conviction .pdf.

United States Department of Labor, Bureau of Labor Statistics. *Employer Costs for Employee Compensation.* Quarterly report. Accessed December 23, 2011. http://www.bls.gov/.

United States Department of Labor, Bureau of Labor Statistics. *Employment Situation Summary.* Monthly report. Accessed December 23, 2011. http:// www.bls.gov/.

United States Department of State. *Rights of the People: Individual Freedom and the Bill of Rights.* Accessed December 23, 2011. http://infousa.state.gov/ government/overview/borpreface.html.

United States Sentencing Commission. *Federal Sentencing Guidelines Manual.* November 1, 2011. Accessed December 30, 2011. http://www.ussc.gov/ Guidelines/2011_Guidelines/Manual_PDF/2011_Guidelines_Manual _Full.pdf.

United States Sentencing Commission. *Sentencing Table.* Accessed December 30, 2011. http://www.ussc.gov/Guidelines/2011_Guidelines/ Manual_PDF/Sentencing_Table.pdf.

Vermont Committee on Jury Policy. *Reports and Information.* Accessed
    November 30, 2007. http://www.vermontjudiciary.org/Committes/
    ChrgeDes/jurypolchrgedesig.htm [page no longer available].
Vidmar, Neil. "The Performance of the American Civil Jury: An Empirical
    Perspective." *Arizona Law Review* 40 (1998): 849–99.
Vidmar, Neil, ed. *World Jury Systems.* Oxford: Oxford University Press, 2000.
Vidmar, Neil, and Valerie P. Hans. *American Juries: The Verdict.* Amherst, NY:
    Prometheus Books, 2007.
Vidmar, Neil, and Jeffrey J. Rice. "Assessments of Noneconomic Damage
    Awards in Medical Negligence: A Comparison of Jurors with Legal
    Professionals." *Iowa Law Review* 78 (1993): 883–911.
Whyte, Luke. "The 3 Most Crowded State Prison Systems in America."
    CorrectionsOne, October 27, 2009. Accessed January 8, 2012. http://
    www.correctionsone.com/jail-management/articles/1959168-The-3-most-
    crowded-state-prison-systems-in-America/.
Williams, Glanville Llewelyn. *The Proof of Guilt: A Study of the English Criminal
    Trial.* 3rd ed. London: Stevens & Sons, 1963.
Wilson, Scott. "Obama Signs Fair Sentencing Act." *Washington Post*, August 3,
    2010. Accessed January 3, 2012. http://voices.washingtonpost.com/44/
    2010/08/obama-signs-fair-sentencing-ac.html.
Wolfram, Charles W. "The Constitutional History of the Seventh
    Amendment." *Minnesota Law Review* 57 (1973): 639–747.

STATUTES: UNITED KINGDOM

Administration of Justice (Miscellaneous Provisions) Act, 1933, c. 36.
Contempt of Court Act, 1981, c. 49.
Criminal Justice Act, 2003, c. 44.
Juries Act, 1949, c. 27.
Suicide Act, 1961, c. 60.

STATUTES: UNITED STATES—FEDERAL

Antiterrorism and Effective Death Penalty Act of 1996. Public Law 104–132,
    provision on remedies in federal courts codified at 28 USC § 2254.
Civil Rights of Institutionalized Persons Act. Public Law 96–247 (May 23,
    1980), codified as amended at 42 USC § 1997.
Fair Sentencing Act of 2010. Public Law 111–220 (Aug. 3, 2010).
Prison Litigation Reform Act of 1995. Public Law 104–134, §§ 801–810 (1996),
    codified as amended at 11 USC § 523; 18 USC §§ 983(h)(3), 3624(b), 3626;
    28 USC §§ 1346(b), 1915,1915A, 1932; 42 USC §§ 1997.
Prison Rape Elimination Act of 2003. Public Law 108–79, codified as amended
    at 42 USC §§ 15601–15609 (2006).

STATUTES: UNITED STATES—STATES

Alaska. *Statutes: Education, Libraries, and Museums: Public Schools Generally.* Title 14, c. 3.

California. *Code of Civil Procedure,* § 170.1, as amended 2010.

Illinois. *Compiled Statutes: Citizen Participation Act.* 735 ILCS 110.

Mississippi. *Code of 1972, As Amended.* Title 63, c. 3.

Ohio. *Revised Code: Commissioners of Jurors,* c. 2313.

Ohio. *Revised Code: Crimes—Procedure,* c. 2901.

South Carolina. *Code of Laws: Public Officers and Employees: Government Volunteers.* Title 8, c. 25.

JUDICIAL DECISIONS: HONG KONG

Re Lau Ko Yuen Tom, [1998] 4 HKC 735.

JUDICIAL DECISIONS: UNITED KINGDOM

Bushell's Case, [1670] 124 ER 1006 (CCP).

R v Abdroikof, [2007] UKHL 37.

R v Commissioner of Police of the Metropolis *ex parte* Blackburn (No.1), [1968] 1 All ER 763 (CA).

R v Dolby, King's Bench, 1823, reported in Barnewall, Richard Vaughan, and Cresswell Cresswell, *Reports of Cases Argued and Determined in the Court of King's Bench,* vol. 2 (1824), 104–12.

R v Fricker, [1999] EWCA Crim. 1773.

R v Khan, [2008] 3 All ER 502.

R v McKenna, [1960] 1 All ER 326.

R v Schot, [1997] 2 Cr. App. R. 383.

R v T, B, C & H, [2009] EWCA Crim. 1035.

R v Twomey, [2011] EWCA Crim. 8.

R v Young, [1995] QB 324.

Ward v James, [1966] 1 QB 273.

JUDICIAL DECISIONS: UNITED STATES—FEDERAL AND STATE

Apodaca v Oregon, 406 US 404 (1972).

Apprendi v New Jersey, 530 US 466 (2000).

Batson v Kentucky, 476 US 79 (1986).

Berghuis v Smith, 130 S. Ct. 1382 (2010).

Blakely v Washington, 542 US 296 (2004).

Bordenkircher v. Hayes, 434 US 357 (1978).

Brown v Plata, 131 S. Ct. 1910 (2011).

Caperton v Massey, 129 S. Ct. 2252 (2009).

Carter v Jury Commission of Greene County, 396 US 320 (1970).

Clark v US, 289 US 1 (1933).

Coleman v Schwarzenegger [district court]. Order. No. CIV S-90-0520 LKK JFM P (ED Cal. July 23, 2007). Accessed January 22, 2012. http://www .clearinghouse.net/chDocs/public/PC-CA-0002-0008.pdf. *See* Coleman v Schwarzenegger and Brown v Plata.

Coleman v Schwarzenegger, 2009 WL 2430820 (ED Cal., August 4, 2009), *stay denied,* 2009 WL 2851846 (ED Cal., September 3, 2009), *stay denied,* 2009 WL 2915066 (US Supreme Court, September 11, 2009). *See* Brown v Plata.

Cunningham v California, 549 US 270 (2007).

Duncan v Louisiana, 391 US 145 (1968).

Duncan v Perez, 445 F2d 557 (5th Cir. 1971).

Duren v Missouri, 439 US 357 (1979).

Ewing v California, 538 US 11 (2003).

Farmer v Brennan, 511 US 825 (1994).

Fay v People of State of New York, 332 US 261 (1947), *rehearing denied,* 332 US 784 (1947).

Gall v US, 128 S. Ct. 586 (2007).

Gallagher v Delaney, 139 F3d 338 (2d Cir. 1998).

Gitlow v New York, 268 US 652 (1925).

Hernandez v New York, 500 US 352 (1991).

Hopkins v Oxley Stave Co., 83 F 912 (1897).

In re Debs, 158 US 564 (1895).

In re Fahy, 2009 WL 567997 (Review Department of the Cal. State Bar Court, no. 05–O–05123), March 6, 2009 (not reported in Cal. Reporter).

Johnson v Pataki, 691 NE2d 1002 (NY 1997).

Kimbrough v US, 552 US 85 (2007).

Local 36 of International Fishermen and Allied Workers of America v US, 177 F2d 320 (9th Cir. 1949).

Lockhart v McCree, 476 US 162 (1986).

Lockyer v Andrade, 538 US 63 (2003).

Marshallo v US, 298 F 74 (1924).

Miller v California, 413 US 15 (1973).

Mitchell v Harmony, 54 US 115 (1851).

People v Beatty, 80 P3d 847 (Colo. App. 2003).

People v Gitlow, 136 NE 317 (N.Y. 1922), *affirmed,* 268 US 652 (1925).

People v Huey, 505 A2d 1242 (Conn. 1986).

People v Keenan, 758 P2d 1081 (Cal. 1988), *cert. denied,* 490 US 1012 (1989).

People v Kriho, 996 P2d 158 (Colo. App. 1999), *rehearing denied* (September 2, 1999), *cert. denied* (Colo., March 20, 2000).

People v Williams, 21 P3d 1209 (Cal. 2001).

People v Woodlief, 90 SE 137 (N.C. 1916).

Plata v Schwarzenegger. Findings of Fact and Conclusions of Law re Appointment of Receiver. No. C-01-1351 THE (ND Cal. October 3, 2005). Accessed January 8, 2012. http://clearinghouse.wustl.edu/chDocs/public/PC-CA-0018-0007.pdf. *See* Coleman v Schwarzenegger and Brown v Plata.

Rabinowitz v US, 366 F2d 34 (5th Cir. 1966).

Railroad Company v Stout, 84 US 657 (1873).

Ring v Arizona, 536 US 584 (2002).

Rita v US, 551 US 338 (2007).

Rochin v California, 342 US 165 (1952).

Shannon v US, 512 US 573 (1994).

Sherrill White Construction v South Carolina National Bank, 713 F2d 1047 (1983).

Singer v US, 380 US 24 (1965).

Smith v Texas, 311 US 128 (1940).

Sparf v US, 156 US 51 (1895).

Spears v US, 129 S. Ct. 840 (2009).

Steckler v US, 7 F2d 59 (1925).

Strauder v West Virginia, 100 US 303 (1879).

Tanner v US, 483 US 107 (1987).

Taylor v Louisiana, 419 US 522 (1975).

Turney v State, 936 P2d 533 (Alaska 1997), *appeal from conviction following remand,* 2000 WL 422363 (Alaska App. 2000), *denial of habeas corpus petition affirmed sub nom.* Turney v Pugh, 400 F3d 1197 (9th Cir. 2005).

TXO Production Corp. v Alliance Resources, 509 US 443 (1993).

US ex rel. Wheeler v Williamson, 28 F Cas. 682 (ED Penn. 1855).

US v Anderson, Crim. No. 602–71 (DNJ 1973).

US v Antwuan Ball, US District Court for the District of Columbia, Case Number 05–cr–0100 (2007–2008).

US v Armstrong, 517 US 456 (1996).

US v Bailey, 444 US 394 (1980).

US v Battiste, 24 F Cas. 1042 (CCD Mass. 1835).

US v Biaggi, 909 F2d 662 (2d Cir. 1990).

US v Booker, 543 US 220 (2005).

US v Canania, 532 F3d 764 (8th Cir. 2008), *cert. denied,* 129 S. Ct. 609 (2008).

US v Cox, 627 F3d 1083 (8th Cir. 2010).

US v Dougherty, 473 F2d 1113 (DC Cir. 1972).

US v Duncan, 400 F3d 1297 (11th Cir. 2005), *cert. denied,* 546 US 940 (2005).

US v Dunnigan, 507 US 87 (1993).

US v Gelb, 881 F2d 1155 (2d Cir. 1989).

US v Greenspan, 26 F3d 1001 (10th Cir. 1994).

US v Grier, 475 F3d 556 (3d Cir. 2007), *cert. denied,* 552 US 848 (2007).

US v Heicklen, Grand Jury indictment, US District Court for the Southern District of New York, Case Number 10–cr–01154–KMW (November 18, 2010). Indictment dismissed, April 19, 2012.

US v Hiveley, 61 F3d 1358 (8th Cir.1995).

US v Hopper, 177 F3d 824 (9th Cir. 1999), *cert. denied sub nom.* McKendrick v US, Ries v US, Reed v US, 528 US 1163 (2000), *cert. dismissed sub nom.* US v Reed, 529 US 1063 (2000).

US v Horne, 474 F3d 1004 (7th Cir. 2007), *cert. denied,* 551 US 1123 (2007).

US v Hurn, 496 F3d 784 (7th Cir. 2007), *cert. denied,* 552 US 1295 (2008).

US v Ibanga, 454 F Supp. 2d 532 (ED Va. 2006), *vacated and remanded by unpublished per curiam opinion,* 271 Fed. Appx. 298 (4th Cir. 2008).

US v Jackson, 436 F2d 39 (9th Cir. 1970), *cert. denied,* 403 US 906 (1971).

US v James, 203 F3d 836 (10th Cir. 2000) (unpublished opinion, cited by page reference, in "Table of Decisions Without Reported Opinions").

US v Juarez-Ortega, 866 F2d 747 (5th Cir. 1989).

US v Krzyske, 836 F2d 1013 (6th Cir. 1988), *reconsideration denied,* 857 F2d 1089 (6th Cir. 1988), *cert. denied,* 488 US 832 (1988).

US v Morris, 26 F Cas. 1323 (CCD Mass. 1851).

US v O'Brien, 130 S. Ct. 2169 (2010).

US v Polizzi, 549 F Supp. 2d 308 (EDNY 2008), *vacated and remanded sub nom.* US v Polouizzi, 564 F3d 142 (2d Cir. 2009).

US v Rosenthal, 454 F3d 943 (2006).

US v Settles, 530 F3d 920 (DC Cir. 2008), *cert. denied,* 129 S. Ct. 999 (2009).

US v Snipes, 611 F3d 855 (11th Cir. 2010), *cert. denied,* 131 S. Ct. 2962 (2011).

US v Spock, 416 F2d 165 (1st Cir. 1969).

US v Thomas, 116 F3d 606 (2d Cir. 1997).

US v Watts, US v Putra, 519 US 148 (1997).

US v White, 134 Fed. Appx. 880 (6th Cir. 2005), *rehearing en banc granted, opinion withdrawn,* 503 F3d 487 (6th Cir. 2007), *opinion en banc* 551 F3d 381 (6th Cir. 2008), *cert. denied,* 129 S. Ct. 2071 (2009).

US v Wilson, 28 F Cas. 699 (Cir. Ct. ED Pa 1830).

Washington v Lambert, 98 F3d 1181 (9th Cir. 1996).

Wayte v US, 470 US 598 (1985).

Weeks v Angelone, 528 US 225 (2000).

Wellons v Hall, 130 S. Ct. 727 (2010).

Williams v Florida, 399 US 78 (1970).

Williams v New York, 337 US 241 (1949).

Wisconsin v Leitner, 646 NW2d 341 (Wis. 2002).

Witte v US, 515 US 389 (1995).

Index

ABA. *See* American Bar Association (ABA) survey
Abolitionists, fugitive slaves and, 78. *See also* Fugitive Slave Law
Acquitted-conduct sentencing, 134–39, 169–70
Adams, John, 5, 93, 158, 163
Administrative costs, 19–20. *See also* Cost assessment, of jury system
African Americans, racial bias and. *See Duncan v. Louisiana* (1968); Fugitive Slave Act
Amar, Akhil Reed, 63
Amendments, to U.S. Constitution: First, 47; Fifth, 5, 94, 132; Sixth, 5, 50, 88, 89, 135; Seventh, 5; Eighth, 178, 185; Fourteenth, 5, 47
American Bar Association (ABA) survey, 31–32, 39, 63, 69–70, 97
American Legislative Exchange Council, 29, 34
Amish, rejection of jury duty by, 38
Appeals, 10–11, 26

Appellate court, 11, 46, 53, 102, 120; sentencing and, 127–28, 129, 135, 137–39
Attorneys, 21–22; eligibility for jury duty, 115–17
Authority figures, 29, 33–36, 37, 43, 61. *See also* Judges

Barry, Dave, 50
Batson v. Kentucky (1986), 96
Bayard, Nicholas, 45
Bazelon, David, 104, 107, 160, 164
Bentham, Jeremy, 112, 113
Bias, in judges, 55–57. *See also* Racial discrimination
Bill of Rights, 89
Blackstone, William, 82–83, 104, 119, 160
Blue ribbon jury, 82, 112
Boulder County, Colorado, 67–68
Bribery, 54
Bright, Myron, 138, 154

Brown v. Plata (2011), 175, 176–78, 179–82

Bureau of Labor Statistics, 16, 17, 20

Burger, Warren E., 175–76

Burns, Robert, 65

Bushell's Case (1670), 76, 78, 87–88, 111; Penn and, 79, 113; political principle of, 92–93

Butler, Paul, 39, 152, 162, 168

California prisons: inadequate medical care in, 179–82; overcrowding in, 175, 176–78

California State Bar Court, Review Department, 116–17

California Supreme Court, 104–5, 121, 155

Camden 28 case (1973), 80, 91, 162, 166

Capital punishment. *See* Death penalty

Casper, Jonathan, 58

Center for Jury Studies, 23, 24

Charles II, King of England, 44

Chesterton, G. K., 57

Citizens, jurors as, 29, 166. *See also* Democratic citizenship myth

Civic responsibility, 66–68

Civil cases, nullification in, 85

Civil injunction, 79

Civil legal action, 7

Cocking, Dean, 148

Colledge, Stephen, 111–12

Colorado Court of Appeals, 127–28, 136

Commercial regulation, 3–4

Common-law jury systems, 5, 51. *See also* English jury system

Community: conscience of, 159; fair cross section requirement, 94–96; juries as representing, 3, 45, 68–69; participation of, 97; values and interests of, 47–48, 80, 99

Condorcet jury theorem, 49

Congress, U.S., 125, 127

Connecticut Supreme Court, 136

Conrad, Clay, 161–62

Conscience, morality and, 153, 158–59, 163

Conscientious objection, 38

Constitution, U.S., 5, 29; Amendments to (*See* Amendments, to U.S. Constitution)

Contempt of court, 79

Cooley, Steve, 156, 177

Cost assessment, of jury system, ix, 13–27, 62, 64–65; administrative, 19–20; consulting industry, 22–23; further legal proceedings, 25–26; ignoring jury summons and, 36; juror hardship, 26–27; juror time, 14–19; not readily quantifiable costs, 23–27; rules of trial procedure and evidence, 24–25; of study, research, and skills development, 23–24

Court Statistics Project, 14

Criminal cases, 7; jury deliberation in, 9–10

Criminal Courts Review, 6, 50, 62–63, 102; on nullification power, 77, 105–6, 160; on reluctance to perform jury duty, 33, 35

Criminal history, sentencing and, 126–27, 155

Crook, Frances, 85

Death penalty, 38, 50–51, 104; as unjust punishment, 82–84, 162, 167

Death threats, against jurors, 54

Democratic citizenship myth, ix, 61–71; cost of jury system to promote, 62; jury duty as education in, 62–66, 100; jury duty as fostering community, 68–69; jury duty as participation in government, 66–68

Department of Justice, U.S., 153, 183

Department of Labor, U.S., 16, 17, 20

Diamond, Shari Seidman, 58

Discretion, responsibilities and, 145–56; discretionary support trust, 147–48; of jurors, 157–58; of prosecutor, 152–56

Dispensing power, of jury. *See* Nullification power

Douglas, William O., 97

Drug prosecution, sentencing in, 85

Duncan v. Louisiana (1968), vii–viii, 101–2, 163, 168–69; nullification power in, 89–91, 102, 158, 160

Dwyer, William L., 6, 35, 63, 68–69, 97; on juror's fear of reprisals, 121; on jury nullification, 76–77, 79–80, 85, 91, 160

Economist survey, 31, 63

Education, in citizenship, 62–66, 100. *See also* Democratic citizenship myth

Eighth Amendment, 178, 185

Eisenberg, Theodore, 56

Eleventh Circuit Court of Appeals, 120

English jury system, 3–5, 6, 25, 31, 38, 51; bribery in, 54; *Bushell's Case* (1670), 76, 78, 79, 87–88, 92–93, 111, 113; civil legal actions and, 7; Colledge case, 111–12; death penalty in, 82–84, 104;

intimidation in, 55; juror expertise, 53; Lilburne case, 77, 78; Official Secrets Act and, 81; Penn and Mead case, 75, 79, 113, 161

Entering judgment, 10

Evidentiary standard, 124, 138–39, 169

Examination, of witnesses, 8–9

Excluded reasons, 148, 149

Exempt categories, jury selection and, 114–17

Expert knowledge, 52–53

Extra burden, social role and, 149

Fair cross section requirement, 94–96

Fairness: of juries, 54–57; of justice system, 31; legitimation of government and, 96–97

Federal Sentencing Reporter, 176

Fifth Amendment, 5, 94, 132

First Amendment, 47

Fisher, Clarkson, 80, 160, 162

Fisher, George, 153

Fourteenth Amendment, 5, 47

Fugitive Slave Act (1850), 78–79, 148–49, 150–51

Gammage, Robert, 55–56

Gates, Henry Louis, Jr., 39

Georgetown University School of Law, 70

Gertner, Nancy, 106, 124, 129–30

Government: community conscience and, 159; jury as legitimation of, 96–98, 100, 131, 133–34; jury as safeguard against, viii, 87–98, 101; jury duty as participation in, 66–68; obstruction of jury by, 141–42. *See also* Authority figures; Judges

Grand jury, 6, 94, 112
Grant, William, 167
Group decision making, 49.
    See also Trial outcomes,
    juries and
Guilty plea, 7
Guilty verdict, 9

Habeas corpus. *See* Writ of habeas
    corpus
Houston, Paul, 64

Illinois Citizen Participation Act, 66
Incorporation doctrine, 89
Injustice, in prisons. *See* Prison
    conditions, injustice in

Jefferson, Thomas, 54, 63
Joiner, Charles W., 118
Jonakait, Randolph N., 35, 49,
    51, 52, 80
Judges, 9, 39, 54; bench trials and,
    43; bias in, 55–57, 99; competence
    of, 49, 51–52; as government
    officials, 29–30; low level of trust
    in, 63; nullification power and,
    88–91, 118; public opinion
    of, 31, 32; sentencing and,
    x, 10, 54, 124, 129–30,
    136–38, 141, 154; summing-up
    by, 21; survey of, 43–44
Judicial Conference of the United
    States, 25
Jurors: competence of, 48–52;
    expertise, 52–53; fair cross section
    requirement, 94–96; hardship of,
    26–27; intimidation of,
    54–55; misconduct of, 25, 26;
    oath and promise of, 159–63;
    responsibilities of (*See*
    Responsibilities, of jurors);
    unsound behavior, 50–51

Jury: blue ribbon, 82, 112; death-
    qualified, 38; deliberation by,
    9–10; fairness of, 54–57; as legiti-
    mation of government, 96–98; as
    peers of defendant, 44–47, 95, 99;
    political roles of, 71, 101–3, 142,
    163; representing "the people,"
    93–96, 102; as safeguard against
    government, 87–98
Jury duty: conscientious fulfillment
    of, 157–72; morality and
    conscience in, 158–59; oath and
    promise of, 159–63; as recourse
    role, 157–58
Jury duty summons. *See* Summons,
    for jury duty
Jury equity, 81. *See also* Nullification
    power
Jury obstruction, in trial process. *See*
    Trial process, jury obstruction in
Jury Patriotism Act (proposal), 34
Jury selection, 111–17; exempt
    categories and, 114–17; *voir dire*
    process and, 8, 15, 21, 111–14
Jury system: constitutional
    commitments to, 5–6; workings
    of, 3–7; worth of, 99–107
Jury system costs. *See* Cost
    assessment, of jury system
Jury-trial consulting industry, 22–23
Jury trial procedure, 6–11
Jury yield, 16, 17
Justice system, 29, 69–70, 97; juror
    responsibility and, 166–69;
    noncompliance to jury summons
    and, 33; public attitudes toward,
    31–32, 38–39

Kadish, Mortimer R., 37, 149,
    150–51, 157, 158
Kadish, Sanford H., 37, 149, 150–51,
    157, 158

Kalven, Harry, Jr., 43–44, 56–57, 90
Kriho, Laura, 122
Krzyske, Kevin Elwood, 118–19, 122, 160

Language, 45–46
Leipold, Andrew, 103
Levine, James, 52
Lilburne, John, 77, 78
Lincoln, Abraham, 29, 66

Madison, James, 107, 159
Martin, John, 39
Masschaele, James, 4
Mead, William, 75, 79, 161
Medical care, in prisons, 179–82
Merritt, Gilbert, 136
Miller v. California (1973), 47–48
Minow, Martha, 52
Mistrial, 9
Morality, conscience and, 153, 158–59, 163
Moral responsibility, 163–68. *See also* Responsibilities, of jurors

National Center for State Courts, 14, 19–20, 23, 24; on juror hardship costs, 26–27
National Education Association, 64
National Prison Rape Elimination Commission, 183
National will, nullification and, 103
North Carolina Supreme Court, 136
Nullification power, ix, 99–100, 158, 166–67; *Bushell's Case*, 76, 78, 79, 87–88, 92–93, 111, 113; in civil cases, 85; concealed from jury, 117–20; judicial ambivalence regarding, x, 88–91; juror's oath and promise, 160–62; legitimation of government and, 96–98, 100, 131, 133–34; as license for unjust acquittals, 106–7; long history of, 75–86; moral responsibility and, 164, 165; national will and, 103; as path to anarchy, 104–6; Penn and Mead case, 75, 79, 113, 161; people of color and, 82; as "perverse verdict," 77; as "pious perjury," 83, 104, 119, 160, 167; prison conditions and, 174, 175; safeguarding against government, 98, 100, 166; sentencing and, 136–37, 141, 142; unjust laws and, 78–82; unjust punishments and, xi, 82–85, 167, 170, 172; as unwieldy and inconsistent instrument, 103–4; *voir dire* process and, x, 113–14, 122, 161

Oakley, Justin, 148
Obama, Barack, 171
Obscenity, standards for, 47–48
Obstruction, of jury. *See* Trial process, obstruction of jury in
Obstruction of justice, 131
O'Connor, Sandra Day, 56
Official Secrets Act (Britain), 81
Owen, Stephen, 81

Peers, jury as, 44–47, 95, 99
Penal codes, 125. *See also* Prison entries
Penalties, for ignoring jury summons, 34–35, 36, 37
Penn, William, 44, 75, 79, 113, 161
People v. Williams (2001), 160
Peremptory challenges, 8
Perjury, penalty for, 131
Persons of color, 95–96. *See also* Racial discrimination
Perverse verdict, 77
Pious perjury, 83, 104, 119, 160, 167. *See also* Nullification power

Pointing, Clive, 81
Police, recourse role of, 151–52
Political roles, of jury, 71, 101–3, 142, 163. *See also* Nullification power
Pratt, Charles, Lord Camden, 94
Price-fixing case, 97
Prison conditions, injustice in: inadequate medical care, 179–82; juror responsibility and, 173–85; overcrowding, 175–79; systemic rape, xi, 182–85
Prison Litigation Reform Act (PLRA, 1996), 178–79
Prison Rape Elimination Act (PREA, 2003), 183–84
Prohibition era, 79–80, 84
Prosecutor, 7; recourse role of, 152–56; repeat-offender statutes and, 154–55
Public attitude surveys, 31–32

Racial discrimination, 55, 94, 106–7, 168–69. *See also Duncan v. Louisiana* (1968)
Rape, in prisons, xi, 182–85
Recourse roles, 150–58; jury duty as, 157–58, 168; of police, 151–52; of prosecutor, 152–56. *See also* Social roles
Repeat-offender statutes, 154–56
Research costs, 23–24
Responsibilities, of jurors, x–xi, 163–72; deviation from role and, 148–50; discretion and, 145–56; means and ends, 147–48; moral responsibility, 158–59, 163–66, 167; police role and, 151–52; in practice, 169–72; principles of, 163–66; prosecutor role and, 152–56; recourse roles, 150–56, 168; social roles and, 146–47,

149; "three-strikes" law and, 154–56. *See also* Nullification power
Rice, Jeffrey, 57–58

Scheflin, Alan, 157
Selection, for jury duty, 111–17; exempt categories, 114–17; *voir dire* process and, 8, 15, 21, 111–14. *See also* Summons, for jury duty
Sentencing hearing, 10, 54, 123–24
Sentencing process, 167; acquitted-conduct sentencing, 134–39, 169–70; factors and elements of the offense, 128–30; further offenses and, 130–34; judges and, x, 10, 54, 124, 129–30, 136–38, 141, 154; juror's assessment, 139–40; jury obstruction in, 123–42; nullification power and, 136–37, 141, 142; repeat-offender statutes and, 154–56; sentencing guidelines, 125–28, 170–71
Seventh Amendment, 5
Sexual harassment case, 46
Shadow jury, 22
Sixth Amendment, 5, 50, 135; nullification power and, 88, 89
Sixth District Federal Court of Appeals, 135
Skills development costs, 23–24
Snipes, Wesley, 128, 131
Social community, jury duty as, 68–69. *See also* Community
Social roles, 145, 146–58; deviation from, 148–50; recourse roles, 150–58, 168; role of police, 151–52; role of prosecutor, 152–56
Spanish language, 46, 52, 53
Sparf v. US (1895), 88, 91, 157
Special jury, 82, 112
Spooner, Lysander, 167

State Department, U.S., 66, 67
State-of-the-States Survey, 14
Strauder v. West Virginia (1879),
    44–45, 47
Stuntz, William, 45
Summons, for jury duty, 7–8; cost of,
    14, 16, 20; normative factors in
    rejecting, 38–40; obeying or
    disobeying the law and, 36–38;
    penalties for ignoring, 34–35, 36,
    37; public noncompliance with,
    32–39
Supreme Court, U.S., 50, 51, 97,
    139, 175; appeals to, 11; *Batson v.
    Kentucky* (1986), 96; *Brown v. Plata*
    (2011), 175, 176–78, 179–82; on
    community conscience, 159;
    Duncan v. Louisiana (1968), vii–viii,
    88–91, 101–2, 158, 160, 163,
    168–69; incorporation doctrine
    and, 89; *Miller v. California*
    (1973), 47–48; on prison rape,
    182; public opinion of, 31; on
    role of prosecutor, 152, 153; on
    sentencing, 127, 130, 131; on
    separation between people and
    government, 29; *Sparf v. US*
    (1895), 88, 91, 157; *Strauder v.
    West Virginia* (1879), 44–45, 47;
    Taylor v. Louisiana (1975), 91,
    94–95; on *voir dire* process, 21;
    Williams v. New York (1949), 133;
    Witte v. US (1995), 132–33
Surcharge, social role and, 149

Taylor, Gregory, 156
Taylor v. Louisiana (1975), 91, 94–95
Theft cases, death penalty for, 82–84
"Three strikes" laws, 154–56
Tocqueville, Alexis de, 62–64, 65
Trial outcomes, juries and, 43–59;
    community values, 47–48;

competence, 48–52; consistency,
    57–58; fairness, 54–57; juror
    expertise, 52–53; jury as peers
    and, 44–47; myth of improved,
    43–59. *See also* Sentencing
Trial process, obstruction of jury in,
    24–25, 111–22; concealment of
    nullification power, 117–20;
    exempt categories for jury
    selection, 114–17; pressure on
    jury, 120–21; threat against jury,
    121–22; *voir dire* process and,
    111–14
Twain, Mark, 50
Tyler, Tom, 36–37

*United States Sentencing
    Commission*, 125
US v. Antwuan Ball (2007–2008),
    139–40, 142, 169
US v. Hurn (2007), 135–36
US v. Krzyske (1985), 118–19,
    122, 160
US v. Morris (1851), 78–79,
    161, 166
US v. Polizzi (2008), 91
US v. Putra (1997), 134–35
US v. Watts (1997), 134–35, 136
US v. White (2008), 135, 136
US v. Wilson (1830), 164
Unjust laws, nullification and,
    78–82
Unjust punishments, 171–72; death
    penalty as, 82–84, 162, 167;
    nullification power and, xi, 82–85,
    167, 170, 172. *See also* Prison
    conditions, injustice in

Van Dyke, Jon, 157
Vaughn, Chief Justice, 76, 87
Verdict, unanimity in, 9, 10
Vidmar, Neil, 57–58

Vietnam War protestors, trials of,
  117; Camden 28 case (1973), 80,
  91, 162, 166
Voir dire process, 8, 15, 111–14; cost
  of, 15, 21; death penalty attitudes
  and, 38, 162; nullification power
  and, x, 113–14, 122, 161

Weinstein, Jack, 91, 119, 160
White supremacy, 39, 168
Williams v. New York (1949), 133

Wisconsin Supreme Court, 136
Witnesses: examination of, 8–9; role
  of, 147, 149, 150
Witte v. US (1995), 132–33
Writ of habeas corpus, 11,
  25–26, 76; fugitive slaves and, 79,
  149

Yale Law Journal, 87

Zeisel, Hans, 43–44, 56–57, 90

About the Author

MICHAEL SINGER, MA, PhD, JD, is professor at the Dickson Poon School of Law of King's College London, England. He was previously law professor at the University of Pennsylvania and George Washington University, and is a member of the State Bar of California. His many previous publications include *The Law of Evidence* (with Jack H. Friedenthal) and *The Legacy of Positivism*. He holds a juris doctor degree from Stanford University, bachelor's and master's degrees in mathematics from Cambridge University, and a doctorate from London University.